Queenie

Memories of a Grandma

A book for the family by Anita Louise

Queenie Memories of a Grandma

ISBN-13: 978-1539918936

ISBN-10: 1539918939

Email: anitalouisewriting@gmail.com

Contents

Queenie, Memories of a Grandma.

It is said that within each and every one of us there is a book to be written. The story I have to tell is about my Grandmother. Growing up in our extended family in Goff's Oak I recall her interests and stories with fondness. Many a time she was told to write a book, but she never did, now I am attempting to unravel her story for future generations to enjoy. Like many others before, her 'ordinary' life was quite extraordinary. It is interesting to look at what impacted upon her throughout the years, shaping and moulding the person I remember with admiration and love.

Recalling Queenie's life has been like sewing a tapestry. Each memory a thread, some have been clear and vibrant giving easy colour and definition. Others have thinned and faded over time making the pictures difficult to recreate. As the memory distorts over time, care has been taken to only include memories considered to be true and accurate. Consequently, this has created small holes in the story which will never be filled.

The Early Years

Hilda Louisa Wombwell was a Christmas baby, born on the, wintry, 25th day of December 1898. She was the second born child to Albert and Elizabeth (Lizzie) Wombwell and came into the world seven years after her big sister Nellie.

She was born at The Cedars, Theobalds, in Waltham Cross where Albert and Elizabeth were living. John Saunders Gilliat Esq. MA. MP. JP. was in residence at The Cedars. It was a glorious manor house positioned within the Theobalds Estate. It stood in its own grounds and gardens, under the shadow of the spectacular cedar trees. There were separate quarters for staff and servants on the site but exactly where the family lived is a mystery. In 1912, a decade or so after Queenie and her family had left, the house burnt down leaving only the remains of the conservatory and a small part of the servants' quarters. Nothing of the house was ever rebuilt and eventually, in 1921, the park was left to the people of Waltham Cross to enjoy. With only a fragment of the former house in Cedars Park today.
Theobalds Estate was centuries old and very impressive. It was known as the Royal Palace of Theobalds. In 1607 Robert Cecil inherited the estate from his father. When Robert was a boy Elizabeth I visited on more than one occasion. She often stayed for up to a month at great expense to his father. Robert Cecil grew up to serve both Queen Elizabeth I and later James I. When James made his way down from Scotland to London to become King he stayed with Robert Cecil at the Palace of Theobalds. Cecil served the King as spymaster and went on to become 1st Earl of Salisbury. The King became a regular visitor and fell in love with the palace. Four years after James came to the throne, he asked Cecil to exchange estates. Cecil the Earl of Salisbury was given Hatfield Palace. When James I died, his son Charles I inherited Theobalds Palace. Following his execution in 1649, Theobalds Palace was listed by the commonwealth as a property to be disposed of. So in 1650 much of the property was demolished and then re-built after the restoration.

Major changes took place in the Georgian period when George Prescott bought the Palace. He decided to demolish the palace and build three smaller houses on the estate. One of which was the stately Manor known as The Cedars. The area boasted many royal connections and for that reason Albert began to call his little daughter Queenie. It stuck and she was known to everyone, throughout the generations, simply as Queenie.

Nellie, Queenie on Lizzie's knee and Albert at The Cedars

Times were hard for people during the 19th century. Under the rule of Queen Victoria Britain had witnessed great strides in the improvement of both drinking water and sanitation. The situation in both Cheshunt and Waltham Cross had been dire. Both areas were susceptible to flooding and raw sewage posed a major health hazard to a large proportion of the population. Finally, in 1850, the board of health began to deal with the problem. The village of Cheshunt was given clean water pumped from a deep well into a reservoir and a newly established sewage farm which served both areas.

By the time Queenie was born the areas of Cheshunt and Waltham Cross had begun to change for the better. Lady Meux of Theobalds House laid the foundation stone of the Cottage Hospital in October 1889. The hospital was built in Church Lane, Cheshunt and opened eight months later in 1890. Major advances were being made in the world of medicine. A basic understanding of both health and hygiene was slowly being established. Many families were still living in abject poverty in the rat infested tenements of the towns and cities across the country but young Queenie had every opportunity to thrive.

Queenie was a child taking her first faltering steps into the brave new world of Victoria's Empire at a time when many people saw Great Britain as truly great. The country was on the very cusp of automation and technology. By the time Queenie was born gas was

Wombwell Wedding. 16-8-1902 at Abbey Lodge, Waltham Abbey.
The wedding of Charles Wombwell (born1878) to Elizabeth Peace.
Top row second left Albert Wombwel with wife Lizzie standing in front of him. Beside her Harriett Wombwell. Seated, far left Louisa Wombwell (Martin) with sisters Alice and Ada. Seated beside the bride is David Wombwell next to his third wife Emma, their daughter Elizabeth sits far right. Seated on the ground far left are Queenie and Nellie.

already lighting the streets of Cheshunt, making it safer. The world was waking up to the suffrage of women and women were beginning to stand up for themselves and loudly fighting for their rights.

It was a time of progress and change. No more so than with the death of Queen Victoria in 1901 and the coronation of Edward VII, the former Prince of Wales. Bertie, as he was known, came to the throne overweight and self-indulged. At first he had little interest in the country and his supporters were few, but Bertie had an easy charm. From the austerity of the Victorian era Bertie became a breath of fresh air. He transformed the gloomy rooms of Buckingham Palace with white and gold. Bertie became the People's King; he opened hospitals and was seen by his public. He was the first monarch to be interested in real people and not class, sparking an era of rapid social change.

Queenie's father, Albert Wombwell, was born in Langley, Essex. He was descended from a long line of Wombwells in the area. Like many of the Wombwell family, young Albert began his working career as a farm labourer, moving from village to village following the seasonal work. He married Elizabeth (Lizzie) Rebecca Watts in 1890 and fate brought them first to Cheshunt, where Nellie was born in 1891, and then to Theobalds, where Queenie was born. At the time of Queenie's birth, Albert was working as a labourer at the Royal Gunpowder Mills in Waltham Cross. It was dangerous work and Albert made the decision to move back into agriculture. By 1905 Albert had returned to his farming roots and relocated his family to Beaumont Farm in the hamlet of Beaumont, where he and Lizzie worked and raised their unusually small family of two daughters. Most families of the time were large. Little was known of contraception and nature took its course.

As the years progressed siblings from both sides of the family made the move away from Essex and into Hertfordshire. Lizzie had a sister and brother-in-law, Jonah, living in the hamlet of Beaumont. Jonah worked on the Grant Estate gardens at Beaumont Manor and this contact may have been a catalyst to Albert's move.

The current Beaumont Manor had been rebuilt in 1806

One of Queenie's treasured postcards...
Schoolgirls of the time.
It would be lovely to know the significance of this postcard.
Is Queenie one of the little girls standing in the field?

on the site of the former medieval house. The estate was bought by Major George F. Grant, the whisky family, in 1899 and a little community began to grow up. Accommodation in the form of Beaumont villas were built and a tiny corrugated iron church was erected. A football field and cricket pitch were provided by the estate for the people of the hamlet, along with a small clubhouse. The area of Beaumont was becoming a country idyll and Queenie was lucky to be growing up in it.

In 1865 the "Scheme of the Beaumont Charity" had been formed by Major Grant's predecessor. It oversaw the poor relief for the Waltham Cross area and the Parish of Cheshunt. It was responsible for the distribution of monies to the needy from all the local churches. Britain was divided by poverty. Unemployment was high, 25% of the country was living in poverty and 10% of people were living below subsistence level, with families unable to scrape together enough funds to feed themselves adequately. Many families were so poor that the children ran bare foot in the streets. Life for Queenie was different. Rural life was physically tough and arduous but with a little land people could grow a few vegetables and keep some hens. Families like the Wombwell's could feed themselves and create a stable life for their children.

The way parents reared their children was changing. There was a gradual move away from the "seen and not heard" philosophy of the strict Victorians, where children were considered to be miniature adults to be taught and disciplined. For the first time children had their own clothing of informal comfortable smocks. Traditional child rearing was being challenged in favour of a new relaxed approach to motherhood. Happily for Queenie, parents were encouraged to spend time nurturing their children, enjoying their innocence and encouraging their thinking.
For the first time books written specifically for children were available along with toys and games. Queenie would have enjoyed The Water Babies' a book with a moral tale of a badly treated chimney boy, Treasure Island, Black Beauty and Alice's Adventures in Wonderland. It was recognised that play and exercise were essential for a growing child. What better time to be a youngster! Growing up on the various farms of Beaumont, Queenie must have enjoyed the new freedoms of the time.

Albert was very close to his sister Louisa. They had left Essex at a similar time and Louisa had lived with Albert and Lizzie at The Cedars. She was six years his junior and soon became a favourite and close aunt to Queenie. Back in 1905 when Queenie was only six or seven Aunt Lou sent a postcard to little Queenie expressing her joyful anticipation of tea with her on the lawn at Beaumont Farm. Queenie kept all her postcards in a special book. Year-on-year she received warm birthday wishes and good health from family and friends. It is obvious from the pretty pictures and the loving notes that Queenie was doted upon.

Education for all 5 - 11 year olds had only been compulsory since 1880 and free for all children since 1891. Prior to that, life was grim for youngsters. Children were expected to go out to work as soon as they could. Many worked twelve hour shifts in abhorrent conditions during the industrial revolution. It took forty-one years of argument and debate in Parliament before anything changed. When the Factory Act 1878 was passed it outlawed work for the under 10s and restricted the length of the working day to six and a half hours for under thirteens. This left a void in many children's day and the government replaced labour with learning.

It is unclear where Queenie was educated. In 1870 Parliament announced through the first Education Act that there had to be a school in every town and village. School Boards of local people were set up to build and run these new schools. The local Board of Health formed an Attendance Committee to insure every child went to school.

Most schooling at the time was provided by Board Schools which in 1902 came under the authority of the LEA (Local Education Authority).They were instructed to develop elementary schooling for the youngest children and set up secondary and technical schools for the education of the older children.

The oldest school in the area, Dewhurst, was founded in 1640 by Robert Dewhurst for the free education of boys. This very early education of the poor was to enable them to read the Bible, become more civilised, and enable them to support themselves and their families. Most churches provided Sunday school and taught reading through Bible study for a couple of hours.

Alternatively poor children were sent to a Dame School. These were run by one woman in her home, cramming in as many children as she could in the one room. It was more a child minding service than an educational establishment. Parents paid a few pennies to have their child learn the alphabet. One such establishment was in the little cottage opposite Goff's Oak House with the proprietor Susan Norris.

At the time Queenie attended school there were a number in the area for primary aged children. The British School in College Road was a mixed school for 263 pupils. There was a National Infants at Turnford for 65 and Churchgate for 144 pupils. A National Girls School also at Churchgate for 130 and another mixed National School at Wormley for 227 pupils. St. James Church School in Goff's Oak was another mixed school for 103 children. In addition there were many private schools which came and went as fast as their proprietors. Many were run by the daughters of wealthier families. Miss Paul and her sister ran a day school in Cheshunt Street and later in Church Lane. Halt House in Flamstead End held a more prestigious private school for the education of young men. For a short time classes were held in the room of a house on the Beaumont Estate. All had facilities to teach children the rudiments of the three Rs. Reading, writing and religion were taught in a rigid and formal fashion. Much was learned through repeated affirmations and by rote.

Elizabeth (Lizzie) Wombwell

By the time Queenie went to school in 1903 the modern system of education in Britain had been born. School clothing was changing, especially, for girls. At first Queenie would have worn a soft knitted cotton liberty bodice under her loose fitting smock dress, with a protective white pinafore over the top. By 1908 schoolwear was gathering a more formal, uniform look. Gym slips were becoming popular and the older girls were beginning to wear a shirt and tie, with a calf length skirt and tailord jacket.

Living at Beaumont, Queenie walked with her family to the Methodist Chapel at Goff's Oak each and every Sunday, come rain or shine. Whether she attended school in this area or in neighbouring Wormley we will never know. What we do know is that she was educated to a higher level. From 1907 scholarships were provided by the LEA for the brightest working class children who passed the scholarship exam. A culture of betterment was developing.

In 1910 Queenie's friend Mabel, from Green Hall, Bramfield, writes of them both going back to school. Gaining qualifications is of importance to her peers, and another school friend Mollie writes in 1915 of taking up a French course at the Polytechnic. At the time there was a mixed senior school at Gews Corner and an Art and Technical School in Turners Hill. The

Public Library in Cheshunt provided evening classes at the School and offered people the opportunity to better themselves. Additionally the Reverend John Teague Greenway ran correspondence courses from the Vicarage in Goff's Oak. He had 372 people on his books. Opportunities for further education were beginning to open up and young people were encouraged to make use of it.

It is clear that Queenie's early years were happily spent on the various farms in Beaumont with Mum, Dad and big sister Nellie. Over the years Albert was moved from farm to farm within the Beaumont area. With each move he improved the yield of the land. His good reputation was growing fast amongst the rural community. The family's address changed from Beaumont Farm in 1905 to Beaumont Manor Farm in 1906. Then in 1907 to Beaumont Green Farm and finally, in 1908 to Charity Farm, Beaumont. At the time Nellie was working in service as a ladies maid to Lady Grant up at the manor. She wrote a postcard to Queenie on the 23rd June 1910. It captures the close relationship the sisters had.

My Dearest Sister

Hope you will like this postcard trusting all are well. Will you ask Mother if she will see about my blouse, when she goes to the Cross, as I have not heard or received parcel yet. I cannot understand it.

Much love and heaps of kisses.

Trusting to see Mum on Sunday

Your loving sister Nell.

Farm work was hard; it was heavy work for both men and women. Everyone was expected to pull their weight. Up before dawn in all weathers, there were animals to be fed, cows to be milked and crops to be tended.

The life of a farmer's wife was a tough one. Up with or before her husband Lizzie would have been expected to get the range scrubbed, blackened and lit first thing. Hot water was essential on the farm and the large black pots and kettles took an age to boil. As soon as the range was lit the heavy pots would have gone on, and a constant supply would have been carried from the pump or well to be heated on the stove for use throughout the day.

By about 7.00am, dressed in layers of restricting, heavy clothing, Lizzie would have been down on her hands and knees scrubbing the hard stone floors of the kitchen. The flag stones of the farmhouse would have been a constant battle. With every step into the kitchen came mud and animal dung from the yard. Having worked up a sweat from her labours she would have freshened up. Cleanliness of the body was considered most important to staying healthy. Bathing was generally for children and men, and most women made do with a strip wash in a bowl of warm water at the washstand.

By 8.00am breakfast would have been on the table.

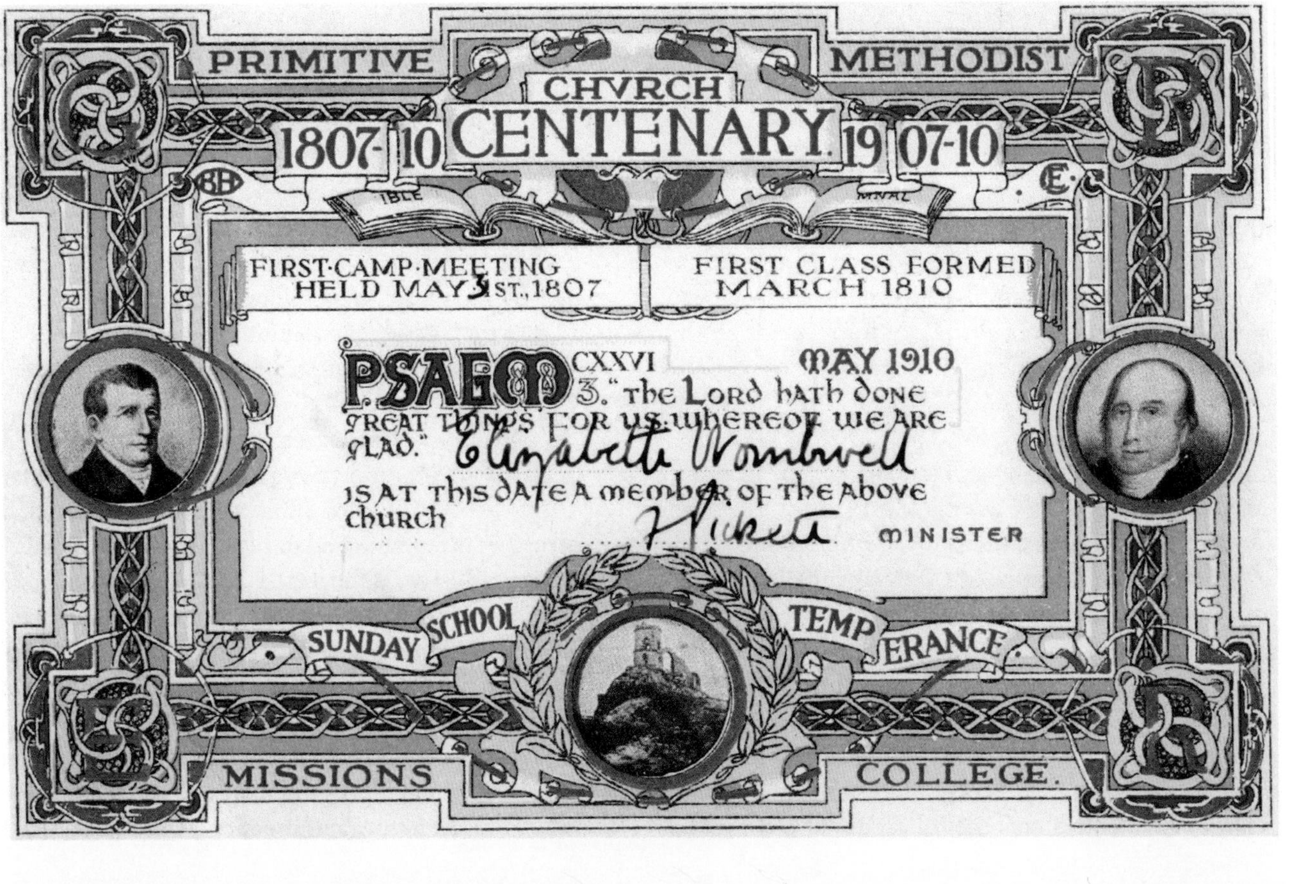

Albert would have already checked his livestock and done some of his jobs, and he would be ready for some food. Typical for the time, a farmer's breakfast was a wholesome hash of bacon, onion, and potato cooked to a tasty but rather grey mash. There was always a big pot of steaming tea and hunks of rustic bread. After breakfast Queenie would have been packed off to school and Albert would be back to his farm toils. Lizzie's day would be a constant round of chores. With water to be fetched and heated, the range needed to be fed with a steady supply of dry wood. Kindling needed to be found, along with logs that needed to be cut and stored. Beds needed to be made, rooms swept, clothes washed and food prepared.

Typically, lunch was served at 1.00pm. Often it was a big pot of stew that had been put onto the range after breakfast and left to slowly simmer whilst the chores were done. Life was certainly hard on the farm even with the introduction of the farm tractor and the steady flow of labour saving inventions; it was still labour intensive and manual for the majority of farmers. Despite the hardships of the times Queenie grew up cosseted and loved. Her life on the various farms was free and easy. She was clothed, well fed and educated.

By 1910 the country had a new monarch in George V, with Queen Mary at his side the world was moving on. From the excesses of Bertie's reign, George and Mary upheld the virtues of the upper middle classes and stood for family values. Under the guidance of Prime Minister David Lloyd George, the Liberal reforms saw the emergence of the welfare state as we know it. It was realised that illness and old age were greater causes of poverty than idleness. Some councils began to offer free school meals for poor children, the over seventies were being paid a small pension and there was talk of sick pay.

Albert's success in farming was growing and in 1911 he was appointed Farm Bailiff to Lady Meux. Queenie, now 13 years old, was moved to Poyndon Pits Farm in Silver Street, Goff's Oak. Goff's Oak was much larger than the small Hamlet of Beaumont but still only a sleepy village of farms and workers cottages set in rolling fields and woods. With its Smithy in the centre by the village pond and the windmill up Common Road, Goff's Oak must have drawn quite a few outsiders to swell its modest numbers. The roads to and from Cuffley, Goffs Oak and Cheshunt were just dusty dirt tracks, gravelled and potholed. Most travel was done by foot, trudging these well-worn lanes with the help of a pony and trap if you were lucky. Young Queenie, living her simple life in Goff's Oak, was slowly developing into a young lady.

The Methodist Chapel and the Wombwell Family

In order to begin to understand Queenie you need to look back, as for all of us, into her family history. Although not overtly religious Queenie had a deep-rooted faith that had permeated through the generations from her early Essex family. Their Methodist beliefs gently moulded them into adventurous, open-minded individuals with great faith. Throughout her life Queenie attended chapel on a regular basis, a routine fixed from birth. Every Sunday morning, from a very young age she would walk with her parents from their home in Beaumont to the little chapel on Common Road in Goff's Oak, a little chapel that was to become an important cornerstone in both her grand-father's and father's lives.

The original brick and slate chapel at Goff's Oak was built in 1868 only thirty years before Queenie was born. The area of Cheshunt was long considered a stronghold for the Methodist nonconformists. There were few meeting places for 'free church people' as these nonconformists or dissenters were known. It is said that the owner of the estate in Goff's Oak grudgingly gave the small plot of land for the erection of the 100 seat chapel at Common Road. The money to build it was raised, as is often the way, by the sheer hard work of the few.

One of these founders of the Chapel was John King. Born in Suffolk he had moved to Hertfordshire sometime before 1861. At this time he was living at number 2 Cuffley Hill Road with his small family, and working as an agricultural labourer. Ten years later he was living in Goff's Lane and by 1881 he had moved into Rose Cottage on Halstead Hill with his wife Mary, young son Harry and daughter Eliza known as Grace.

John's 27 year old unmarried daughter Grace worked from home as a dressmaker. John King was a hardworking man; he worked various jobs throughout his long life. A gardener in his fifties, a horseman in his sixties and at the age of seventy-six a cattleman on a farm. John King lived to the ripe old age of ninety-eight. He was a religious man and totally dedicated to the work of the chapel. Throughout the years he supported the chapel financially and was a trustee of the Goff's Oak Methodist Church for 53 years. It was through John King that the Wombwells developed a stronger connection with the chapel at Goff's Oak.

When the chapel first opened its doors in 1868 there were only six hundred people living in the small rural community of Goff's Oak. It was part of the Enfield

Circuit; the Enfield Minister had three churches under his guidance and spread his time between them.

The ethos of the Methodist Church must have captured the hearts of the simple farming community at Goff's Oak. Its nonconformist views on rules and authority challenged the religious assumptions of the Church of England. With its methodical pursuit of biblical holiness the Methodist message was simple. It preached work hard, save for the future, and give generously; temperance was recommended and gambling inappropriate. With its warm and welcoming nature it is not surprising that the numbers soon swelled. Albert traipsed his wife and two daughters across the muddy fields to services three times every Sunday. Such was the chapel's success that in the early 1900s, when Queenie was just a tot, the membership of the Methodist Chapel at Goff's Oak outnumbered that of Bush Hill Park Chapel despite it's higher population. At the time the chapel at Goff's Oak was congratulated on its excellent Sunday school attendance. Raising a generous five shillings most months. Queenie was inevitably part of its success with her regular attendance. Soon big sister Nellie was playing the Church organ. She thought nothing of the long walk through the farm tracks from Beaumont, out to Crouch Lane and then onto Common Road and the chapel. She played the organ most Sundays until her Father died in 1935 and she could not face it again.

By 1911 Albert and his family were living in Goff's Oak at Poyndon Pits Farm in Silver Street. In the small tight-knit community Albert would certainly have known John King and his family. They lived at Rose Cottage in Halstead Hill and were virtually neighbours. Both men had rural upbringings. Their roots were in agriculture. Both men had worked the land as labourers. The relationship between them must have grown and their common interest in the Methodist Chapel cemented it.

It appears that the Methodist ideology was deep-rooted within the Wombwell family long before Albert Wombwell walked his family across the fields to pray. Since before 1712 Wombwells have been living and working in Essex. It is in this North Western corner of Essex that interest in the Methodist Church amongst agricultural workers was one of the strongest in the country. It was highly likely that members of the large Wombwell family would have joined the growing trend in those very early years.

The Primitive Methodists as they were known came into the area via missionaries from Norfolk in around 1839. They rapidly spread into North West Essex, East Hertfordshire, West Suffolk and South Cambridgeshire. The early meetings were held outdoors. Many lay preachers were local agricultural workers. They understood the area and its hardships; they understood their congregations and how they lived. This brought religion closer to the people, and the preachers' words were more relevant. The founder of the English movement, John Wesley (1703-1791), was a highly successful evangelist and preached in the open air. He encouraged people to personally experience Jesus Christ and he believed that the carnal nature of humanity could be cleansed through faith.

From delivering sermons from the back of a cart in all weathers, the early Essex preachers began to move their congregations into barns. The Methodist movement became stronger and more organised; funds were diligently raised through bazaars and charity teas. Benefactors were found and in time chapels were built in Clavering in 1844, Langley in 1862 and Chishall in 1868. It was said by a Langley clergyman at the time that before the chapel was built the members of these small rural communities were living in total ignorance of religion and many of them were wicked and no better than wild heathens.

Once the chapels were built the pews filled and the Wombwell family name can be found on the roll books of both Clavering and Langley Chapels. This holds a certain status as the seats had to be paid for. In both Chapels the Wombwells have six/seven seats making them amongst the largest family groups in the parish to be represented in the Chapels.

Surprisingly the Chapels in these poor rural communities had no trouble filling their pews. But they did have some difficulty in collecting class fees for Sunday school. A luxury few could afford for their children. Those too poor to pay for a seat were called 'hearers' and were allowed to stand at the back of the Chapel and listen to the service. It is said that at the time there were three times as many hearers in the congregation as those with seats. The small Chapels of Clavering and Langley must have been full to bursting.

Early Wombwell Family Tree

JOHN WOMBWELL married **MARY** HARE, then in 1750 married MARY CANE
b. 1712 d. 1784 — b. 1712 d. 1749 — b. 1720 d. 1754

John b. 1734 | Richard b. 1736 | **JAMES** b. 1739 | Thomas b.1744 | MARY b. 1753 d. 1763

JAMES WOMBWELL married **SARAH** ROGERS, then in 1787 married SARAH COLLIS
b. 1739

Sam b. 1760 | Sarah b. 1762 | William b. 1764 | Josiah b. 1771 | Elizabeth b. 1773 | **JOHN** b. 1774 | Ann b. 1777 | George b. 1777 d. 1850 | Zachariah b. 1780

William b. 1787 | Sarah b. 1790 | Sarah b?

JOHN WOMBWELL married **HONOR** KING
b. 1774 d. 1845

George b. 1795 | Sarah b. 1797 | Honor b. 1798 | William b. 1800 | Hannah b. 1802 | **JOHN** b. 1804 | Eliza b. 1805 | Maria b. 1807 | Charles b. 1812 | Emma b. 1811 | Ellen b. 1814 | Peter b.1816 | Peter b. 1818 | Joseph b. 1820 | Elizabeth b. 1823

JOHN WOMBWELL married **SARAH** Corbey
b. 1804 d. 1871

Honor b. 1831 | Charles b. 1833 | William b. 1835 | Arthur b. 1838 | John b. 1842 | **DAVID** b. 1846

DAVID WOMBWELL married **ELIZABETH** Anne ABRAHAMS
b. 1846 d. 1923 — b. 1848/9 d. 1887

ALBERT	Frank	Harriett	Louisa	Charles	Samuel	Ada	Alice	Frank
b. 1868	b. 1879	b. 1873	b. 1875	b. 1878	b. 1880	b. 1882	b. 1884	b.1886

DAVID WOMBWELL second marriage **EMMA** Barleyman
b. 1853 d. 1912

Elizabeth

JOHN KING

DAVID WOMBWELL third marriage **ELIZA (GRACE)** KING

David Wombwell's Story

Albert's father, Queenie's grandfather, David was born in 1846. David was the youngest of six children born to John and Sarah Wombwell. John, like so many of the Wombwell family, worked as an agricultural labourer in Essex. He lived with his wife Sarah in Water Wick, Lower Green, Langley where all his six children were born. At the age of 15 David was still living at home with his mother, father and siblings. At this time he was working the land alongside his father and older brothers.

David Wombwell

Ten years on David was married to Elizabeth Abrahams and living in Upper Green, Langley with his baby son Albert. David and Elizabeth went on to have eight more children, with only one child dying in infancy, little Frank born in 1879.

Still working as an agricultural labourer David moved his family to Manor House, Little Chishall, were three of his children were born. Barely a year after their youngest child Frank number two was born in 1887, Elizabeth died. David must have been devastated. He coped as best he could with his young family for two years until he remarried in 1890 to Emma Barleyman. Albert was a young man of about twenty. It was around this time that he made the decision to leave home with his sister Louisa and start his own life in Hertfordshire.

David and Emma went on to have a daughter of their own and called her Elizabeth. In 1891, David still lived in Great Chishall with his wife, baby daughter and five children from his first marriage.

David shared his home with his father-in-law William Barleyman, and Emma's half-brother Joseph. With seven children and three adults under the same roof, living conditions must have been quite snug. This was a common sign of the times but it is not surprising that Albert made the decision to leave and begin his own life.

Father-in-law William, at the age of 75, was still employed. Son Charlie, aged 13, and stepson Joseph, aged 12, had all followed in their father's footsteps. There was little else for them to do and all the males, young and old, worked together on the Essex land.

Inscription at Goff's Oak Methodist Church

After 22 years of marriage Emma died leaving David, now 66 years old, alone once again. David became a regular visitor to Goff's Oak and eventually a resident. Not only were Albert and Louisa in the area but his son Frank was also living and working in Goff's Oak. David soon became a respected pillar of the community. He had become treasurer to the Methodist Chapel and kept the accounts for eight or so years. It was through this involvement with the Chapel that he met John King and his daughter Grace.

Three years after Albert had moved to Goff's Oak his twice widowed father David married for the third time to John King's daughter Grace. The family bonds strengthened between the Wombwell and King families. In 1914 John King took David Wombwell into his home and he lived with his new father-in-law and bride in Rose Cottage, in Goff's Lane, until he died in 1923 only two years after his father-in-law. David took the Methodist Chapel to his heart and they took to him. Many a time he would take on the duty of lay preacher and address the congregation. Following his death a memorial tablet was erected by his friends and can be seen in the church today. It bears the following inscription:-

In

Loving Memory

Of

DAVID WOMBWELL

WHO WAS A DEVOTED MEMBER
AND CLASS LEADER

OF THIS CHURCH:

BORN 5th APRIL 1846, DIED 20th AUG. 1923

"HE FOUGHT THE GOOD FIGHT."

David was buried at Chishall alongside his first wife, Elizabeth. His third wife Grace was most upset. She wanted her husband to be buried in Cheshunt, which she claimed was his wish.

Over the years John King was very good to the Wombwell family. It is said that he helped David's daughter Louisa financially and that he treated all of David's children as he would his own grandchildren. On his father's death, Albert took up the mantle of benefactor to the Chapel and did much to extend the influences of the church.

Growing Up

Growing up from child to teen Queenie would have been fully aware of the distinct fashions for each milestone. Long hair was worn halfway up in the later teen years. It acknowledged the first step into adulthood when young women would be expected to wear tight restricting corsets and a hat on top of their tightly wound hair. Out of desperation Mary Crosby invented the first bra in 1913; she joined together two handkerchiefs with a satin ribbon. This scandalous design took some time to perfect and be accepted by the masses. Life in the early nineteenth century was full of etiquette and rules but younger women were furiously striking out and fighting for their rights. Whether Queenie was aware of it or not the likes of Emmeline and Christabel Pankhurst were big news. They were attempting to change attitudes toward women with public displays of defiance. They were trying to make a difference by interrupting political meetings and being arrested. Women wanted to be heard!

Three years after the Wombwell family moved to Goff's Oak War was declared. Volunteers were sought to fight but not conscripted. Men working the land could not leave so easily as others. The country still needed to be fed and Albert who was in his forties stayed behind, working twice as hard whilst the younger men were away fighting.

Queenie and her family lived at Poyndon Pits Farm for four years and it must have been whilst living in Goff's Oak that Queenie took her first job. For the poor and the working classes work for women was a necessity. Everyone was expected to contribute to the household. It was however different for middle-class girls who, after being educated to a higher standard, chose to work. With Britain at war the working world for women was about to open up. Suffrage took a back seat whilst Britain fought but women wanted to help. They even marched through London in protest, demanding their right to serve.

Nursing was seen as an acceptable path for women but working in many of the other auxiliary services was not fully supported by most men. But still young women did their bit, working in jobs predominately done by men. The world was becoming a different place.

Women were moving out of the home and into a wider world. Their views were changing; they were mixing with people from all walks of life. Social barriers were being eroded forever and a generation gap was beginning to grow. Young women were no longer fulfilled by a family and a home as their mothers had been. Higher education for girls was acceptable and some saw this as a route to finding a husband. For the first time women were looking for a family and a career. They craved individuality from men and Queenie would have been no exception, even living as she did on the many farms cocooned in the Hertfordshire countryside. Queenie was most certainly a free spirit and determined to make her own way.

With the world at war telecommunications were of massive importance. Sometime after completing her education Queenie began work as a telegraphist or telegraph operator, sending messages through Morse code. Her first job was at Wormley Post Office were she probably worked the dual role of sorting clerk and telegraphist, which was common practice at the time.

During the 19th century there was vast expansion in the Post Office. Adult literacy had increased dramatically and this, along with the penny postage, created an increase in the volume of mail. The Post Office was aiming to offer a cheap service to the masses and the Postal Union employed women as cheap labour. At the time this brave step was both novel and experimental.

Each day Queenie would have trudged the dirt lanes from Goff's Oak to Wormley until Albert moved his family for the final time to Cuffley in 1915. Travelling from Cuffley to Wormley in all weathers would have been near impossible and a change was needed. Queenie's experience and tenacity landed her a job with the Great Northern Railway at King's Cross Station. The train from King's Cross terminated at Cuffley. The line and station had been planned for Goff's Oak but Cuffley was decided upon, much to the annoyance of the Goff's Oak residents. The line was opened on the 4th April 1910 and provided a lifeline to the people of Cuffley. Each morning Queenie would have trotted off to work in the City.

Telecommunications began in England in 1870 when the National Telegraph Service was first established. By 1880 control of the telegraph service had passed on to the Post Office. Three years later the Central Telephone Exchange was established at Oxford Court, London. By 1904 The Wireless Telegraphy Act conferred licensing powers to the Postmaster General. By the time Queenie started work the entire service had been taken over by the Post Office and was providing the country with its first unified system. During this time of rapid growth, 450 new exchanges were opened. Albert was one of the first to have a telephone in Cuffley being number 4 on the exchange. It was an exciting time for people.

In the telegraph office at King's Cross men and women were working the same roles but fraternisation between the sexes was totally unacceptable. In many places of work there was strict workplace segregation. Women worked completely separate from men and the two groups never met. The women were escorted in and out of the building at times when males could not see them.

Sending messages by Morse code was very slow. Each word had to be laboriously spelt out letter by letter. Queenie soon learnt her trade and before long she was very adept at receiving and sending messages through the series of dots and dashes. It was a skill she was never to forget. Her nephew Albert Cooke went on to work for the railway and years later Queenie could still send him secret messages across the room by blinking out the dots and dashes with her right and left eyes. I remember as a child thinking "What are they up to?"!

Nellie Wombwell a young lady of the times

The First World War brought many changes to society. Clothing, for example, was becoming far more relaxed. The sombre mood of the country combined with the economics of the period dictated a move away from the lavish clothing and jewellery previously enjoyed by the young women of the time. For the first time women's hair was cut short and practical. Dress protocols for formal occasions and events became more relaxed and some women even wore trousers for work. Quite outrageous! In order to use less fabric skirts and dresses got shorter. By 1915, mid-calf was seen as acceptable, the shortest hemline ever worn. With these shorter shirts came shorter knickers. Traditionally bloomers were modestly worn well below the knee. Now they were creeping up to the thigh and above!! Queenie, a young working woman in the city and still a teenager, would have been influenced by the London fashions. I am sure she would have fully embraced these changes as quite forward and modern, blissfully unaware of just how racy things were going to get in the decades to come.

Queenie as a young lady

As the war ended the plight for women's equality began again in earnest. Nothing was to stay quite the same for women again. Women were asserting themselves, their attitudes had moved on and they were no longer accepting that they were just an extension of their husbands' egos. In 1918 Parliament gave the vote to women householders over the age of thirty. But it was not until 1928 that Queenie would have been given the vote. When the so-called 'Flapper Vote' gave the vote to all women over the age of twenty-one, Queenie took this to be a privilege and only once missed an election, when in the 1970s she and her 'adopted brother' Cecil Harriss were delayed back from a continental holiday and the polling station (which she had in the billiard room end of Goff's Oak House) had just closed, and they were unable to cast their votes in the local election. To her horror her party lost by just two votes. She found it really hard to forgive herself.

Scenes from Goff's Oak and Wormley just as Queenie would have known them.

GOFF'S OAK VILLAGE IN THE EARLY 1900's

THE ORIGINAL GOFF S OAK IN THE EARLY 1900's

GOFF S LANE IN THE EARLY 1900's

Queenie, now a young lady of nearly seventeen, was working in the hustle and bustle of London and living with her mother and father at Lower Hanyards Farm in Cuffley. This sleepy hamlet was not much more than a cluster of eight farms. Their black tarred wooden boarding and weathered tiles were a Hertfordshire characteristic. The original hamlet of Cuffley had no more than six cottages, a small green with a pump, the Plough Inn and a hideously ugly corrugated-iron Church. There was little to inspire a vibrant young woman. There was no Post Office or shop and bread was delivered daily from Northaw. All other provisions were either brought in from Enfield via the train or from Potters Bar via pony and trap.

Not only did the train provide a lifeline to the Cuffley residents but with it came the arrival of day trippers and holiday makers. Cuffley was marketed for its clean country air. Posters invited people to enjoy the rural surroundings and natural charms of the Great Wood. They had the opportunity to leave behind the city smog and sample the rustic delights of Cuffley. This sleepy backwater of Hertfordshire bustled with life at the weekends. The Wombwells were in a perfect position, close to the station, at Lower Hanyards Farm to exploit the situation. Here, they could invite ramblers and revellers in for tea and cake and charge them a penny or so.

Inspired by the weekenders passing through the kitchen of Lower Hanyards and fuelled by the antics of the newly formed Girl Guide Movement, Queenie, full of adventure and fun, along with Aunt Lou's daughters, her younger cousins Rene and Barbara, would sleep overnight in the large white bell tent on the farm or pitch the tent under the stars in the Great Wood.

A year after they had arrived in Cuffley, on 3rd September 1916, the now historic Zeppelin was shot down over Cuffley. These deadly air ships loomed out of the night sky as big as battle ships. There was no real civil defence against them. There were no sirens wailing a warning instead boy scouts blew bugles whilst policemen on bikes blew whistles or whirled rattles. At the time Albert Wombwell was a special constable. All special constables were informed of the impending raids and asked to be on the lookout. Albert was one of the first on the scene when the airship ripped through the night skies with Lieutenant Robinson in hot pursuit. In a blaze of flames it fell through the skies shattering into thousands of pieces of shrapnel close to Hill Farm on Plough Hill. It was reported by a resident as far away as Dunstable that the light burning from the Zeppelin 20 miles away in Cuffley was so bright that "on looking out of his window he could clearly see the apples on his tree at the bottom of the garden."

This was the first airship to be brought down over Britain and the crowds flocked to see the wreckage and find a piece of the airship to take back home. The trains from King's Cross were fit to bursting! It is reported that a thousand people travelled out from London to Cuffley in the overcrowded carriages. Only to be replaced by another thousand on their return. The roads into Cuffley from all directions were nose to tail with cars and buses. Soldiers were billeted into local homes during the clean-up of the airship wreckage. It is said that every scrap of food and milk was used up for the flocks and flocks of visitors and troops. The little village of Cuffley was well and truly on the map. Queenie like many others picked

Lower Hanyards

over the wreckage in the hope of finding something. She was not disappointed, finding a copper shell case which was later made into a table lamp.

3787 C THE WRECKED ZEPPELIN. CUFFLEY, 3RD SEPT., 1916. ROTARY PHOTO. E.C.

Aunt Lou, Albert's sister, Louisa Martin, lived at Brick Wall farm, the smallest farm in the village. All that remained of the farm after a fire in 1900 was the 200 year old barn and this was now part of Lower Hayards. Next to the barn were two army huts and this is where Louisa first lived. Later she lived with her family in the converted barn known as "The Cabin". Aunt Lou was an inspiration to the impressionable and youthful Queenie. Seizing the untapped potential of the needs of the Cuffley folk Aunt Lou set up a much needed makeshift shop at her home. It is said that the barn and adjacent land were given to Louisa by her step grandfather, John King. But was it his to give or did he buy it for her from Albert? "The Cabin", as it was known, sold mostly dried goods and basic essentials. Molly Hughes in "A London Family Between the Wars" writes…'by sheer chance I discovered a kind of shop in Cuffley, lurking among the many outbuildings of the old farm near the station (Lower Hanyards) where you could 'obtain sugar, candles, matches, and all those things that one runs out of at critical moments'. Life could be a bit colourless in Cuffley and Queenie was drawn to the buzz of "The Cabin". Here she would help Aunt Lou at the weekend running errands and serving in the shop and café, which offered tea to visitors in the large barn room.

One particularly important person in Queenie's life was drawn to the Cabin and Lower Hanyards Farm. The Harriss family moved into Tolmers Road with their only son Cecil. The family had just returned from a trip to Canada. Cecil's father had tuberculosis and the holiday was to be a restorative rest for him. Cecil, a sickly boy with asthma and eczema, was often sent down to the farm for fresh eggs and milk. He loved the clean healthy air and the exertion of outdoor life. He took an interest in the animals on the farm and became a regular visitor. Queenie enjoyed his company and they soon became the best of friends. When Cecil's father died leaving his mother widowed and all alone, it was Albert Wombwell

In the field at the back of Brook Farm, Nell leads the horse whilst Louisa rides. Albert stands with his dog.

Cecil Harriss as a boy with Albert Wombwell

who helped her through the grief. He took the young Cecil under his wing and when his mother died whilst he was still a young man the Wombwell Family unofficially adopted him and Cecil became part of the family. Cecil never married or had a relationship. He appeared to have no interest in sex and as far as we know lived a happy but celibate life. The relationship between Queenie and Cecil was always purely platonic. In all the years that we have known them, neither my mother nor I, have witnessed anything inappropriate. When out meeting new people Queenie would always introduce him as her brother and that was the type of relationship they had. Amicably squabbling and bickering over unimportant issues, they were good companions for each other.

Aunt Lou as forward thinking as ever realised another need in her neighbours. The phone, a new and exciting technology that was catching on fast. One was installed at the farm and soon she was charging 6d for a call. Molly Hughes used the service. "I knocked at the ever open farm door, and was given a chair near to the telephone." she wrote. Louisa's niece, Olive, later went on to run the first telephone exchange in Cuffley. As a child Olive lived in a hut by the Cabin with her parents. Like Queenie she helped her aunt with this early telephone exchange in the Cabin which went on to have 40 subscribers.

Life in Cuffley could be a bit dull. The population in the hamlet had grown following the excitement of the airship to that of a small village but it was still so sparse that everyone knew each other. It was such that 'Albert Wombwell, Cuffley' was sufficient address on any post. The hamlet was divided by the haves living on the Ridge Way and the have-nots living elsewhere in Cuffley. Albert and his family placed themselves nearer the haves.

This dull existence must have bored the vibrant young Queenie but once again Aunt Lou came to the rescue. The Cabin became the ideal venue for entertaining the villagers. It is said that the 1921 Christmas dance was so popular that you had to jostle for floor space. Albert and his sister Louisa converted the Cabin to become a Village Hall complete with living accommodation. It became the hub of the village providing a meeting room for all manner of organisations and societies. The community was brought together with the lively shows put on in the Cabin during the evening when all the teas had been served and the shop was closed. Queenie was involved with her aunt in these productions. She would help with costumes and props, sewing into the early hours. The dancing club met regularly and unusually it had no social class distinction, just a good deal of fun for everyone. Queenie, like many of the Cuffley population, thoroughly enjoyed the distraction these early events brought to the village.

The Twenties

Albert Arnold Fletcher, Bert as he was known, was born on the 6th of October 1900, the youngest child to Ellen and Arnold James Fletcher. Arnold James was a professional man from Great Berkhampstead. He was a self-employed carpenter with his own account. As a young man he had moved to Cheshunt probably in search of work. Here he and Ellen went on to have four children, Constance, Charles, George and Albert Arnold (Bert). Later, when Albert Arnold was a small boy, the family moved to Little Cote Cottage, Goff's Oak. The simple village life of Goff's Oak was all that he knew.

Growing up as he did in the small village of Goff's Oak, Bert the country lad would have known Queenie. He was 11 years old when the Wombwells moved into Poyndon Pits Farm at the end of Silver Street. Queenie was 13 years old. At this time Queenie's father was Farm Bailiff for the Meux Estate. After a rudimentary education at Saint James School, young Bert went on to work as a farm assistant. The paths of the two Alberts must have crossed on a regular basis.

The position of Farm Bailiff carried a certain authority and Albert Wombwell received respect from many villagers. He worked his way onward and upward to Cuffley where in 1921 he established himself as a tenant farmer at Lower Hanyards Farm, it was here that Albert Wombwell employed young Bert as a farm assistant.

From the innocent friendship of two rural children, love blossomed between Bert and Queenie. The era saw the beginnings of a sexual revolution. Writings of Sigmund Freud advocated sex as central to the human experience. For the first time women were recognised as sexual beings with impulses and desires the same as men. Sexual liberation encouraged women to stake claim to their bodies. Before too long Queenie found herself in trouble with a baby on the way. A hasty wedding had to be arranged and it was very likely that Queenie turned to her Aunt Lou for comfort and support.

So it was that on the 29th of October 1921 a five-month pregnant Queenie walked into Hatfield Registry Office to marry her sweetheart Bert Fletcher. A simple affair, the only witnesses were brother-in-law Harry Cook and favourite Aunt, Louisa Martin. It is uncertain who was there to share their special day. We do not know if their parents attended or not.

After the initial shock of the situation Albert Wombwell must have forgiven his youngest daughter. Maybe Aunt Lou intervened to smooth things over. Albert found the couple a humble home on Lower Hanyards Farm. The adapted army huts that had once provided a home for Aunt Lou now housed the newly married Queenie.

As the 1920s rolled in Queenie found herself newly married, and before long a mother to baby son Donald Jack Albert Frank Fletcher. The little family lived happily in the draughty wooden hut on her dad's farm. A home not much more than a basic room or two, it was heated by a small cast iron stove.

With war ended Britain was reeling from its losses. Nearly one million citizens had lost their lives for their country. Those that returned faced unemployment and two decades of economic gloom. But the world still moved on. The roaring twenties had arrived and finally there was some liberation for women.

Queenie must have felt the constraint of motherhood. Her contemporaries were removing their corsets, donning slinky dresses, cutting their hair to their chins, and applying a little rouge. They were dancing the night away at the new London clubs, restaurants and dancehalls. Married life in the sleepy village of Cuffley must have been at its dullest. The wireless radio was the marvel of the 1920s. The BBC began to broadcast in 1922 and for those lucky few who could afford to own a radio it became a great companion. Queenie enjoyed her father's radio. She was entertained by the echo of crackly upper class voices from far away. From topical news and world affairs, to plays, documentaries and music, the radio educated and entertained the nation. In the evening Queenie would gather her family round for their favourites. Queenie especially enjoyed Stage Door, Variety Band Box, Workers Playtime and Dick Barton Special Agent.

Queenie settled into motherhood and in December 1926, with a four-year age gap, she gave birth to a baby girl, Pamela Jill Elizabeth Fletcher. Still living at "The Chalet", Station Road, Bert had now been promoted to Farm Bailiff. He was managing the land for Albert and helping to create a successful farm with his father-in-law.

By and by, with the help of her dad, Queenie and Bert moved into Brook Farm a stone's throw from Lower Hanyards. This rented farm provided the couple with their first real home. It gave Bert the opportunity to be his own man and work his own land. At last Queenie had a place of her own. She took to the chores of the farm as naturally as her mother, brightening it up with a lick of fresh paint here and there, and filling the farmhouse with jugs of bright flowers, fresh from her own garden.

The Life and Times of Albert Louie (Lewis) Wombwell (1868- 1935)

Queenie's father, Albert Wombwell, was a country boy born and bred. He was brought up by his father David Wombwell and mother Elizabeth Anne Abrahams. The family lived in various remote villages in Langley and Clavering. They were nestled amongst the chalky hills of Essex. In the mid-eighteen hundreds the Essex countryside was both poor and harsh. There was no resident Squire to support education amongst the poor and many of the population were illiterate. A Clergyman of the day complained of the general poverty of the area's inhabitants and the lack of support he received from anyone. "Our wealthiest residents" he said, "being only middling farmers, one half of whom are dissenters, and the land owners residing at a distance have given me but little encouragement".

Albert Wombwell

Elizabeth (Lizzie) Wombwell

Needless to say schooling in the area was sparse. Schools came and went; many were no more than Dame Schools. The majority of families did not see the benefit of encouraging their children to learn to read and write. Education took them away from paid work in the fields and required a penny or two for the privilege. Like many families of the time David and Elizabeth must have been torn. Albert was their eldest son and was required to pull his weight but it is likely that he spent some time at the local British School. This dissenters or chapel school reopened in a new building in 1879 when Albert was about eight. Whatever education he had, it was to put Albert in good stead for a fulfilling future.

Rural life did not provide many opportunities for the good people of Essex. For the majority of simple country folk the only work to be found was on the land. Like generations of Wombwells before him, by the time Albert was thirteen years old, he was working the fields alongside his father. Up at first light he would be out working in the cold country air. Albert would have needed a lot of brute strength to carry out his duties as farm work was labour intensive, seasonal and combined working the land and tending to the animals. Many of the jobs were smelly and hard, much was paid piecework so the faster one worked the more one could earn. It was a hard time.

For years Albert and his father David toiled together, working amongst the local men. Kinship grew between them all. Fathers, sons and grandsons laboured together with the sole aim of earning a few coppers and feeding their families.

In 1885, for the first time in their lives, the working men of Clavering were entitled to the vote. This was a momentous occasion and a real honour for them all. At the time Albert was only a young man of 17 years but his father, uncles and comrades would have enjoyed the privilege. There was great excitement amongst the men. It is not surprising that nearly 300 agricultural labourers attended a Tory meeting held one evening in an oil lit barn. There was lively debate between the Tory and Liberal supporters. In the polls the Liberals won. Which sparked fury and rioting in Radwinter, Newport, Stansted and Clavering in the Fox and Hounds Public House.

The Fox and Hounds, Clavering

The landlord, George Coleman, gave a full and frank account of what had happened. He reported that the pub was packed. At closing time he had to push the last of the drinkers out onto the street. An argument then broke out between two brothers. Tempers were running high after the election and a stone was thrown, breaking a pub window. The crowd then tried to force their way back into the pub. The stone throwing continued on for nearly 45 minutes. Have-a-go hero George Miller, lodging at the Fox and Hounds, tried to stop the riot but he was hit back with a stick. He reported to have seen the defendants standing outside on the road throwing mud and stones at the windows. All the windows in the taproom were smashed. The roof and walls were also damaged. The house was a complete wreck. One big stone flew through a window and almost hit a sleeping baby. The landlord's pregnant wife became distressed and had to be carried upstairs. Eventually, the village bobby, PC Frederick Faulkner, summoned reinforcements and eight men were arrested, one of whom was Charles Wombwell.

PC Faulkner's report was indecisive. He said that he could not see what was happening or who was doing what. By the time the case went to trial some of the men had alibis. Their mates swore blind that they were elsewhere... "drinking down at the Prince of Wales". Three were acquitted through lack of evidence, one of whom was Charles.

Charles was surely related to Albert, there were so many Wombwells in the area. He may have been an uncle or cousin. In such a small community as this, it is possible that David and even Albert were drinking in the Fox and Hounds on that very night.

Albert's life continued much as it had. His routine followed the same path. Up early and out in the fields working until the light faded. Until, sadly, his mother died in 1887 before his youngest brother, baby Frank was one year old. Albert, now a young man of 22 years, was living with his father and eight siblings. He supported his father as best he could up to the point when his father David took a new wife. The situation at home must have changed suddenly. David's new bride, Emma Barleyman, moved in. She brought her elderly father William and thirteen year old half-brother Joseph to live in the house. Living conditions must have been seriously cramped in the little tithe cottage.

Work on the Essex land was becoming more difficult to find. Harvests were increasingly poor following atrocious weather from 1875 onward and the whole country was gripped by an agricultural depression. Cheaper imported wheat was flooding into the English ports, and landowners were finding it increasingly difficult to sustain a living. 60% of a families wage was needed for food alone. They needed every penny, there was no saving for a rainy day! These were hard times for agricultural workers and pushed many young men out of Essex in search of alternative work. Whether it was because of this lack of work, or the situation at home, we do not know but Albert made the decision to leave and look for work elsewhere. Little sister Louisa followed him and together they made their way down to western Essex and the Hertfordshire border.

Albert's sweetheart from Chishall, Elizabeth (Lizzie) Rebecca Watts, followed him and in 1890 they married somewhere in Hertfordshire. From a similar working-class background to the Wombwells, Elizabeth's father James and her brothers all worked as agricultural labourers in Essex. Like the Wombwell family the Watts family also had ties with the Methodist Church and their name can be found on the roll at Chrishall. Ten years on and James and Hannah Watts had followed their daughter and were living at 17 Cross Road, Waltham Cross. James was labouring in a market garden and Hannah had her own account, working from home as a dressmaker and running repairs for people.

By 1891 Albert and Lizzie were living in Clifton

Cottage, Eleanor Road, Cheshunt, with their 18 month old baby daughter, Nellie. Albert's 16 year old sister Louisa was living with them and working as a general servant. Head of the family, Albert, was employed as a powder labourer in the Royal Gunpowder Mill at Waltham Abbey. The work was physically hard and extremely dangerous. Wages were little better than an agricultural labourer and living costs were higher in the town. Albert must have found life tough at the time.

Explosives had been made on the site in Waltham Abbey since the early seventeenth century. Gunpowder made on the site had been used in combat as early as the battle of Waterloo and later in the Crimean and Boer wars. During times of peace the explosives were used for construction, mining, quarrying, tunnelling and railway building. It was a busy factory employing many people from the area to do this dangerous work. Accidental explosions were commonplace even though steps were taken to minimise them.

In 1865 the War Office Chemist, Sir Frederick Abel, developed and patented gun cotton. Later in 1889 he went on to assist in the development of the propellant Cordite. This paste-like product incorporated two unstable explosives into a safer dough. Although Cordite was relatively safe to handle it was still dangerous to work with and in 1890 there was yet another explosion at the Royal Gun Powder Mill killing two men.

Safety was an ongoing issue, and Albert would have witnessed many explosions in his time at the Mill. The Government and bosses reviewed safety for its workers regularly. In 1870 the assistant superintendent produced his "Handbook for Gunpowder Production at Waltham Abbey". Rules from this book were hung in every household and each week the foremen were instructed to reinforce the rules to the men. Working conditions were still extremely dangerous. The men worked surrounded by volatile explosives. It took merely a particle of sand or grit to ignite the gunpowder. Explosions could be massive. They rippled through the spaced outbuildings and rocked the whole of Waltham Abbey, blowing out windows and causing damage to buildings and sometimes homes. Injuries were commonplace and fatalities inevitable. One such accident must have been witnessed by Albert and took place on May 7th 1894.

The Gunpowder Mill report reads: *'At 4.08 p.m., again on the South or Quinton Hill Site, the Nitro-glycerine Washing House blew up, followed seconds later by the Nitro-glycerine Store 61 yards away. Both buildings were surrounded by high brick-revetted traverses. The total quantity of nitro-glycerine which explodes was in the region of 3,700 lbs. the four men who were killed were the 22 year old chemist-in-charge, William Bennie, William Ingram, the foreman plumber, George Sucking, the charge man and George Frost, a workman. 20 other people were injured by flying debris, but none seriously.'*

The Waltham Abbey Church Monthly reported that the funeral took place on the 11th May and went on to record:

"The escape of men and lads who were at work close to the scene of the fatal disaster was simply miraculous, and although many were injured by the falling debris, none were greatly harmed. Much praise is due to the heroic men who, in the face of imminent peril, went into danger houses, and under God's good providence, secured the preservation of the town from further damage and terror. The men who met with this violent death, we are glad to record, were earnest, consistent Christian workers and ready for that sudden summons from the captain of their salvation."

Albert was given a bible with the words:

Albert Wombwell

Waltham Cross

In remembrance of our dear friends

Mr W Bennie

Mr W Ingram

Mr G Suckling

Mr G Frost

May 7th 1894

Having contacted the Royal Gunpowder Mill, I have discovered that they have no record of Albert Wombwell, but this I was told is not unusual. They were most interested in the Bible and its inscription as it is the only one that they know of to date. It is interesting to consider that Albert was involved in a way which entitled him to a commemorative Bible. Was he injured? If so, it was never recorded by the Mill. Or was he one of the brave men who risked their lives to save their colleagues?

Measures to improve safety were ongoing at the Mill. In 1881 electric light was installed improving working conditions and safety. Ten years later, when Albert was working in the factory, the telephone was put in. Then in 1894 the Sandhurst Hospital was built within the grounds. It was cleverly positioned so that casualties could be brought in via the complex network of canals and waterways used by the Royal Gunpowder Mill to transport goods.

In 1898 when Queenie was born, her father Albert was still working at the Royal Gunpowder Mill. The address on the birth certificate was simply, The Cedars. This impressive manor house stood within the park and was part of the Meux Estate at Theobalds. The Meux family lived in Theobalds House, built by George Prescott a year after he had The Cedars and two other manor houses built on the estate. All accommodation on the estate was primarily for its workers and it is uncertain whether Albert was doing additional work for the Meux family at the time.

In her early days Lady Meux, a former banjo playing barmaid, was a scandalous lady and popular with the gents. Her parties were notorious. She entertained Edward VII and Winston Churchill in the room above Temple Bar. She had brought it from London by horse and cart and had it rebuilt brick by brick to make an impressive entrance to her elaborate home at Theobalds. Lady Meux made many alterations and modernisations to Theobalds House. She had an indoor roller skating rink and a swimming pool built. In the grounds she had her own menagerie of exotic animals. Her wild parties went on into the early hours and it is said that she often invited tradesmen of humble birth. Albert knew Lady Meux but we do not know how well!

Sometime before 1905 Albert moved his family out of Cheshunt to Beaumont. The work at the Royal Gunpowder Mill was no easier and he returned to his roots, the land, finding work in this country hamlet. His sister-in-law and her husband Jonah lived within the Manor at Beaumont. Jonah was employed on the Grant Estate and it may have been this link that orchestrated Albert's change in direction. It was also around this time that his older daughter Nellie, now in her teens, began to work for Mrs. Grant as a Lady's Maid. This is where she met the love of her life, Harry Cook. He drove the car for the Grant family, until he was called up to serve in the First World War.

Moving from rented house to rented house Albert worked many of the farms in the Hamlet of Beaumont, one of which, Beaumont Manor Farm, was a fine double-fronted house built in the eighteenth century. His address changed over the years but the work most likely remained the same. Although it was hard and dirty it required skill and knowledge. Albert proved himself to be a skilful farmer. He was moved from farm to farm to improve productivity and efficiency. The Edwardian era was "the Golden Age" for farmers, with steam engines beginning to ease the load for the wealthy. There were machines that could do the work of five horses and a threshing machine that could do work that took a team of men two days in just two hours. The life of a farmer was slowly beginning to change.

Eventually Albert's reputation took him to Goff's Oak where, in 1911, still a young man in his early-thirties, he was employed by The Meux Estate as a Farm Bailiff. Lady Meux had died a year earlier, in 1910. During the Boer War she took a keen interest in the battle of Ladysmith and out of her own pocket she had six naval guns made. The War Office declined her gift so she had them shipped directly to the Naval Officers in South Africa. On his return home Sir Hedworth Lambton called in on Lady Meux to thank her personally for her generous contribution. Lady Meux was so taken with the Officer that on her death she left him Theobalds Park estate with the one condition that he changed his name to Meux. Which he duly did!

Along with the post of Farm Bailiff came a farm and Albert moved his family into Poyndon Pits at Goff's Oak. The position was one of high regard. Albert was agent to the landowner. His tasks would have included managing staff and collecting rents. He may also have been responsible for enforcing evictions and checking on poachers and rustlers. The job was important to the Estate and a reliable, responsible person was essential for the role. Many of the nouveau riche employed a bailiff to tend their farms. It may have been that Sir Hedworth Meux fell into this category. His background was with the military, not the land and he would have needed a reliable manager to look after his estate.

Albert proved himself through and through. A respected figure in the village and beyond, he walked around the farms and estates dressed in a lounge suit, standard wear for working men, and a heavily starched shirt with a turned down collar and knot tie. He sported a bristly moustache that got bushier with age. Which in later life he slurped his soup through. His greying hair was cut short and his head was covered when he was out in public. It was possible to tell a person's class by their hat. Everyone wore one. Gentlemen wore top hats, the working classes wore cloth caps but the middle classes could be spotted by their stiff bowler or smart Homburg. Pictures show Albert wearing a straw boater around the farm in the summer months and a bowler hat when out on business. His aspiration was certainly one of middle class and he had a mind to improve his lot.

From the successes of Goff's Oak Albert was able to move to Cuffley where, as a gentleman in his early forties, he began as a tenant farmer at Upper Hayards and later gentleman farmer at Lower Hanyards farm.

'PHONE: POTTERS BAR 104 x 5.

A. L. Wombwell.

LOWER HANYARDS FARM,
CUFFLEY,
HERTS.

During the years of agricultural depression many tenant farmers were offered cheap rents and some were even offered to purchase the freeholds of their farms. The Theobald Estate was slowly being dissolved. The contents of the house started to be sold off along with the farms. Cedars Park was gifted to Cheshunt after the First World War and eventually the house was sold by Sir Hedworth Meux's widow in 1929. Over the years Albert acquired a sizeable chunk of Cuffley's farm land. Whether he owned it or sub-let the farm house is unclear. Hill Farm where the Gray family lived and Albert farmed was opposite the Plough public house. It was merged with Hanyards Farm to the north and eventually Lower Cuffley Farm to the south, or as it became known, Lower Hanyards. I believe Albert must have had a hand in this merger as it happened shortly after his arrival in Cuffley.

Lower Hanyards was a charming farm with its cosy cottage and attractive black boarded barn. It stood back from the road on the left of the station behind a large duck pond. Much of the 160 acres of land were situated on the opposite side of the road. Albert and Lizzie made it their home. Lizzie created fragrant beds of colourful flowers on either side of the footpath up to the farmhouse door. She tended the small orchard behind the house and became famous for her fruit wines and tonics. In the whitewashed dairy she made her own butter and creams. Lizzie enjoyed her home crafts and diligently worked to create a warm and welcoming home for her husband and growing girls.

The small community of Cuffley never boasted a police station. Instead it kept law and order through the work of special constables who were entrusted to keep their own communities safe. These citizens were appointed by the local authorities on a part-time basis and paid "reasonable" expenses. Albert, an upstanding and respected resident of Cuffley, volunteered for the part-time post. Special constables were granted the same powers, authorities, advantages and immunities as full-time officers. They could be issued with "articles" or weapons whenever the authorities considered it necessary. At the beginning of the Great War specials were organised into a body of men, with the primary function to prevent German infiltration of the Nations water supply. On the night of September 3rd 1916, specials across the Country were informed of a likely raid and ordered to be on high alert for an air attack. It was Albert Wombwell who was first on the scene when the infamous airship crashed amidst a plume of flames and smoke onto his land, the field behind Hill Farm. The next day when crowds of sightseers flocked from the station to get a glimpse of the crash they forced their way through his cornfield and stack yard. Albert had to mount his horse and control the unruly mob on horseback.

A couple of years after the war, Albert attended the home of writer Molly Hughes. One evening she was startled by an intruder who was prowling around the garden seeking entry into the house. Her son ran off to alert the constable and Molly went next door to her neighbour, Mr. King, the builder. By the time Albert arrived Mr. King had everything under control. He had apprehended the culprit, ready for the authorities to take over. Such excitement had given them an appetite so Molly set to and fried sausages for them all.

In the twenties only a small minority of people had telephones. Albert was one of the first in Cuffley with the number 4. He was truly upwardly mobile. In 1914 only 20% of the population were deemed middle-class. To be middle-class you had to have at least one servant. Albert had been brought up with the Victorian attitude that only you were to blame for your poverty. To become successful took sheer hard work and thrift. From the working-class roots of agriculture Albert through his own diligence and probably a degree of good luck gave the outside world the persona of middle class. He drove one of the few cars in Cuffley and dressed in a middle-class fashion. He moved in their circles and joined their associations.

For many years Albert was a Freemason. Freemasonry originated in the early 16th century when working masons gathered together to protect their trade. Modern Freemasonry of the 1700s became highly fashionable. There was a shift from including working masons only to include 'speculative' Freemasons such as aristocrats and artists. By 1717 the first Grand Lodge was opened in London and fast became a 'Gentlemen's club'. This fraternal organisation of men only was set up to promote religious and political tolerance, through charitable works. This brotherhood of like-minded individuals had to believe in God, act with morality and abide by the law of the land. Self-knowledge was taught through a series of ritual dramas which had to be learnt and performed to the Lodge members. The Lodge had to swear allegiance to a Grand Lodge and be chartered by them. Each lodge had its own secret password, handshake and sign by which to recognise its members. The Freemasons' icon of a square and compass surrounding the letter G is highly symbolic. God is represented by the G, the square for square actions with all men and the compass to create boundaries in life. The principles of brotherly love, relief and truth are still relevant in today's Masons. Albert involved himself fully. He would meet regularly at the Enfield Lodge, number 1237 where he was a steward. His name is found in the Mimmine Lodge 4932 under Founders and First officers. This lodge was consecrated in 1927 and it is highly possible that Albert had a part to play in it. He occasionally went to Cheshunt Great House, where the Gresham Lodge and later, its daughter Lodge, the Gaddesden, met. Albert attended all the Freemason events with great enthusiasm. On ladies' nights a young vivacious Queenie would be invited to join him. She loved the opportunity to dress up in a glamorous gown and socialise with the haves in a beautiful ballroom for the evening. She could leave the humdrum of domesticity and step into a world of pomp and ceremony where she could apply her impeccable manners and act like a lady for a few hours. She loved it!

Albert took his charitable responsibilities seriously. He donated money to the Methodist Chapel in Goff's Oak on more than one occasion and volunteered his services to the Barnet Union Board of Guardians. He joined the committee and was bestowed the honour of being able to visit the Wellhouse Hospital at any reasonable hour.

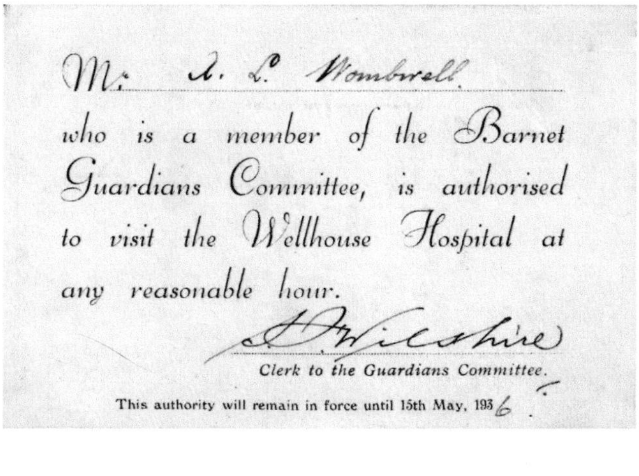
Mr. A. L. Wombwell
who is a member of the Barnet Guardians Committee, is authorised to visit the Wellhouse Hospital at any reasonable hour.

A. Wilshire
Clerk to the Guardians Committee.

This authority will remain in force until 15th May, 1936.

In 1838 the Wellhouse Hospital started life as the Barnet Union workhouse when it was open to 200 inmates. In 1886 an infirmary block was added to the east wing and another to the south in 1901. In 1915 the Guardians began work on a new Hospital. The adjacent Mansion of Pickering Lodge, with its lovely gardens and tennis lawn, was acquired to provide the hospital with a nurses' home. As the Guardians began work war broke out and it was impossible to get the labour required to finish the job. The Army Council stepped in and took over. The project was completed in 1916 when it became Barnet War Hospital.

During its two years of service as a War Hospital, almost 6,000 wounded and sick soldiers were treated. With war over, in October 1919, the Army Council handed the hospital back to the Guardians. Generously the Army Council allowed the Guardians to purchase all the equipment from the War Office for 10% less than its value four years previous. The Guardians renamed the hospital Wellhouse Hospital in honour of the Physic Well that was once on the site. The famous diarist Samuel Pepys visited the well twice to take the waters. The therapeutic qualities of the mineral spring were well known across the country.

The Wellhouse had room for 204 beds in six wards, on three floors. This included a thoroughly modern maternity and labour ward with nine beds. The hospital had been designed with the view to extend its wards in the future to house 600 beds. The wards were washed in a soft shade of pale green and each had a comfortably furnished day room for recovering patients to use. South facing wards led out onto a sunny veranda were patients could sit and look out across the open countryside. All the medical facilities were the latest and patient comfort was paramount. The kitchens were powered by steam and boasted hot plates. It was the most up-to-date of hospitals.

The Wellhouse Hospital was officially opened in 1920 by Lord Hampden, the Lord Lieutenant of Hertfordshire. Controversially the Guardians put forward the idea of making spare beds available to private patients. This did not sit well with the hospitals work house roots in helping the poor. But in 1922 the Hospital set aside a ward for paying patients charging them a minimum of 2 guineas a week for their stay and treatment. In 1930, with the abolishment of the Poor Law Unions and the Board of Guardians, Hertfordshire County Council took over the administered control of the hospital and Albert and his colleagues were out of a job.

Albert, a jovial, portly gentleman in his sixties, sporting a bushy moustache and a welcoming smile, had many friends and acquaintances. Albert drove one of the few cars in Cuffley. He was one of a very small minority to own a car in the country. Even in 1940, five years after his death, only 1 in 10 people owned their own car. When Albert first started to drive no formal instruction was required. It was not until 1934 that the driving test came into being for new drivers. Albert gained his licence as a matter of course through "Granddad's Rights" and he proudly carried it in his wallet along with his AA Membership card.

In 1923 Albert and a business partner "Nielson" bought Northaw Great Wood. No mention is made of Nielson on the Sale Agreement; he must have had his reasons for this. It is possible that it was Nielson's money and Albert's knowledge that made the deal. We may never know! But in April 1923 John Henry Mohun Ashfordby Trenchard Esq. sold Northaw Great Wood for the princely sum of £8,500 to Albert Lewis Wombwell of Lower Hanyards Farm. And so it was that Albert became part owner of Northaw Great Wood.

Recorded as early as Norman times, the 500 acre trackless site of rough pasture belonged to the Abbey of St Albans for hundreds of years. The Abbey leased it to various nobles until the dissolution of the Monasteries when it became the property of the Crown. Henry VIII and Elizabeth I granted it to the nobility. Extending almost seven miles it provided the aristocracy with the perfect location for hunting and sport. During much of the 16th century the wooded common was used by the locals to graze their animals and pollard the hornbeam for fuel.

Following the Enclosure Act in 1806 the common of Northaw became privately owned for the first time and the land was managed for profit. Many of the overgrown hornbeams were cut down in 1811 and replaced with Scots pine and oak. Eventually much of the wood was sold, making way for the Ridgeway toll road to be built. One lot was sold to William Bush and became the site of Cuffley Camp an outdoor centre for youngsters, but the largest lot remained with the Nyn Manor Estate and was sold to Patrick Thompson who later mortgaged the wood to Dr Trenchard. The wood then passed to him on Thompson's death and it was from him that Albert and his partner Nielson bought this broadleaved woodland.

By the time Albert got his hands on the Northaw Great Wood the oaks were mature and ready for felling. Between the pair of them, Albert and Nielson must have made a tidy sum from the timber. Towards the end of Albert's life the wood was depleted of nearly all its mighty oaks and its value greatly reduced. Albert still had the Great Wood in his possession when he died but no mention is made of it in his will. Possibly he had put wheels in motion when he sold Lower Hanyards farm knowing that the proceeds would return to Nielson!? The Great Wood was sold to Hertfordshire County Council, as a public open space, in 1937 two years after Albert's death. Today the wood is leased to Hatfield Rural Council who manages it for the enjoyment of people near and far. It is a popular destination for families and amateur naturalists. The site is of Special Scientific Interest and receives many visitors and much interest.

Albert had established himself as a confident and upstanding farmer and businessman. In the phone book he was listed as A L Wombwell, Farmer. From 1925 up until his death he was a councillor for Northaw. He was on the Housing Urgency Subcommittee, the Fire Brigade and Ambulance Committee and the Plans and Town Planning Committee. For ten years he served the Council with diligence and commitment.

Probably using the money raised through his venture with Nielson and the influential contacts he had made. Albert was able to acquire a plot of land and an acquaintance Mr. Cooper drew up the plans for a pair of semi-detached houses in Tolmers Road. In 1900 only 10% of the population owned their own home. In 1913 "The Cuffley Tenants Ltd" began building in Cuffley. Whether Albert was involved with this enterprise we may never know but they did build a cul-de-sac of eight two-storey semi-detached cottages off Tolmers Road. Towards the end of the 1930s the number of people in their own homes had still only risen to 27%. The majority of families lived in rented homes. Albert's houses were, reputedly, built from old bricks reclaimed from Hatfield Brewery. They had a front room, a main room and a kitchen out the back. A steep staircase rose to a small landing and two bedrooms with a fashionable bathroom accessed via both. The story goes that one of the newly built semis was for Nell and the other for Queenie. When the houses were finally finished Nell and Harry moved into number 24. Queenie was, by this time, settled into Brook Farm and never got her house. It is said that Nell and Harry paid a nominal rent and of course Albert Wombwell helped his daughter Queenie and her husband Bert on the farm but Queenie was always a little sore that she did not get her little house in Tolmers Road. The second semi was rented out to Alice Dellow, Albert's sister. Albert had bigger ideas and he had plans drawn up for houses to be built in Waltham Cross or Waltham Abbey. But there is no evidence that these were ever built before his death.

Lizzie, Albert's dependable companion and loving wife, was a sick woman. She died in 1933 after a prolonged illness. For years she was bedridden, a frail and sickly woman often seen, wrapped in lace shawls, sitting up in bed. Sadly Lizzie suffered a brain tumour which left her weak and very ill. Eventually she was admitted to the Wellhouse Hospital where she died.

Following his loss Albert decided to sell up and have one last adventure. He disposed of all his assets, put his furniture into storage with Queenie at Brook farm, and prepared to travel to Canada to stay with his younger brother Charlie. On the 25th June 1934 he travelled alone to Canada for a two-month trip of a lifetime. It was a great success. Albert loved the wide open expanse of Charlie's property. He helped on the land and enjoyed his brother's company for eight long lazy weeks of holiday.

Albert Wombwell

Albert and Charlie Wombwell in Canada

Upon his return Albert moved in with Queenie and Bert, where he had self-contained accommodation within the main house. Surrounded by his familiar belongings he created a cosy home for himself. He brought with him a crystal radio, which he set up in the warm farmhouse kitchen where the family would cosy up and listen to the news and light entertainment of the day. A jolly Granddad to Jack, Pam and Nellie's son, little Albert, he quickly settled into life on Brook Farm. But this comfy life with his daughter and her family was short-lived. In December 1935 Albert was taken ill. The doctor was called to his little room upstairs but sadly Albert suffered a heart attack and died at home aged 67. His larger than life presence left a gaping hole in the lives of Nell and Queenie.

Lower Hanyards farm had been demolished sometime in the 1930s to make way for Tolmers Gardens and the Cuffley Hotel, which was built on the site of the farm pond where Jack and Pam had played. Much had changed in the years of the Wombwell's residence and much of this had been down to Albert and his sister Louisa's insight. The village had certainly grown and prospered since the early days of Albert's arrival and Albert had grown and prospered with it. He died a wealthy man!

In his will Albert left one hundred pounds to each of his surviving siblings. A probable total of £600 or £700. £100 was donated to the Methodist Chapel and £100 went to Mrs Cooper, the wife of one of the Executors to the will. Albert also left £100 to an unknown Enfield lady, a Miss Corbett, who it appears was mentioned in his previous will. Not so surprising from this ladies' man! The bulk of the estate was to be sold and divided equally between his three grandchildren and put in trust until they reached the age of 25. When the business was completed a generous £1,000 was raised for each of them. The estimated total value of his estate was a staggering £4,000. Quite a sum for the day, when you consider that a new built semi in the mid-1930s could be bought for approximately £400. Queenie was quite put out. She had hoped for something and received nothing. It was a blow that she never quite forgave him for.

Looking at it from the outside, one can see the legacy Albert left his youngest daughter. He was an impressive father and a positive role model. He came into the world with nothing and left having succeeded as a businessman, and proved himself to be a generous man. Queenie may have been hurt at the time but consciously or unconsciously she was to go on to accumulate her own wealth and become her own generous person.

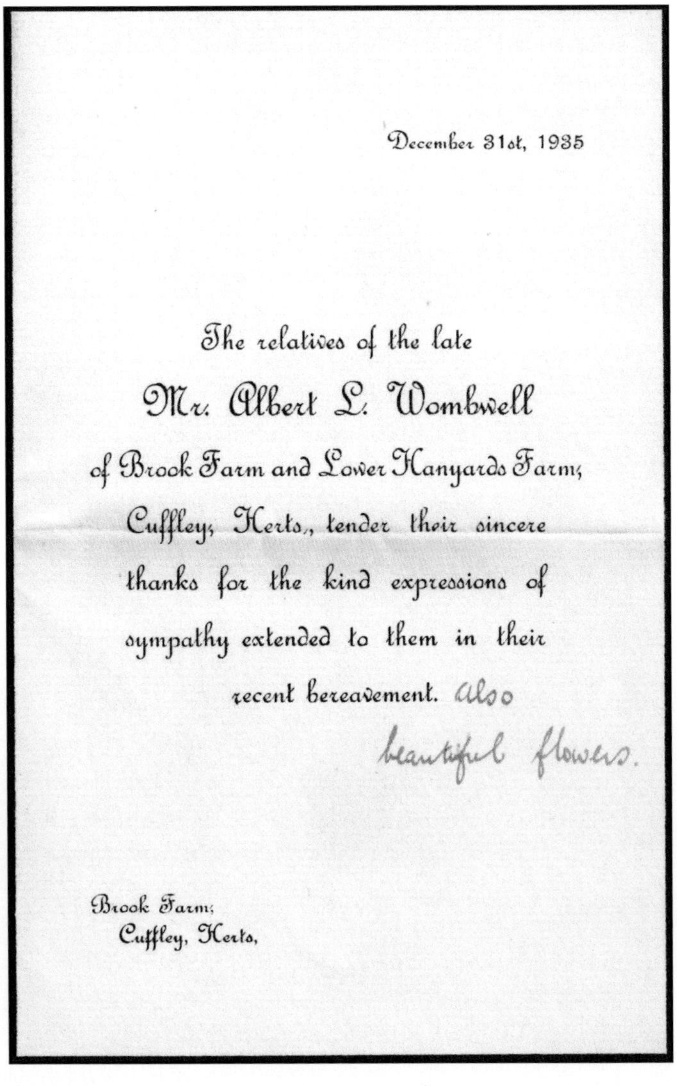

December 31st, 1935

The relatives of the late

Mr. Albert L. Wombwell

of Brook Farm and Lower Hanyards Farm, Cuffley, Herts., tender their sincere thanks for the kind expressions of sympathy extended to them in their recent bereavement. Also beautiful flowers.

Brook Farm,
Cuffley, Herts.

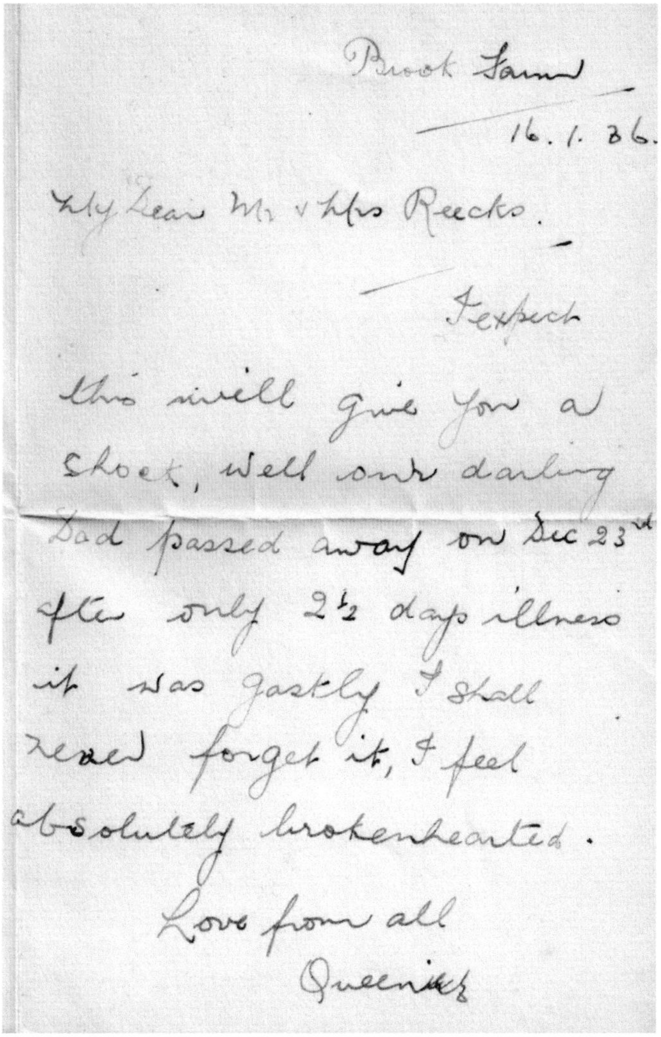
Brook Farm

16.1.36.

My dear Mr & Mrs Reecks.

I expect this will give you a shock, well our darling Dad passed away on Dec 23rd after only 2½ days illness it was gastly I shall never forget it, I feel absolutely brokenhearted.

Love from all

Queenie

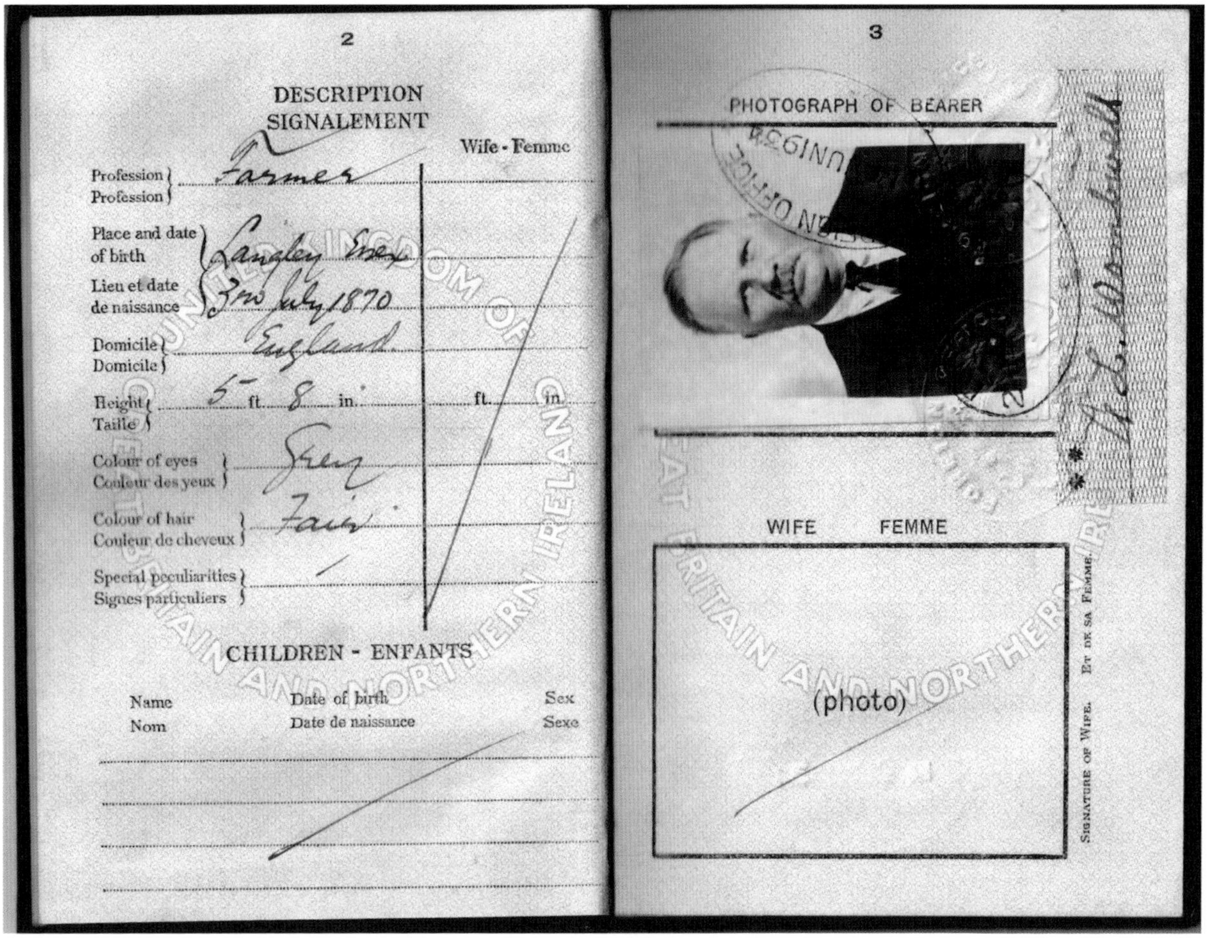
2

DESCRIPTION
SIGNALEMENT

		Wife - Femme
Profession / Profession	Farmer	
Place and date of birth / Lieu et date de naissance	Langley Essex 3rd July 1870	
Domicile / Domicile	England	
Height / Taille	5 ft. 8 in.	ft. in.
Colour of eyes / Couleur des yeux	Grey	
Colour of hair / Couleur de cheveux	Fair	
Special peculiarities / Signes particuliers	—	

CHILDREN - ENFANTS

Name / Nom	Date of birth / Date de naissance	Sex / Sexe

3

PHOTOGRAPH OF BEARER

A. L. Wombwell

WIFE FEMME

(photo)

Signature of Wife. Et de sa Femme.

THE VARIETY ARTISTES' FEDERATION

INCORPORATING

Actors, Revue Artistes, Concert Artistes, Circus Artistes and Entertainers of all descriptions.

Founded Feb. 18th, 1906. Registered Trade Union, No. 1378.

Affiliated to the World's League of Artistes (embracing Austria, Belgium, Checko-Slovakia, France, Germany, Great Britain, Hungary and Russia).

Telegrams and Cables— "ARTIFEDERA, LESQUARE, LONDON."
Telephone— Temple Bar 6950.

OFFICE HOURS
11 to 4
SATURDAY, 11 to 1

18, Charing Cross Road,
London, W.C.2.

17th January, 1936.

Mrs.Queenie Fletcher,
Brook Farm,
Cuffley,Herts.

My dear,

Your letter of the 13th inst. which we received at home yesterday evening, believe me, was a very sad shock to Mrs.Drewe and myself, and I hardly know how to express ourselves in respect of the Passing of our esteemed friend, your respected Father, and can only add that you have one consolation, namely, that he has left behind a memory which I can best describe as that of a respected English Gentleman, with a kindly Christian disposition.

Would you care to come along and see us at the Flat one Sunday afternoon? Our 'Phone number after office hours is Maida Vale 8443.

With all kind wishes.

Faithfully yours,

A. V. Drewe

No Comms. recognised as Official unless signed by the Hon. Chairman or General Secretary.

73552 1/10/35

ARNOLD JAMES FLETCHER married ELLEN

Constance Charles George **ALBERT**

QUEENIE WOMBWELL married **ALBERT** (BERT) ARNOLD **FLETCHER**

DONALD **JACK** ALBERT FRANK **PAMELA** JILL ELIZABETH

Queenie, a Wife and Mother

Queenie doted on her children but she was a busy Mum and a hard-working wife. Her life was kept busy and full with the duties of the farm and her cash side-lines. More often than not she had campers or circus guests staying on the farm. The children were often left to their own devices. Queenie gave them the liberty to explore the relaxed informality of Cuffley country living, much like the freedoms she had enjoyed as a child. Jack and Pam spent their days on the farm out in the fresh air, building their bodies and their imaginations through the rough and tumble of the great outdoors.

Pamela and Jack enjoying the Chuck Wagon

Bert was a great Dad, gentle and doting. He helped Jack and Pam build a chuckwagon with some old wood and a pair of rusting wheels. The children had endless fun hauling it around the farm and setting up camp with all manner of disused pots and pans that they found around the farm.

When World War II threatened, Bert built a sturdy dugout for his family. Using a natural hollow created in the bank of a now dry river, he was able to build a strong shelter with old railway sleepers to protect them. Early one evening young Jack was playing under the old oak tree on the farm when there was a threat from the sky. He jumped to his feet in terror. Scared of what might happen, he threw himself around the corner to the dugout. In his blind panic he slipped on the wet grass and landed face first in a smelly cow-pat! Poor Jack, Pam never did forget that unfortunate incident and often teased him about it. Like most families there was a bit of sibling rivalry and Jack got his own back by tormenting the cockerel which, on seeing Pam return home from school each day, would go for her aggressively. She would have to stand at the big farm gate and holler and cry for her Dad to come to the rescue. Until one day she realised that the old cockerel was not so bright. She learnt that if she turned her school hat back to front the tormenting beast did not recognise her and let her pass unmolested. Most of the animals on the farm were as friendly as could be. Pam had one hen in particular which was as docile as they come. Pam could wrap the bird up in a dolly's blanket, tuck her into the doll's pram and take her for long walks around the farmyard.

Pamela

Little Jack Chops Wood !

Pam had a little Shetland pony called Ruby which she loved to ride. To commemorate the coronation of George VI, the villagers organised a parade to Northaw. Queenie loved to dress the children up. She had no problem in finding a circus outfit for young Jack to wear and got to work in making something for Pam. The two entered the parade with Ruby adorned in ribbons and Jack wearing a feather in his hat. Pam rode on the little pony's back and Jack walked beside her leading the way to Northaw, and proudly they won a prize.

Pamela rides as Jack leads Ruby to Northaw

Bert was a kind and generous man. He was an intelligent, reflective soul looking for a simple, quiet life. Queenie was quite different. She was an extrovert, always seeking excitement and looking out for something more. Their lives may or may not have been lit with passion but the household was always harmonious. There was a mutual understanding of companionship and loyalty between the two of them.

Bert was a true countryman, out on the land through all weathers. He had a good reputation for animal husbandry and was well respected amongst his peers, and it gained him a photo in "The Farmers Weekly" of November 29th 1935. The caption read…"This cow owned by Mr A Fletcher, Brook Dairy Farm, Cuffley, Hertfordshire, gave birth to triplets at her second calving". A proud day for all the family.

Albert loved all his animals. During spring orphaned or sickly lambs would be brought into the kitchen. The open fire, with its seats on either side of the big hearth, would be stoked to a warm glow. Bert would tuck the little creature into a piece of old sack and lay it in a box close to the fire to warm up. Queenie would tempt it with a bottle every hour or so until it was strong enough to join the flock. Bert would cover the lamb with a fleece from a less fortunate beast and introduce it to a grieving ewe as her own. Bert would keep a watchful eye as

November 29, 1935

Farmers Weekly

MARKETING SC

TOMATOES: Union Expect of Chan

THE National Farmers' Union has decided to prep scheme for tomatoes.

Preliminary details have been discussed by the Fruit, Committee since the withdrawal of the suggested Fruit M

The Glasshouse Produce s mitted the original proposa of the market was to a cer supply of tomatoes from t

Accordingly a conference Channel Island growers, co-operate in the workin

THE FARMERS WEEKL will insist on this co-ope success of the scheme. T proceed with the scheme passed in the Channel Islar

It is understood that th as far as they would commi were willing to submit to t

When the draft scheme further conference with th will be held. In the m Advisory another a

This cow, owned by Mr. A. Fletcher, Brook Dairy Farm, Cuffley, Hertfordshire, gave birth to triplets at her second calving.

WASTAGE IN PIG LITTERS

Recording Scheme Shows Loss of 23 per cent

Statistics which are expected to be of value in solving the problems of breeder are being obtained in Recording Scheme intro- Pig Industry

mind the losses that occur between birth and weaning, litters in which eight or fewer pigs are born are economic, as the average number in such cases is bound to

Bert Fletcher's triplet calves

slowly, slowly the mother accepted her surrogate.

Bert Fletcher

Shooting was Bert's favourite pastime. He spent as much time as he could out with his friends, Mr Cheshire, the local butcher, and Dallyn, the Welsh farmer from Northaw. Bert's dogs were his pride. A patient teacher, his gun dogs were always perfectly disciplined and obedient to the last. Rover, a Labrador mongrel, was one of his best loved dogs. When he was sick Bert fed him on best steak from Cheshire's the Butchers. Nothing was too good for his animals. Bert was rewarded with their loyalty and a dog was never far from his heel.

Bert Fletcher with his dogs at Goff's Oak House

Along with his gun dogs and terrier for retrieving rabbits, Bert had his ferrets. These smelly creatures were often smuggled into the house inside his jacket pocket, and he would play with them and torment his little daughter Pam amidst fake screams of terror. It was the pink eyes that she did not like. As she squealed for him to take them away, Queenie quietly looked on with an amused glint in her eye and a wry smile on her lips.

Young Jack helping out on the farm

Queenie's creativity filled her spare time. She spent hours tending to her flowers, bringing them into the drab farmhouse to create colour and brightness where there had been none. Food was always important and like her Mother, Queenie would preserve the excesses of the seasons. The big boiling pans would be found ready for the jams and chutneys which were laboriously made and stored in jars for the future.

Jack Fletcher, dressed up for a Masonic fancy dress party

Photo by A. E. Hunt, Potters Bar.

One of the charming scenes in the Display given by pupils of Miss E. Jolley.

Pamela standing second left

1935...

A talented seamstress, Queenie enjoyed making soft furnishings for the home and clothes for herself and the children. She still helped Aunt Lou when she could with the village productions. Queenie loved to get involved. She took delight in any excuse to dress the children up for parties and events. Her Father Albert was a respected Mason and she often accompanied him with the children to fancy dress parties held in top London Hotels. Much to the delight of Queenie the children often won a prize. The photo of four year old Jack dressed as Jackie Coogan, a child star of the day, was blown up to poster size and proudly hung on the kitchen wall for as long as I can remember. Pam recalls the rabbit outfits. Queenie used an old white blanket to make them both fluffy jump suits with big floppy ears. The two of them bounded around the ballroom of the Grosvenor Hotel on all fours and came home with another first prize.

When Pam was born Queenie was delighted. At last she had a "little doll" to dress and fuss over. It seems that as soon as Pam could walk she was enrolled into Miss E. Jolley's dance classes. Each week the boys and girls met at the Cabin hall for instruction in the performing arts. Now Queenie had a project. There were costumes to be designed and made. With her make do and mend attitude she acquired material from old frocks and linens and turned them into masterpieces fit for the stage. Pam remembers her Mother as she warmed the metal curling tongs on the gas ring in the farmhouse kitchen prior to a performance. Pam endured "hours" of preening and pulling as Queenie teased her hair into a mass of Shirley Temple ringlets.
Queenie was full of pride to see her daughter's name appear in the Potters Bar Gazette on Friday 3rd May

CHARMING ENTERTAINMENT AT CUFFLEY
Young Dancers First Annual Display...
A charming and unusual entertainment was given at the Cabin Hall, Cuffley on Saturday in aid of Dr Barnardo's Homes, being the first annual display by pupils of Miss E. Jolly's School of Dancing.
Pam is mentioned more than once...
Pamela Fletcher received hearty applause as a soubrette and as an encore to her song and dance "Over my Shoulder"; she gave "The Guinea Pig".
A very pretty ballet "Balloons" was performed by B Lucas, B Hands and P Fletcher the last named taking the solo part.
.... and Pamela Fletcher delighted the audience with her performance of a difficult classical solo dance.

Queenie would have been so proud of her talented daughter. However it was noted further in the paper under the heading DODGING THE COLLECTION that only £2.8s was raised for Dr Barnardo's Homes. It was written that during the interval collection, the mothers flocked to the dressing room instead of dipping into their pockets! I wonder where Queenie stood in all this.

As Queenie raised her children the face of Cuffley was slowly changing and the population was growing. During the 1930's Aunt Lou attempted to sell the Cabin but a suitable buyer could not be found. From the success of her makeshift business Louisa opened the Cuffley stores and eventually sold the Cabin in 1945 to the residence of Cuffley who renamed it The Victory Centre. Molly Hughes was a patron of the new shop and was less than impressed.
The Post Mistress, she complained, knew everyone's business and when Molly spotted a cat up on the

1935 The wedding of Queenie's Friend Bertha's daughter Audrey
Middle row far right Nellie with Cecil and Queenie standing to his left. In front little Albert and Bridesmaid Pam.

counter licking the cheese she was horrified.
Schooling for the majority of Cuffley children was provided by private enterprise and paid for by their parents. Pam spent her earliest years educated by a silver-haired lady in her bungalow home in Tolmers Road. A small group of children, no more than five or six in number, would spend their day sat around a highly polished dining room table taking instruction on the three Rs from their elderly teacher.

Soon after she was enrolled into the Cuffley School Room, an old tin hut built in the early 1890s where St Andrews Church is today. The room had many uses and the class sat up to collapsible green baize tables. Pam was one of the smaller children in the class. She struggled to sit up to the "big" card table, her neck uncomfortably stretched to see the teacher and write her letters properly. The strain was too much for the little girl and Pam fainted into a dishevelled heap on the floor.

Queenie wanted better for her bright daughter. The world around her was slowly changing. She finally had a vote and took the privilege very seriously. Women were beginning to make a mark on the world. The daring Miss Amy Johnson had flown solo to South Africa in 1932 and technology was starting to progress with the Alexander Palace broadcasting for TV in 1936.
By the tender age of seven, nearly eight, Queenie thought that Pam was old enough to travel on her own to Enfield by train to the Enfield Preparatory School in London Road. From the station, Pam was expected to walk through the park to the big three storey house where Miss Bagshaw would be waiting with her assistant. The school was for girls only and Miss Bagshaw was quite a lady, with high expectations for all her charges. The refined Miss Bagshaw would have a gentile lunch served in the basement each day for the girls. The class would sit around the large refectory table with Miss Bagshaw at the head ready to carve the joint. Her assistant on the other hand was a little less refined and during lessons her temper would often get the better of her, when she would, on occasions, throw wood from the log basket. This certainly made the girls sit up and listen!

Up to this point Jack's education was similar. He was placed in a school in Enfield but unlike Pam who was encouraged to take her education further, Jack was happy to gain the essentials and join his Dad on the farm. He began his working life as a lad taking the pony and trap out from the farm each day with the milk round. There was plenty to do on the farm and Jack

Jack Fletcher 1945 at the farm

was kept busy with the cows, sheep and horses. For a short time Bert had an old carthorse to help around the farm. Later he used the old car to tow the sweep for hay making. Farm technology was moving on but Bert did not have money to spend so he had to be resourceful.

When Pam was ready to move on from the school in Enfield she had her heart set on going to Hornsey High School, where they had a good reputation for art. But this was not to be as the school was in Middlesex and Pam lived out of the catchment area. By this time they were living at Goff's Oak House. There was a lot of toing and froing between Queenie and the authorities. Queenie wrote to the MP Abel Smith to complain that Pam had now been refused a place at Cheshunt and had nowhere to go. By the time they conceded Pam had missed the start of term and was expected to take the entrance exam to the new school all on her own. She passed and was bundled off to the newly built Cheshunt Modern School. A term later than all her new classmates, she arrived without any uniform or proper kit. Queenie was keen for her daughter to receive a good education and was happy to pay three guineas a term for the privilege on top of all the games kit and equipment needed. Queenie took an avid interest in the new school and at its official opening borrowed a cine-camera from her friend Bertha's son. She documented the event with a film which she presented to Mr Moxom the headmaster. Queenie would be pleased to know that it was still in the school's possession at the school's 60th anniversary. Pam took her studies seriously and stayed until she was 17 years old, then proudly left with a school certificate. She loved art and did well in English and French.

With World War II in full flight Pam's first job was with a small firm at Brimsdown, Enfield. The Moulded Rubber factory reused old tires to make army boots and tank parts. Pam worked in the small, newly built lab with the director. She was sent to Enfield Polytechnic in Ponders End for evening classes and occasional day release to learn maths and physics. It took a lot of tenacity during these difficult war years for Pam to get to work and then on to Ponders End to study. Dressed in a white lab coat she spent her working day testing samples of rubber for their stretching points, density and components. One evening Pam left the sample oven on. When she arrived for work the next morning the laboratory was grey with smoke, all the samples had baked to a crisp and were ruined. Thankfully there had not been a fire! Then when war ended, after two years of service at the factory, Queenie decided that she needed Pam back at home to help with the paying guests. Pam was put to work, setting food for the guests, cleaning rooms and painting caravans. She dutifully mucked in, initially enjoying the freedom that came with working at home, but Pam soon got fed up with the domesticity of the routine. Before too long she was on the lookout for a new career. Barclays Bank in Hoddesdon where taking people on. At interview Pam was asked to add up a column of figures. She passed with flying colours and so a new chapter began.

Bert and Young Jack at Brook Farm

The Age of Motoring

Throughout her life Queenie had a love of cars. With the invention of the motor car whilst Queenie was just a child she grew up with each and every development. In the 1920s a family motor car was still only obtainable by the wealthy. It was not until 1939 that the motor car, in the form of the Ford model T, became mass produced and therefore more attainable. She always had a fascination with speed and enjoyed the journey.

In her late twenties, early thirties, Queenie decided that it was high time that she learnt to drive. To the annoyance of her not-so-patient teacher and husband Bert, Queenie over-revved the engine and crunched her way noisily through the crash gearbox of their little yellow coupe. Needless to say her clutch control was poor. Once, on pulling out of Brook Farm onto Cuffley Hill, the vehicle started to roll back. Bert was horrified! He had had enough… He opened the passenger door and jumped out leaving the ever enthusiastic Queenie to sort herself out.

Roads of the time took similar routes to today but they were not all covered in tarmac. Many were still gravelled and potholed. The Cambridge Arterial road was planned in 1914, but with the onset of the First World War, work did not start in North London until 1921. Its construction created much needed work after the war and it reached Turnford in 1924. By the late 1930s this single track highway was a fast and busy route in and out of North London.

Queenie's first solo drive was to the hairdressers in Enfield. Excitedly she drove off with a young Pamela, then aged between 6 and 7 years, bobbing up and down on the seat beside her. Enjoying the liberating freedom of the open road Queenie made her way up Cuffley Hill and through the village of Goff's Oak. She picked up the A10 Arterial road at Cheshunt. Queenie trundled along steadily increasing her speed until she found herself right up behind a lorry. A little uncertain of her route and more than a little unsure of herself on her maiden drive she took comfort in matching her speed with his. The lorry slowed and Queenie slowed, the lorry pulled to the left and Queenie pulled to the left. The lorry slowed to a stop and Queenie so close behind him had nowhere to go. She had no choice but to pull in behind him and stop too. Queenie found herself in a lay-by. Now Queenie had never been confident with reverse gear and not wishing to look foolish she quickly ordered Pamela out of the car to pick wild flowers from the verge as if it had all been carefully planned.

As the years rolled by Queenie's confidence grew. One summer she decided to drive Aunt Nettie and Pam, now in her late teens, down to meet Cecil at Point Clear, St Osyth. The long drive went without a hitch and Aunt Nettie exclaimed, "don't you drive nice, dear". Preparing to park Queenie climbed back into the driving seat, and Pam jumped onto the running board. Queenie engaged the gear and put her foot down heavily onto the accelerator pedal. The car lunged forward at speed straight into the garage door. Cecil was absolutely furious. No one was hurt but this was yet another job… something else for him to fix!

Over the years Queenie's driving became less and less. Cecil seemed happy enough to chauffeur her here and there in the various vehicles she bought. Whilst the Nation was marvelling over the affordability of the Ford Popular in the early 1950s Queenie was setting her sights higher.

West Bay 1951

The old Alvis was one of the earlier vehicles from 1936. It was big and black with spoke wheels and running boards, and had the power to tow the heavy Roll-a-long caravan back and forth to West Bay. The next Alvis was bigger still. It was a coach built shooting break with wooden trim and copious amounts of space to ferry everything to and from Point Clear and West Bay. It was perfect for the holiday Queenie organised to the New Forest and a visit to her best friend Bertha in Poole.

Cecil Queenie and Bert

Just as cars were getting smaller and more compact firstly with the Morris Minor then with the iconic Mini, Queenie opted to buy, in the early 1960s, an Austin Westminster. She decided that this large stylish two-tone blue/grey saloon with its modern comfort was ideal for towing her caravan and perfect for her adventurous travels to Europe. Not content she went on to buy a red/cream Austin Westminster station wagon. Her appetite for large cars was getting a hold on her.

Queenie always thought big and in later years took a liking for large American Chevrolets. She had two, one after the other. The first Impala, bought in 1964, was cream with a metallic blue interior. The second Impala was white with a black interior and purchased around 1970. Both were bought brand new from the motor show. They were showy and brash and Queenie loved the attention that they brought. The suspension was soft and the car wallowed badly, making it highly unsuitable for towing a caravan, but Queenie had it modified at great expense and Cecil was expected to drive the lumbering beast everywhere.

Queenie loved to explore; towing the caravan throughout Europe and enjoying what the United Kingdom could offer. Many times, especially in Dorset and Devon, she would insist that Cecil drive down the most unsuitable dirt tracks, sometimes purely to find out what was down there, other times to find a farm or campsite to stay at for the night. Much to the annoyance of Cecil nine times out of ten they would meet a tractor or farm vehicle at the most inappropriate and narrow point in the road. Muttering and swearing under his breath, Cecil had to attempt to reverse the car and caravan into a small opening between the fields. The track was tortuous with thick slippery mud, and the grass verges and ditches were an unknown hazard. Whilst Cecil manoeuvred back and forth, the farmer just looked on in amazement. After much cursing and shunting, the busy farmer passed with an impatient wave and a less than cheery smile. Queenie, optimistic as ever, brightly smiled him on. Cecil muttered under his breath and dutifully carried on, hoping for somewhere safe to turn around. Cecil knew all too well that he would be passing this way again soon and sure to encounter the same farmer upon his return. There were occasions when Queenie got him into such a pickle that the caravan had to be unhitched and turned around in the middle of the road whilst the Chevy had to be reversed into a field and then hitched up again. Cecil hated this sort of procedure but Queenie took it all in her stride recalling the tale on her return as just part of the adventure.

Queenie often took Pam, Sture and their children out in the car; although a nightmare down winding country lanes the Chevy still had appeal. With its lovely long bench seats at the front and back and no seat belts to concern ourselves with, the family, sometimes seven of us, would pile in and take off for the day, leaving after breakfast and returning late into the evening after an exhausting but fun time down at the seaside or out into the country.

When Queenie took Mark and I away late on a Friday evening for the weekend we could top and tail on the long back bench and sleep for most of the way, stopping for pancakes, or an all-day breakfast, at Queenie's favourite, the 'Little Chef'. We could have exactly what we liked. I remember ordering a strawberry milkshake and being sick after 10 minutes in that wallowing car. I have never drunk another milkshake to this day.

Queenie's old poodles were not so keen; they often rested on the back parcel shelf dozing in the warmth behind the glass. With every curve and bend in the road they would slide the full width of the Chevy. On warm sunny rides they would sit in the back with Mark and me. With paws on the armrest, nose pointing out of the part open window, they would smell the rushing air, ears flapped back and eyes half closed.

With the growing years using this big car for local trips became unnecessary. Queenie invested in a little automatic Mini estate. This was much better for Cecil to use to pick up the bread at Brooke Bakery or take Queenie down to the bank. On one occasion he needed to finish off his own business and gave Queenie the car key to let herself in. When he came back to the car he could not find her anywhere. He looked up and down the street. Where could she be? Can you imagine his embarrassment and horror when he spotted Queenie sitting bold as brass in a stranger's car wondering where the hell he had been! Tempers were high that day. And for a few days after!

Austin Westminster and Caravan

THE WOMBWELL CIRCUS CONNECTION

GEORGE WOMBWELL (founder)
b. 1777 d.1850
1st wife **MARY**, 2nd wife **ANNE MORGAN**

HARRIET m. **JAMES EDMONDS**
b. 1815 d.1890 — b. 1815 d. 1878

JAMES WOMBWELL

JAMES WILLIAM
b. 1855 d. 1919

(EDMOND) **EDWARD HENRY** m Elizabeth Bostock
b. 1858 d. 1940 — b. 1859 d. 1927

FRANK CHARLES m. Susannah Baily
b. 1866 d. 1912 — b. 1868

WILLIAM WOMBWELL m. HANNAH GIBSON
b. 1800

EMMA m. **JAMES BOSTOCK**
b. 1839 d. 1909 — b. 1814 d. 1878

GEORGE WOMBWELL JR.
(BUSTER/ THE GOV'NOR)
b. ~1811 d. ~1891+

Queenie's Circus Connections

Queenie's love of the Circus was a passion that grew from the legacy left by her great, great, great, great-uncle George Wombwell, founder of the Bostock and Wombwell travelling show.

George Wombwell 1777-1850

George was born near Saffron Walden on the 24 December 1777 in the small village of Duddenhoe End, at Wenden Lofts, Essex. A few weeks later he moved with his family to Langley.

Young George always had an interest in animals. As a boy he would tend to the sick and injured creatures he found, nursing them back to health as best he could. At times he sought advice from the local doctor. Over the years he learnt a lot about their needs.

It is believed that George's first marriage was to a young woman called Mary. What happened to her we do not know. His second marriage was to Anne Morgan (born 1788- died 3 Oct 1876) who was reputedly the widow of a circus owner called Morgan. She had children by Morgan but it is unknown if she had children with George. None have been found in my search.

In 1800 George moved to London where he set up a cordwainer's shop in Old Compton Street, near Covent Garden, where shoes and other goods were made from fine Spanish leather. His work took him down to the docks to purchase leather as it came off the ship. It was here in 1804 that George spotted two of the largest boa constrictors that he had ever seen as they were unloaded from a ship in from South America. He bought the pair for the princely sum of seventy-five guineas. George was a canny man. He exhibited the "two wonderful Siboya serpents" in Soho, taking them around all the

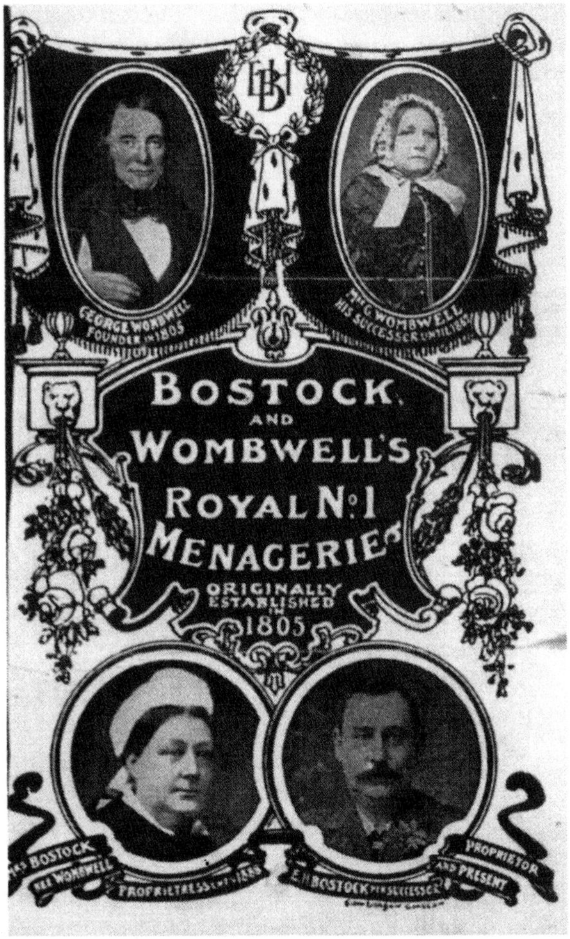

local taverns and charging people to view them. In three weeks he had reclaimed his outlay and was making a profit.

Victorian Britain was at her most powerful and influential. Trade throughout the world was at its height. Ships were setting off for distant shores and returning with all things new and exciting. George developed a good relationship with the workers on the docks. They would tip him the wink when ships carrying a cargo of exotic creatures were due to dock from Africa, Australia or South America. George made sure that he was first on the scene, eager to get the best deal for the most wild and dangerous animals that he could.

Later in 1804 George organised his first exhibition at Bartholomew Fair, Smithfield. George secured an office and yard at Commercial Road, London. He became an importer of wild beasts.

His business card read…

WOMBWELL
Wild Beast Merchant
All sorts of Foreign Animals, Birds, etc. bought and sold or exchanged,
at the repository of the Travelling Menagerie

From here he bought and sold animals. In the early days many of the animals he bought sadly died. It was difficult to acclimatise them to the harsh British climate and provide them with suitable food. George bought the very first imported giraffe for the vast sum of £1,000. Just three weeks later the animal was dead. These fatalities were still a source of income. George would make up some or all of his losses by selling them to taxidermists or to medical science. Much of what we know about the natural world has come from the early studies of George's animals.

The Bostock Family 1906

During this era people had a growing fascination for the exotic. Charles Dickens became an ardent fan of George's work and the circus. Wealthy Victorians often had a small private collection of animals from all over the world. George would supply them with interesting stock and his reputation grew.

It was George Wombwell who bred the first lion in captivity. Wallace was born in Edinburgh in 1812 and lived to the ripe old age of twenty-six. He was a fierce lion and inspired Marriott Edgar's poem… "The Lion and Albert". There was an incident in Leeds where a gentleman, Jonathan Wilson rested his hand between the bars of Wallace's cage. Wallace was not impressed and attacked the man by dragging his arm into the cage. The Keeper was able to free Mr Wilson from Wallace but his arm became infected and he died a few days later. When the old lion finally died in 1838, Wallace was stuffed and presented to the Saffron Walden Museum for display, where he still remains.

It is said that the big cats reputedly seen on moors like Bodmin are descendants of the large felines that have escaped from circuses and menageries over the years.

George Wombwell's Lion Wallace

At the yard in Commercial Road, George designed and built the wagons he needed to transport his animals. In 1805 he took his early travelling zoo or "beast show" to the road. It was a great success. George began to make wagons for others and continued to build up his stock with the money he made.

In 1810 he founded the first of his three travelling menageries and toured the towns and villages of Great Britain, entertaining and educating the masses as he went. It was reputedly the finest menagerie that ever travelled. It was never difficult to obtain permission to stay and exhibit. The villagers and townsfolk were always happy to allow the menagerie to set up in the market square. Everyone was so excited by its arrival that at times they would walk miles to join the procession of gaily painted wagons and carts as it progressed slowly along the bumpy dirt tracks to the village or town. The show became so successful that before long the police had to take charge of the thronging crowds that gathered to join them.

Such was George Wombwell's popularity and success

Bostock and Wombwell Menagerie

Bostock and Wombwell on the road 1898

that from around 1820 he held a royal decree from King George IV. It granted George permission to erect and exhibit his menagerie in any market place in Great Britain for any three consecutive days free of charge.

George was a fierce businessman. His main rival was Atkins Menagerie. In 1825 when George was up north showing his menagerie, word came from London that Atkins was to exhibit at the Bartholomew Fair. He was advertising as "the only wild beast show in the fair". George was furious. Immediately he began to pack and load the fourteen wagons for travel. It was an arduous journey. With nearly sixty horses it took a long ten days to slowly drag the massive wagons down to London, the largest and most difficult being the elephant wagon. It was 30' long, 13' high and 9' wide. It had six tyres, each 18" wide and weighing 7cwt. It required twelve horses to pull it on the flat and more than thirty to drag it up the steep hills. The progress was slow and exhausting. By the time George Wombwell's menagerie reached London both men and animals were spent. The elephant was sick and by the morning was dead.

Atkins, keen not to miss a trick, flooded the area with posters announcing that his was the only menagerie with a live elephant. George reacted quickly. Within the hour he had erected an enormous banner on which had been painted… "Come see the only dead elephant in the fair!" Needless to say the dead elephant proved to be a bigger draw than Atkins's live one. Barricades had to be erected to retain the massive crowds. George Wombwell did very nicely!

George enjoyed Royal Patronage for the first time in 1830. When at Thirsk in North Yorkshire, on the 3rd May he was visited by Princess Victoria and her mother the Duchess of Kent.

On 1st November 1834 George was invited to exhibit part of his number one menagerie to their majesties King William IV, Queen Adelaide and their guests in the quadrangle at Windsor Castle.

Bostock and Wombwell horse power

Bostock and Wombwell water stop for the camels and elephant1913

Various other Royal commands followed… 1842, 1847, 1854 and lastly 1869. It was noted in the Windsor Express that all were received with much pleasure by the Royal Parties.

Prince Albert of Saxe-Coburg and Gotha summoned George to the palace to take a look at his sick dogs. The Prince's hounds were dying unexplainably. George realised that the water they were given to drink contained toxins. He recommended that it be changed for another source immediately. The dogs regained their health and no more died. Prince Albert was so pleased he asked George, "What can I give to the man who has everything?" George flippantly replied "The one thing I do not own is a coffin!" A year later George was once again at court and Prince Albert presented him with an oak coffin, which George went on to exhibit to the public for an additional fee!

George Wombwell went from strength to strength, running his three menageries simultaneously. He was a respected and very successful business man.

It is recorded that where a rival may take £90 at the Bartholomew Fair in three days, George Wombwell could take a staggering £1,700. George was very enterprising. It was said of him "His heart was in his work, he spared nothing that would help to move it

Bostock and Wombwell steam power 1913

forward". They say that the elephant tale and others like it may have been sensationalised by the media of the time or by George himself. Even so he certainly had an eye for turning a profit.

Both Wombwell and Atkins Menageries were the chief attractions of the Great Fairs of the time. Wombwell's was considered to be the finest travelling collection of wild animals in the country. When George Wombwell died in 1850 his obituary was published the length and breadth of the country. The Times wrote, "No one probably has done so much to forward practically the study of natural history amongst the masses". George is buried at Highgate Cemetery in London. His tomb is marked by a huge statue of a sleeping lion, his old favourite, the big softy Nero.

George Wombwell's Menageries were known across the country for over 120 years as "wandering teachers of natural history". At the time he was held in high regard. It was said that he brought an interest in wild animals to the people. He learnt how to care for them through first-hand study. He gained animal respect through gentle understanding and handling. George could enter Nero's cage, sit on his back and open his mouth with his bare hands. True trust was needed from both sides. No wonder Queenie was so proud of her heritage.

Menagerie No. 1

Was the original menagerie founded by George Wombwell? When George died in 1850 his wife took over. In 1865 it was George's nephew who took over the helm.

Menagerie No. 2

Was run by George's niece Harriet Wombwell (b.1815-d.1890) who married James Edmonds (b.1805-d.1871). When George died in 1850 Menagerie No. 2 was left to her husband. Both husband and wife ran the Menagerie until their son James Wombwell took over. Later this Menagerie was taken over by the Bostocks.

Menagerie No. 3

Was left to George's nephew George Wombwell Jr. At the age of ten, it was decided by his parents that George Jr. be 'adopted' by George Wombwell. A practise not uncommon in Victorian times. George Jr. lived and worked alongside his uncle, learning the ropes as he went and taking on more responsibility as the years passed. When news reached the royal palace that the menagerie had two new tiger cubs and five new lion cubs being raised by a Newfoundland bitch, Queen Victoria insisted on seeing them. It was George Jr. who had the esteemed honour of putting the baby tiger cub into the waiting arms of the Prince of Wales.

George Wombwell's Descendants

Many of George's family joined the menageries. Some lost their lives. His nephew William Wombwell died at the Coventry great fair at the age of twenty-five. He was killed by an elephant on the 12th June 1849 when he attempted to stop two from fighting. The Wombwell family continued to have connections with the menageries long after George's death.

Captain Fred Wombwell was considered one of the most famous wild animal trainers of all times. Unfortunately, like many Wombwells, fearless Fred liked a drink. One time he entered the cage of two half-grown lions and two half-grown tigers that performed together in an act. One of the lions decided to set upon the inebriated Fred. Thankfully a tiger sprang to his aid; Fred sobered up quickly and made a hasty retreat, with no harm done.

Harriet Wombwell was a lady trainer of daring and skill but she was attacked by hyenas during rehearsals. Her cousin Edmond Bostock, just 15 years old, came to the rescue. Brandishing a big stick and shouting as loud as he could, he managed to scare the beasts away, leaving Harriet with bites to both of her legs and on one shoulder. She was lucky not to have died.

The Fortunes of the Bostock Family

It was in 1839 that, at the age of twenty four, James Bostock (b 1814 - d 1878) left his father's farm after a dispute regarding his stepmother. James found employment with Wombwell's Menagerie No. 2 who was exhibiting nearby. His sound knowledge of horses acquired on his father's farm secured him the position of Wagoner and horse keeper. It was a respectable position. All Wombwell's employees were highly regarded and it was never difficult to find suitable people.

James Bostock was an educated and smartly dressed man and before long he was appointed as contracting and advertising agent to Wombwell Menagerie. He was responsible for organising the itinerary of dates. He would travel ahead, check the site and clarify arrangements, making sure that the next venue was ready for them. James was responsible for securing two of the four royal command exhibitions. The first in October 1847 and the second in October 1854.

Mrs Edmonds's sister, Emma Wombwell (b 1839 - d 1909), was a frequent visitor to Menagerie No. 2. The gallant Mr Bostock set his cap at the young Miss Wombwell and on the 6th October 1852 they married.

Emma was the tender age of fourteen. James was twenty-five years her senior. James and Emma went on to have four sons and three daughters. Three of his sons followed him into the same profession. James William born in 1855, Edmond (Edward) Henry born in 1858 and Frank Charles born in 1866.

James William worked alongside his mother before setting up on his own. But it was his younger brothers Edmond and Frank who made the biggest impact.

Young Edmond loved the menagerie and could not wait to join it during school holidays. By the age of twelve he was travelling with his parents' menagerie, Wombwell & Bostock. He worked with his parents until 1883 when he decided to start his own small independent menagerie, "Grand Star Menagerie". Younger brother Frank joined Edmond until he moved up to Scotland. Frank did not want to be too far from his fiancée and re-joined his mother's menagerie. Back with his mother, Frank married Miss Bailey, and went on to manage the Bostock Wombwell & Bailey Circus.

In 1887, shortly after her husband's death, Emma Wombwell Bostock decided to retire and dispose of the entire show. She was not keen to auction it off, so instead Edmond bought the original family business, lock, stock, and barrel. Some of the stock and plant went to his younger brother Frank, who had decided to try his fortune in America with his Bostock Wombwell and Bailey Circus. Frank went on to become the greatest showman this country has ever produced. In the 1900s Frank C Bostock 'The Animal King' toured his 'Jungle Arena' with different species of animals working together in one big cage. He had a small lion that rode the back of a horse and a tiger that would ride the back of an elephant. At the height of his career he had 1000 animals in various shows all around the world.

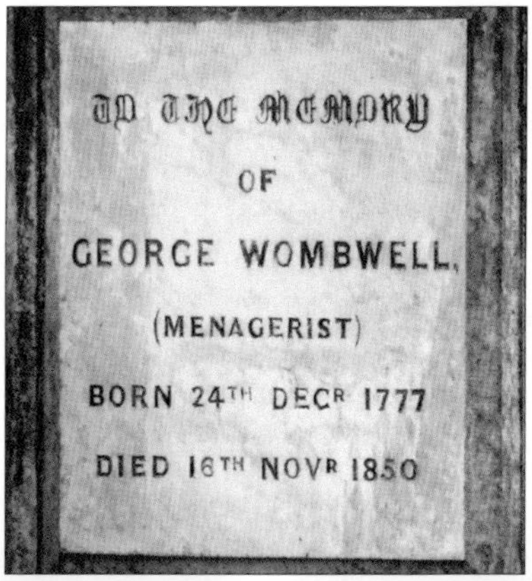

Whether his mother asked him to use the name or not, Edmond was happy to call his menagerie Bostock & Wombwell. The name had such a good reputation everyone across the country knew it.

By 1896 Edmond was suffering from ill health. His mental health was poor, he was entirely unhinged by high winds, not a good scenario when living and travelling in caravans. He made the decision to retire from travelling and left his brother in-law, Mr H F Birkett, in charge. Edmond bought Elgin House just outside Norwich and settled down to retired life for a year. And then he decided to create a permanent zoo and circus.

His first was in Scotland where he secured a cheap rent on the Olympia; Glasgow for five years and moved the family up there. Edmond had cages for the animals built to his own specifications. He had a circus ring constructed in the centre and put in extensive lighting. On 12th May 1897 the Scottish Zoo and Variety Circus formally opened.

After five years of success Edmond Bostock moved his menagerie and circus to the Variety Theatre which he refitted for the purpose. Much money was spent and Edmond took on a partner. But this did not work out well. Edmond briefly retired from Scotland and then, in 1905, he bought back the Olympia and fitted it out with an ice rink… the new pastime of the era. Edmond Bostock opened various venues across the country. His fortunes rose and dipped according to the political climate. One of his son's took over from him and the business interests of the Bostocks turned to other ventures.

Memorial of George Wombwell at Highgate Cemetery

Love of the Circus

Circus people have their own language which is a curious mix of Romany, Italian, rhyming slang and back slang. In the big top they use expressions known only to their small community. Queenie often impressed us with her easy use of back slang. She could rattle off a sentence whilst I was still trying to get to grips with the first word. She was nicknamed Mrs. Feather, a radio character, for her blonde moments but I always found her to be as sharp as a tack. Queenie was always eager to regale her circus related stories to whoever was listening. It was suggested to her that she should write them down but unfortunately she never did.

Over the years Queenie got to meet many interesting circus people. Initial introductions were made through her father, probably when she was quite young. Both Albert and his father David Wombwell must have known one or two of the Bostock and Wombwell showmen and women but exactly who is uncertain. George Wombwell Jr. was a very distant cousin to David. It is said that Albert did meet him but by the time Albert was born George Junior's success in the menagerie was beginning to fail.

George Jr. was George Wombwell's nephew. In an interview with the Daily Mail in 1891 he told of his birth one windy night in a converted elephant wagon. He told them that it had been said that he was "born to be a wild beast".

When George Jr. was only ten years old his uncle, the famous George Wombwell, adopted him and he joined him on the road with the menagerie. His uncle was successfully running three menageries and George Jr. helped with the lions, tigers and elephants. His proudest moment was when he accompanied his uncle to his third royal command at Windsor Castle. Queen Victoria and Prince Albert were keen to see the newly-born tiger and lion cubs. The little bundles were put into a wicker basket and taken to the stables along with their foster mother, a Newfoundland bitch. The royal party were enthralled by the tiger cubs as they jostled for milk from their foster mother. The young Prince of Wales asked if he could hold one. His father the Prince Consort asked if it would be safe and with pride George Jr. put the baby tiger into the waiting arms of the excited six-year-old.

With the support of his uncle, George Jr. was able to learn the skills needed to run a successful menagerie and when his uncle died in 1850 George Wombwell left menagerie no.3 to George Jr. Building on the success of his uncle, George Jr. became a renowned lion tamer. He was known from Land's End to John O' Groats. But after something like twenty years of prosperity, due to a series of setbacks, the fortunes of this famous showman, known as the Guv'nor, began to decline. The order of events is unclear but it appears to have begun in the small border town of Peebles. This remote spot was battered by high winds as the Guv'nor drove the menagerie along the treacherous road to town. Six wagons were blown over that day, everyone was heartbroken when the wagons had to be left with the animals still inside! As they looked out toward the town they could see the sky alight with fire. The stables where the Wombwell horses were housed were ablaze! Thirty horses were injured and twelve lost their lives that night. It was a massive blow for the menagerie as advance bookings were not honoured and money was lost.

But this was just the beginning of a string of bad luck. A mysterious ailment struck the menagerie. Despite every effort the carnivorous animals kept dying. George Junior replaced them time and again, trying stock from London, Liverpool and Bristol, but the result was always the same and the beasts perished. Eventually a specialist recognised that it was a form of rinderpest but the damage was done. Eight out of his nine splendid lions were dead and George was in debt.

Then on a bleak road out of Huddersfield a snowstorm struck. The elephant wagon got stuck in a cutting and to the dismay of everyone it had to be left. The next day they went out to retrieve the beast but the snow was so thick that the men could not get within a mile and a half of the elephant. It was twelve long days and very cold nights before the wagon could be reached. A report came back to the Guv'nor … the elephant had lain down to eat its mash. But the next day George Jr.'s brother-in-law announced that the animal was dead! George Jr. lamented, "A menagerie without an elephant is nothing!" Only weeks before he had been offered £650 for the animal. Such was the value of this impressive beast. The loss of the elephant was the end of the show and George Jr. was forced to sell the menagerie at Columbia Market in the 1870s. He was just able to cover his debts.

After the collapse of his business George Jr. was able to make a meagre living by touring with numerous circuses where he would play in the band. Eventually he got past it and some twenty years after the sale of the Menagerie, George Jr. was living the life of a destitute. With his wife in an infirmary, he was living in a squalid basement room in City Road, Shoreditch. His only source of income was to take his patched up cornet to the local public houses and play for pennies. He was asked, "Was drinking your ruin?" "Never", he replied, "I am often offered but always I refuse. I could do better", said the eighty-year-old, "if I had all my teeth and my cornet was not patched with cobblers wax!"

The only certainty is that Albert Wombwell had a strong relationship with the famous showman Bertram Mills and his two sons, Cyril and Bernard, but it is unclear quite how or when this came about. Bertram was not born into a circus family. His father Halford was a Baptist Preacher, a funeral director, coach builder and writer for the Undertakers Journal. Did the paths of his father David Wombwell and Halford Mills cross? Is this where the two young men met or was he introduced to Bertram through a Bostock Wombell connection?

Bertram was brought up on his father's two farms at Chalfont St. Giles and Harefield, Rickmansworth. Both were for the use of retired funeral horses, where they could spend their final years put out to pasture. It is here that Bertram developed his passion for horses. By the age of fifteen Bertram was working for his father washing coaches. A year later he was driving a four-in-hand from London to Oxford and sporting his signature blue cornflower in the buttonhole of his black tailcoat. Bertram worked for his father until the outbreak of the First World War, when Bertram joined the Royal Army Medical Corps and rose from the ranks to Captain. On leaving the army Bertram became interested in the Circus and made a wager that he could form a circus company and within a year become as good as any. Bertram was as good as his word and in 1920 Bertram Mills International Circus was formed. It was a sleek operation with top performers and animals. Bertram famously invited orphaned children to enjoy the show for free and his reputation grew fast. At this point the circus was static and performed each winter season at Olympia, London. Albert and Queenie were keen patrons of Olympia. I suspect that they visited the circus from these early days; they certainly went each year in my memory and often with complimentary tickets. It would have been very plausible for Albert to introduce his family to the great Bertram Mills at Olympia. Albert's circus roots would have been an interesting ice-breaker and topic of conversation. However they happened to meet, Albert and Bertram became very close. By the 1930s Bertram Mills International Circus was by far the best and most illustrious of live shows. Bertram and his sons made the decision to take the circus on the road and their first tenting season, in 1930, began at Luton and it is highly likely that Queenie accompanied her father with eight-year-old Jack and four-year-old Pamela.

Manzano

Lower Hanyards farm became the ideal spot for showmen to rest up. It was ideally placed with its rail links into London. Albert was asked by one of the Mills men to find room on the farm for Arturo Manzano. In Spain he had been a renowned bullfighter and horseman. The Mills Circus first invited him to perform the act 'Arturo Manzano on horseback with two bulls', and a short High School horse routine in 1932 at their third tenting season. Following that he then joined them for their 1932-33 Olympia season and did the same the following year. Mills arranged for a gaily painted living wagon to be brought to the farm for Arturo and his wife to use whilst the Olympia Seasons were on. Mrs Manzano spoke no English and this self-contained existence was probably easier for them than living in London digs. Albert and his family made them very welcome and they soon became close friends. The Manzanos were so grateful for the hospitality that they had been shown that Arturo's wife gave little Pamela an exquisite pair of Spanish gold and gem earrings.

Through Bertram, Cyril and Bernard Mills, Albert met all manner of showmen and women. He offered accommodation on the farm when it was needed and entertained the occasional act, often inviting them to take tea at the farmhouse.

One afternoon, when Pamela was only seven or eight, a gentleman arrived with a troop of performing midgets. They performed in their own mini circus riding mini horses and proudly presenting all the usual acts like trapeze, juggling, etc. There were about six or seven little men at the farmhouse that afternoon and Pamela was invited to join her grandfather in entertaining these unusual guests. With the curiosity of an innocent child, Pamela was fascinated by these little people. Fully grown yet no taller than her. She studied their bright eyes full of fun and their lined faces, etched with years of life. She thought of them as playmates and was happy to take them on a tour of the farm when her grandfather asked. After tea the little men scrambled to their feet happy to get out into the fresh air and explore. Pamela was enchanted. These pocket people had led such an unusual life in the circus that in some ways they had never grown up and played like children. A couple of the men grabbed the farm shovels leaning against the wall and jumped onto them like pogo sticks and started bouncing around. Pamela watched them with interest then raced off out into the yard with the little men in hot pursuit. She clambered, nimble and light as any youngster, over the familiar five-bar gate into the field. The little men followed closely. She turned to check on their progress and was mortified to see the smallest of the group in floods of tears. His little legs were far too short to reach the first bar of the gate and he was sobbing all alone on the other side.

Throughout her life Queenie knew many showmen and circus people; she was fascinated by their transient lives. I think she felt a strong kinship with these misunderstood nomads and when her father died in 1935 Queenie took up the mantle of providing accommodation to the friends she had made and continued to visit the circus whenever she could. Such was the draw that some years she would go with the family on as many as four or five occasions!

Bette Stebbing became a very close friend to Queenie. Born on Christmas Eve to an aspiring opera singing mother and a show business father, Bette and her two brothers grew up fast in this high energy environment. They worked together on a number of acts, many including horses, riding and clowning. In 1925 Bette was married, at the tender age of sixteen, to Big Jim Fossett, the name Fossett being one of the most famous names in the world of circus. They were one of the oldest circus owning families. Their original circus was founded by Robert Fossett in 1852 in Ireland. This Irish family of redheads was large and talented. Many were renowned equestrian riders and others were well known for their clowning. Fossett acts were sought after by many prestigious circuses and years later it was said that every circus in the country had a Fossett in it.

Bette Fossett

Over the decades this large family spread their wings. Some of the extended family left Ireland to begin circuses of their own. Robert's sons, Bobby, Teddy and Johnny Fossett, whilst in their early twenties, were recognised as the youngest recorded circus proprietors. Teddy continued to run a Fossett Circus in Ireland. Bobby ran the Sir Robert Fossett's Circus, 2nd cousin Little Tom ran Fossett's Circus and Big Tom Fossett ran Ringland's Circus, all famous circuses in the United Kingdom. The Fossett family was immense; it is said that as many as five generations of Fossetts worked together in some circuses.

Big Jim and Bette had their own caravan parked down behind the cowshed at Brook Farm. When they were not working with their riding act they would stay in their scruffy wooden home on the farm. Big Jim and Bette had two children, Jimmy and Belle, who both went into show business. By the time the Fossett family were staying at the farm Jimmy was already performing with his mum, dad and Uncle Billy. Billy was a similar age to Jimmy and they worked together on various routines with combinations of riding, tumbling and acrobatics. Bette and the family had a popular clowning routine called 'The 4 Kranks', which they performed at the prestigious London Palladium. Touring with a family was not easy and young Belle was sent away to live with her Aunt Jessie's family. Jessie was also a similar age to Belle and they went to school together in St. Anne's near Blackpool. On the rare occasions that Belle joined her parents at Brook Farm, she would spend time with Pam. Both families got on well and made friendships that endured the years. Bert and Big Jim often slipped out for a pint or two to the local pub leaving Queenie and Bette time to gossip over a cup of tea.

The Scott Family

In addition to Big Jim and Bette, Bette's brothers would frequently visit the farm for a night or two. Jack Stebbing had a cowboy act and Billy Stebbing was the acrobatic rider who performed with his nephew Jimmy.

The Scott Family were another family to frequently stay on the farm. They brought their own vans and parked them in the yard. Their stops were often shorter than the Fossetts'; they had other accommodation up north and were often just passing through. The act was called 'The Royal Scotts'. The family wore a smart military costume with pristine white trousers; they were a high-class riding act and much sought after. The act consisted of Mr and Mrs Scott and their three children; Arthur, Elsie and Adie. They brought their beautiful horses with them to the farm and often practised in the paddock.

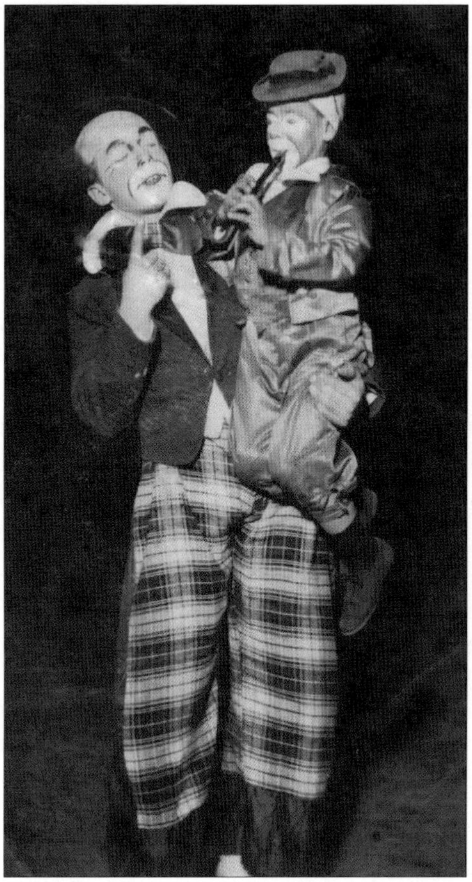

Jack Stebbing

In addition to their horse act some of the Scott family performed with ropes and trapeze. Older sister Adie would climb a rope hanging in the Big Top. She would elegantly hang on whilst brother Arthur twirled the rope at great speed. He spun her at such a speed that her eyes became dangerously bloodshot and literally nearly popped out of her head! In the farm house dinning room Arthur set up a practise trapeze. It hung from the centre of the tall ceiling, over the polished table. Pamela loved to play on it. She would scramble onto a chair and climb up onto the table . Standing in the middle of the table top she would jump up and catch the waiting trapeze where she would dangle, swinging and swaying to her hearts content.

In return for the hospitality shown by Queenie, her circus friends would invite her to the various shows that they were in. Queenie often took Cecil with Jack and Pam to see the daring and the bizarre. At the time, the Circus was quite something. As well as the amazing performances there were all sorts of side shows from around the world to be seen. Pam recalls the Giraffe-necked Women, from Upper Burma, with their long necks extended with rows of hoops, and the Anderson family, three generations of albinos, whose hair was as white as snow. For the people of the 1940s seeing these curiosities for the first time was quite extraordinary. Their only encounter with the wider world was through print and much of that was only black and white. In addition to the annual Christmas invitation to Olympia to see the Bertram Mills Circus, Queenie was invited to Bertram Mills' Ascot winter quarters, where the horses were rested. One year she took Pam; they were introduced to the stable hands and saw some of the beautiful horses.

Memories of the circus at Cuffley are still vivid for some of the villagers, they recall seeing elephants being exercised on Cuffley Hill. These lumbering grey creatures must have been a strange sight plodding along the tarmac. They belonged to Chapman's Circus and were walking from the station along Cuffley Hill toward Goff's Oak. Each year they stayed at the end of Newgate Street Road. They must have turned a few heads in this rural backwater. One year a young elephant refused point blank to go up the hill. When an elephant refuses to budge, no amount of coaxing will entice it. Queenie got involved and offered accommodation for the beast at Brook Farm. The little elephant made himself right at home. After a few days Bert was livid with his new guest

Pam practises her circus skills

and keen to get the animal moved on. Its appetite was enormous and it was eating him out of hay!

Just like their mother both Jack and Pam were captivated by the Circus and Queenie openly encouraged it. The children often stayed a few days with the performers. In the summer of 1937 Queenie took an excited Pam on the train to Skegness where she spent a fun week with the Scott family. The Royal Scotts were performing at the Agricultural Hall, Mum, Dad, and daughters, blond-haired Adie and dark-haired Elsie. Their son Arthur Scott went on to have a famous act with performing sea lions. Pam stayed with the family in digs. The horses were stabled nearby and everyday Pam practised her horse riding skills. She tried her hand at bareback riding and balanced on the back of a patient pony as it walked slowly around the yard, imagining herself in the ring amidst rapturous applause. When Queenie came to collect her the next weekend Pam was keen to show off her new-found skills, elegantly standing on the slow-moving pony as Queenie guided it around. Pam was also eager to introduce Queenie to the elephants housed next door. Queenie had a deep fondness for these placid colossi and needed no encouragement to find them but she got more than a friendly welcome from one who filled his trunk with water from the butt and sprayed a shocked Queenie from head to toe, giving her a right royal soaking!

When Pam was older, whilst she and Queenie stayed with Belle and Bette, she had her one and only time in the Big Top as a performer. It was with Bette's own circus, Coleman Brothers Circus, at Ingotstone outside of Colchester. When, one night, Jack Stebbbing's partner was unable to perform, it was Pam who stepped in to help him with his cowboy act. Jack was an all-rounder. He worked for his sister as an advance agent. He went ahead to book the field, check the access and water supply, pay the council, put up the posters and hand out the free tickets to the local shopkeepers. His cowboy act involved a glamorous assistant, Pam, dressed in a gingham shirt, tasselled leather skirt and waistcoat, standing in the middle of the ring holding pieces of paper. These were held up for Jack to rip up with the precision crack of his long whip. With nerves of steal Pam gently held a cigarette between her lips, in an ear piercing second the cigarette was literary whipped away. The excited audience clapped their appreciation. At the finale Pam threw more paper high into the air to be ripped through by Jack, amidst a shower of confetti she took a low bow to loud applause.

Queenie's son Jack had his own circus adventures falling in love with Adie Scott when she stayed at the farm and following Nancy, one of the Fossett clan, into the circus one year. As a muscled young man Jack, and his friend Tom, joined up as tent masters for a season or two with Coleman Brothers Circus. Jack took his responsibility of the tent very seriously. When, one evening as dusk fell, he spotted a man on the path with a knife, Jack saw red. The guy was trying to cut his way through the thick canvas of the tent. Jack acted on impulse. Without a thought of his own safety he kicked the man to the ground. The guy fell heavily, dropped the knife, and then scrambled back to his feet. Muddied and bruised he ran off into the shadowy night.

During performances Jack was often expected to dress in a cowboy outfit and ride one of the ponies around the ring at the parade. One morning shortly after breakfast Big Jim asked Jack if he would take the previous night's takings to the local bank. "I want you to wear the cowboy outfit and ride the horse into town", announced Big Jim. Jack was a little less enthusiastic with the thought of dressing up but he couldn't argue with Big Jim. So off he went complete with a ten-gallon hat on his head and the takings under his arm. He got to the busy high street when a loud noise, probably a car misfiring, sent the horse into a panic. It reared up; Jack was thrust back in his saddle, and he held on for dear life as the horse galloped off uncontrollably. The takings slipped from Jack's grasp. Coins and notes spewed everywhere. Jack quickly brought the horse under control and rounded back to see everyone bent down helping themselves to the loot. He jumped down from the horse and scrabbled around in the dust retrieving as much of the money as he could find. Some people handed back their stash but it was obvious to Jack that he did not have it all. He had no idea how short he

Belle and Taugh

was. It was no use paying this into the bank without a recount. Sheepishly Jack realised that he was going to have to man up and face Big Jim. With a heavy heart he headed back afraid of Big Jim's wrath. Jack wasted no time in coming clean. He told his unfortunate tale in all its devastating detail.

Big Jim's hard face cracked into an almighty grin. With a weather-beaten hand he gave Jack a hearty thump on the back. "It's alright lad", he said, "don't look so worried. This is the best advert we could have asked for." Needless to say the Circus was the talk of the town for quite some time. Big Jim was right and the big top was packed most nights!

As the years rolled on the Fossetts, Stebbings and Scotts all continued to stay at Brook Farm whenever they could. When Queenie moved to Goff's Oak, her Circus friends followed. When Big Jim died in the 1940's,

Belle and Taugh

Bette was left to ran Coleman Brothers Circus. Her son Jimmy was still performing with the family and Belle was now performing a trapeze act. The family often stayed for months at a time. Queenie and Pam went to see Belle perform at the Wood Green Empire. It was a fantastic evening. The girls' friendship grew and they became very close. By this time the country was at war and they enjoyed going dancing together, taking full advantage of the social life on offer.

The Coleman Brothers Big Top 14-8-1947

With the onslaught of the Second World War it was increasingly difficult for Bert and Queenie to make ends meet on Brook Farm. Rented from the Meux's Estate, the farm was barely making a profit. Queenie and Bert needed to make big changes to their lives. Together they made the decision to move out of the farm and find alternative accommodation. Queenie scoured the east Hertfordshire countryside and went right down to the Essex coast looking for a suitable residence. She was looking for a property that would bring in an income. She had it in her mind to build on her success at the farm. In later years, on our many trips out, she would point out the most memorable to us. Most were quite imposing and she always had a tale to tell. Like the cottage she viewed in St. Osyth. No one answered her calls at the front door so she went around to the back. The rustic stable door to the flagstone kitchen was open ajar. As she approached, a horse swung its head out and whinnied at her!!! It had strolled in from the yard to help itself to a treat. It seems that this was quite a normal occurrence to the owners who patted the horse affectionately as they welcomed Queenie into their home. The tale was a good story to tell but the cottage was not what Queenie was looking for. After a considerable search she finally settled for Goff's Oak House. Bert put the word out that he was looking for work. A talented farmer, it was not long before he was offered a job with A B Stevens, a large family of nurserymen, to set up and run a pig farm.

Goff's Oak House from the lawn

Goff's Oak House the rose arch

Many years previously when Bert's Mother, Hannah, was a young girl, she had worked at Goff's Oak House as a seamstress. Both Queenie and Bert knew of the property as a Goff's Oak landmark. It was owned by Mr and Mrs Vernon, a wealthy flour mill family from Utoxita in the Midlands. When it was offered for rent, Queenie decided that a living could be made from the large and many rooms. She had the experience of her circus friends and the odd camper staying at the farm in Cuffley and she could see the potential in the house. There would be plenty of room for everyone.

GROUND FLOOR PLAN
Not to scale

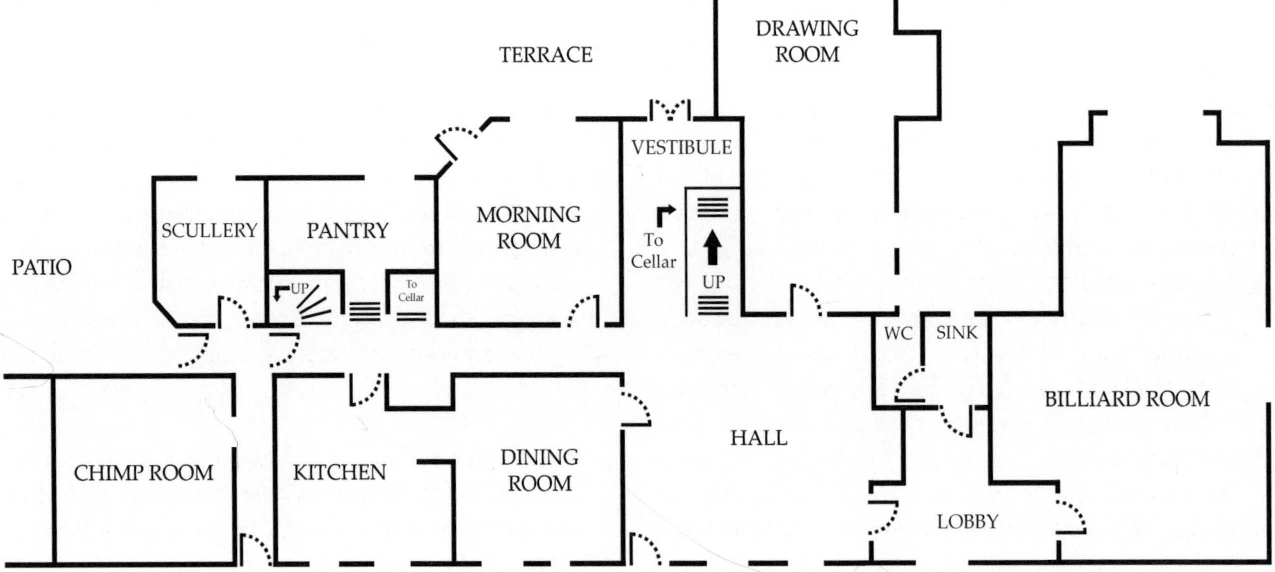

The Hall Inglenook

Together they approached Mrs Vernon with a view to renting for a year. The deal was set. Mrs Vernon's son was to remain in the house whilst he continued his studies to become a vet. Bert, Queenie, Jack and Pam moved into the glorious old manor house; complete with Mrs Grew the scullery maid and the old gardener, in around 1940.

The Morning room

The Hall Arches and Stairway

The Drawing room Fireplace

Pam was excited by the sheer size and number of the rooms! Stepping in through the large front door, the huge hall with its dark panelling and oak archways welcomed. The grand staircase lay in front beckoning you upstairs. A wide oak door to the right took you into the impressive drawing room which looked out over the well-manicured lawns. Both the drawing room and the hall had magnificent dark oak inglenook fireplaces. They had been taken from a grander house many years

The Drawing room and Bar

before (reputedly Theobalds House). To the right of the inglenook fireplace in the hall a wide door led into a small terracotta-tiled lobby, with a kitchenette area and a toilet. From the lobby another door opened up into a very large billiard room. Back off the hall was the dining room and on the same level were the morning room and kitchen. The kitchen had its original big, lead-blackened range and a wide expanse of floor to ceiling dresser. Back in the hall behind the arches, the wide oak staircase ascended, and turned halfway up, where a pair of beautiful full-length stained glass French doors led out onto a large balcony. The stairs continued to a floor of seven well-proportioned bedrooms then up again to the children's nursery and servants' quarters in the eaves. A second narrow staircase descended past the small butler's pantry on the first floor and spiralled down to

The Billiard room Nook

The Kitchen Dresser circa 1970

the kitchen, pantry, scullery, small servant's room and back door, which led out onto the patio. Behind a door opposite the kitchen was another set of stairs. These led down to the cellars. There were three rooms in total, one leading into the other. The first was a little dank and musty. It had cold stone shelving around the edges and a large wire meat safe for perishables. In the floor was a square hole full of water. In bad weather the water level rose and rose causing this cellar to flood. The next two cellar rooms were dryer and used for storage. Under the main staircase was another cellar. This one was originally for wine but proved to be far too damp for use and became riddled with all manner of moulds and rot. The whole house was a child's paradise.

Mrs Vernon had left the house part furnished. A large oval settee in royal blue was positioned in the centre of the entrance hall and a soft, darker, blue velvet chesterfield sat invitingly to the left of the inglenook fire place. A dark oak Jacobean bureau stood in the corner of the room waiting for Queenie to fill. This was just one of the five large reception rooms needing her attention. Luckily Queenie had acquired her parents' furniture. When Albert Wombwell sold up to visit Canada, Queenie had stored it all on the farm and when he died it became hers. Queenie was in her element. Mending and making do, she soon made the splendid rooms comfortable. By the end of May 1941 her first paying guest, Mr Dobson, a professional gent from Manchester, arrived.

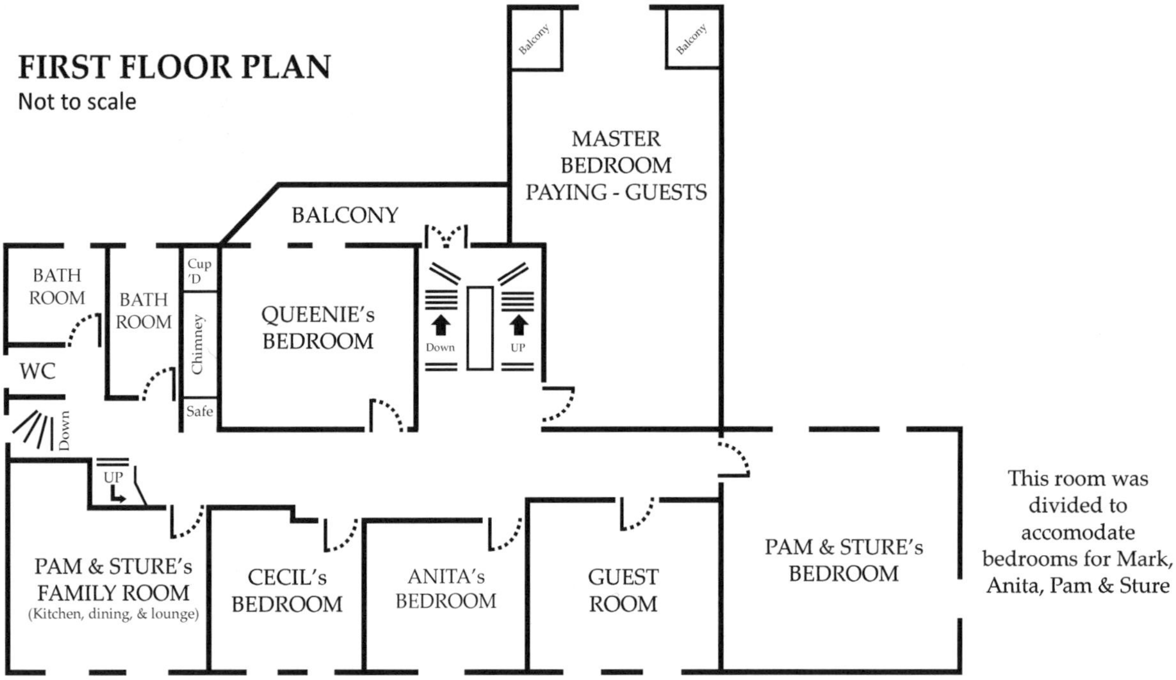

With things going well Queenie could see the possibilities that Goff's Oak House could offer her. Armed with the financial backing of a mortgage for the sum of £3,000 from the Midland Bank in Cheshunt, she approached Mrs Vernon with a view to buying Goff's Oak House. The deal was done and the house was bought lock, stock, and barrel. Mrs Vernon left most of the furniture with one exception. The billiard table, a favourite amongst Jack and the boys, had seen the winning of an important trophy and Mrs Vernon was adamant that it should be given to a serviceman's club as a gift from her family.

The house was poorly lit by wall-mounted, gas mantles and glass globes. Pretty but not practical, they cast eerie shadows along the dark passages. Queenie set to and began to have electricity installed. Eventually the ancient range was removed and a modern, clean and efficient gas cooker was put in its place. Queenie was slowly bringing the property up to date. Her Bohemian style filtered throughout the house. She renovated where she could. She reupholstered all the window seats and made curtains from yards and yards of material. She sought out the auction houses and sale rooms, buying a beautiful French suite in cream and gold for the drawing room. Getting good deals on carpets and rugs, she was always on the lookout for a bargain. She filled the house with an eclectic mix of periods and styles.

Queenie redecorated her bedroom (she and Bert had separate rooms). She bought a brand new suite of bedroom furniture from Maples in London. It was hand painted in a delicate pale green, more suited to a little girl's room. It was beautiful. She made her own curtains. Artistically sewing together swathes of pale green and pink fabrics, imaginatively stitching a pelmet from the offcuts, she created a modern young look.

With World War II in full flight it was essential to keep Goff's Oak House full. Renting rooms became big business. From May 1941 to July 1953 Queenie opened her home to over 450 paying guests. They came from near and far; as far as Cheshire and Manchester in the North; Somerset, Bristol and Cardiff in the West; and Kent and Devon in the South. One guest, a Mrs Michael Cavie, stayed in August 1943; she lived locally in Burton Grange in Cheshunt. Some wartime catastrophe must have befallen the place for her to stay so close to home.

Many came from London seeking refuge from the incessant bombing of the Blitz. In August 1942 Mr R W Hariss brought his family from East Barnet. He wrote in the guest book… ***"a light happy time -- War forgotten!*** Miss Caucutt, a headmistress at Winchmore Hill, stayed over the war years. She travelled out late each afternoon

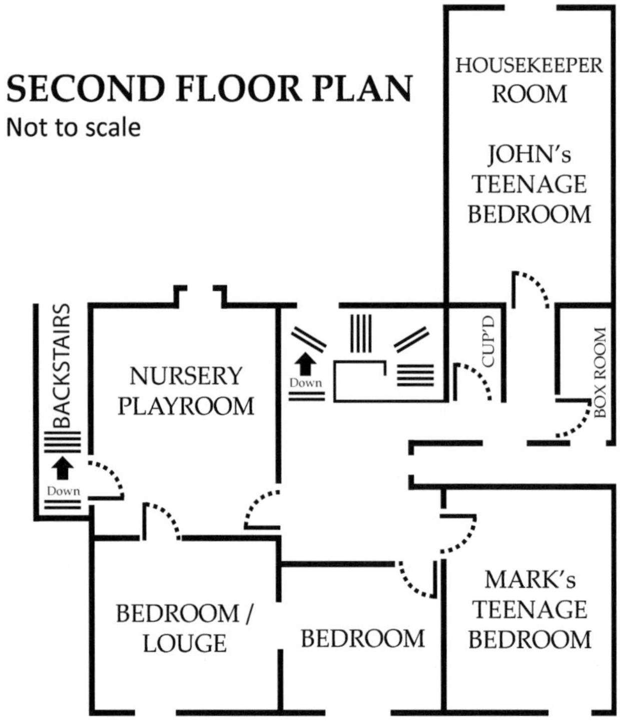

to sleep at Goff's Oak House. In the evenings she sat in the hall inglenook with her torch and book in the darkness of the black out. With her hands nervously shaking, the torch made a rhythmic and uncontrollable banging against the hard cover of the book. At bedtime she took Bert's faithful old black Labrador up to her room for company. One fateful night something spooked the poor old dog; it leapt through the open window and fell to its death. Poor Miss Caucutt must have been scared half to death.

Many visitors came from the filth of the city seeking the peace and quiet of the Hertfordshire countryside. A chap from the Foreign Office stayed and noted… ***"an extremely pleasant working holiday -- with good cups of tea from the old man."*** The 'old man' being Bert Fletcher who loved his tea and was always keen to get the kettle on. Many of the visitors were professional people. Some of the first were teachers working in the area. In June 1944 a gentleman by the name of Addie or Eddie Seamon booked in, his address, simply "BBC London".

Families, friends and neighbours would travel together and rent two or three rooms at a time. Sometimes, when all the rooms were full, they would spill out into the caravan parked in the garden. The compliments rolled in… ***"a home from home." "Most lovely holiday ever spent." "A nice quiet rest." "Very comfortable." "Many thanks for a great welcome and a holiday we shall never forget."*** Recommendation was important to the business and it seemed that everyone was having a good time. Many like the King family, returned several

Dot and Queenie with the children

times over the years.

Small groups of young ladies spent a weekend or a week at a time holidaying in the peaceful tranquillity of Goff's Oak House. The summer of 1944 saw nine young ladies travel together from Hainault, Romford and Barkingside vowing to … ***"be back soon!" "Coming back!" "Coming again!"*** In that same summer Maureen, Rosemary and Yvonne travelled from Fulham to stay for the weekend. They wrote… ***"many thanks for every kindness received from Mrs Fletcher and Uncle Cecil."***

Everyone was welcomed by Queenie's warm hospitality. I wonder if it caused a stir with the residents of Goff's Oak when Mr and Mrs Tomchinsky with their two sons, Peter and Ivan, and Uncle Vladimir de Briger came to stay in July 1943. They were landed gentry or 'white Russians'. With land and status they used their money and influences to escape Russia as war broke out. Queenie would have relished the intrigue. She enjoyed all the interesting stories told by her guests, retelling them time and again with a mischievous flourish, but sadly these tales have been lost through the mists of time.

Both Mr and Mrs Tomchinsky were classical musicians. Mr Tomchinsky paid their way by playing in the Lyon's Corner House band in London, raising the spirits of the visitors with popular wartime tunes as they sipped tea or ate a meal. Queenie found accommodation for them at the top of the house in the attic rooms. The family occupied most of the top floor. Mrs Tomchinsky played the piano and Mr Tomchinsky played both the piano and violin. Queenie together with an army of strong men carted a baby grand piano up the two flights of turning oak stairs to the old housekeeper's room in the eaves. The room overlooked the lawns and Mrs Tomchinsky made this into her studio. Every day she practised her highbrow pieces. Their piercing notes were played with great gusto, echoing down the wide staircase and out through the corridor at full volume. Master Albert Cooke, on visiting his aunt and uncle, shuddered at the hideous sound vibrating down the passageway. The beauty of the notes was completely lost on this youngster. Clamping his hands firmly over his young ears he stomped petulantly back down the stairs as far away from the "terrible noise" as he could get!

Like many of the guests staying at the house the Tomchinskys would gravitate down to the warm family kitchen and sit around the big old table. Queenie would be warm and welcoming and before long Bert would have the kettle on for a cup of tea. Together they would relax and chat about the day's events. When the boys all got back from school Jack would innocently tease the youngest son Ivan. Good friends, the boys' banter was always easy and informal.

Pam and Queenie

With the help of Mrs Grew, Queenie kept the rooms clean and tidy for the many guests. During the war years Queenie encouraged her guests to cater for themselves by bringing their own bed linen and food. She provided them with the use of the butler's pantry upstairs and the main pantry downstairs. Some did require board as well as lodgings and against all the odds Queenie managed to find food for them all. Meat came from either Cheshire Butchers in Goff's Oak or Ripley's in Cuffley. Each week she would travel to Potters Bar to Williams Brothers (which much later became Budgens Supermarket) and buy all other provisions. When bread was short she knocked up a soda loaf to put on the table. Bert was a keen kitchen gardener and provided vegetables throughout the year. With the help of Mrs Vernon's head gardener, cucumbers and tomatoes grew in the two greenhouses. The garden was well stocked with fruit trees and bushes. Even with rationing still in place after the war there was enough for Queenie to create tempting meals for both the family and guests. In 1945 Mr and Mrs Railton commented… ***"very good holiday, plenty to eat."*** An important issue when rationing was in full swing and much of the country was doing without.

Unfortunately, there was one casualty of the War, Albert's parrot. The lovely green bird had been a gift to Queenie's father many years previously. It had lived with him at Lower Hanyards Farm until he sold up and moved in with Queenie at Cuffley after his trip to Canada. On his death in 1935 Queenie took the parrot in and it became part of the family, moving with them to Goff's Oak House and living in the spacious kitchen. The bird was a noisy beast shouting *"ALLO BERT!"* at the top of its voice. Whether this was for Albert Wombwell or Bert Fletcher we do not know but Bert did spend a lot of time chatting to the bird. It was a bright animal mimicking what it heard around him. It would call out *"Have you made the beds?"* and sing *"I Cover the Waterfront", a* tune of the time. Seed for the bird was impossible to find during the war years and Queenie tried to feed him as best she could. All summer she grew tall sunflowers in the kitchen garden. As summer turned to autumn the big yellow heads faded and she took the seeds to dry out. Regrettably it was not successful. The seeds must have been a little damp because the poor old bird became sick. Toxins got into his system and he began to decline. When Pam came home from a day at school, she found Queenie in the kitchen with the bird wrapped gently in a piece of soft warm cloth. She was keeping it warm on the lower rack of the old kitchen range but sadly it died; another statistic of war.

As the war ended a few RAF girls and guys passed through the doors of Goff's Oak House as they made their way back to civilian life. Tired from their duties, it provided them with a night or so of normality.

With Britain still reeling from the ravages of war, the country began to rally around and start to build a future for its returning heroes. Mr Cheshire, the local butcher, was a good friend of Bert's. He and his family decided to host an end-of-war party and asked Bert if he could use Goff's Oak House. The spacious reception rooms were ideal for a grand party and that is what they organised. Jeep loads of young airmen descended from North Weald for the celebrations. Some stayed over after the revelry. It was deemed a great success and remembered long after the event.

When war ended, Jack was married to Dorothy Brooke. Her mother had died whilst she was a youngster and she was brought up in Mill Hill by her father. Mr Brooke was a successful silversmith. During the war he lost a leg and went on to remarry his carer, Herut. She cared for him deeply. Each night she would hoist him onto her back and carry him up the stairs to bed. Dot had worked as a land girl during the war years in Northaw and the surrounding farms. She probably met Jack in one of the local pubs. Jack fell for the lovely Dot. He was soon fed up with travelling to and fro to see her each evening and suggested that they get married and set up home. So in 1944, after a simple wartime ceremony, they were married and a year later Queenie's first grandchild, Paul, was born. Jack built his new family a home in the little black timber cottage at Goff's Oak House. Originally there were two timber cottages standing at the edge of the property but one was completely destroyed by a bomb in WWII and only the second one stood. An elderly couple had occupied it for years. When they passed away the cottage became vacant, and Bert helped his son make it into a comfortable family home. Bert set to and put his skills into practice. He constructed a solid red brick fireplace in the lounge of the cottage, making the room warm and cosy for them during the cold months, and the remaining room was divided to create the space they needed. Dot was welcomed into the

Paul

family with ease. Queenie dotted on her first grandchild and Pam enjoyed the company of her new sister-in-law. They often went out for a drink or to the pictures for the evening.

Pam and Jack had many friends in the village and beyond, and they were always made welcome at the house. Whenever they dropped in, they were always greeted with a cup of tea or a light snack. Queenie's good friend Bertha was living on the caravan site for much of the time and a social soon scene developed between family and friends. There were invitations to dances and dinners. With little TV to watch, going to the movies was big business and a highlight for everyone. Both Queenie and Pam took full advantage of the local buses and trains to travel all over to see the latest films, often going more than once or even twice a week. The evening often began or finished with a drink or two in the local pub. They were never short of company; there always seemed to be someone around to share in the fun.

In 1948 Cecil decided to give up his house, number 5 Cuffley Hill, and moved into Goff's Oak House as most of his free time was spent with Queenie and the family anyway. On weekends he would join them at

Cecil Harriss, man about Town

Point Clear, helping to get the boat out on a Sunday and joining in with all the fun they seemed to have. Living alone as he did and working shifts on the railway must have been a dull existence. It was a sensible decision to have the comfort of his adopted family around him and Queenie made full use of his talents. And so he became her driver and companion.

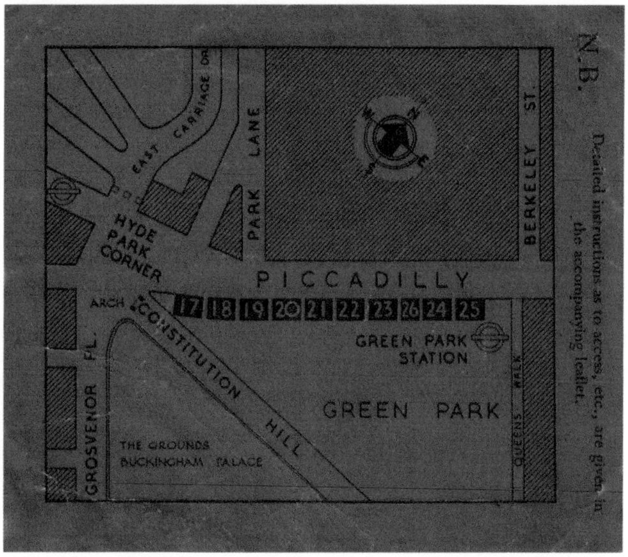

1951 Cecil, Queenie, Jac Wejeis, Pam, Sture and Margaret at Point Clear

With the ever-increasing fortunes of the local nurserymen the Lea Valley had long been an established and respected area for market gardening and growing under glass, with Rochfords being renowned since 1806. Even in 1901 the census showed Cheshunt as having migrant workers from Denmark, Sweden and Switzerland. By 1902 a guide book referred to Flamstead End and Turnford districts as "Rochfordville". Not surprisingly the rooms at Goff's Oak House became home to a variety of young men. Their wealthy horticultural families sent them over to England to gain work experience on the many local nurseries. By January 1951 seven young Dutchmen had booked rooms for a long stay. They became good company for Jack, Pam and their friends. Queenie treated them like her own family, inviting her favourites to join the family on their weekend trips to Point Clear.

Queenie was always one to lead the way where fun was to be had. When Queen Elizabeth II was crowned on June 2nd 1953, Queenie was there! A royalist through and through, she took the train to Green Park Station and sat in seat 9, row F, in stand number 22 erected in Piccadilly. The ticket cost the princely sum of £4. This would be around £100 today. As the procession made its historic way to Westminster it was seen by three million excited spectators lining the streets of London. Many TVs were sold to people wishing to see the Coronation for themselves. TV sales rose to the highest they had ever been and one in four households had a TV in Britain. Families gathered in their front rooms with friends and neighbours to witness history in the making. Descriptions of the Coronation were broadcast in 39 languages by 750 commentators around the world. It was a monumental occasion for Great Britain and Queenie was there.

By the time Sture Eliasson arrived from Tollarp, Sweden, in April 1951, the house was full of guests. Queenie opened the door to him dressed as normal in a pair of men's scruffy old corduroy trousers, her blonde hair tousled from her labours. The hall was dark and foreboding as his eyes adjusted from the bright sun of outside. He could not believe where he had landed up. With lions caged in the yard and a Himalayan bear exercised on the lawn, Goff's Oak House, with all its colourful inhabitants, was a far cry from the small sleepy town of Tollarp that he had just left. When Pam arrived home from a hard day working in the bank, Queenie was waiting. Pam, tired and reluctant, was ushered into the morning room to meet the newest arrival from Sweden. Sture sat in the small room taking in his surroundings and trying to relax. Pam, still in her blue mackintosh from work, popped her head around the door to say a polite hello. Who would have guessed the outcome of this initial meeting!

Queenie with Pam, Sture, Jac and Cecil

The two soon became good friends. Pam took the new boy under her wing. She introduced Sture to her friends and together they explored the local area, riding their bikes into the countryside, enjoying a picnic at a beauty spot or stopping off at the village pub for a swift half. Over time the friendship grew and love developed. When it was time for Sture to return to Sweden after his year of work he asked Pam to go with him.

Pam and Sture Wedding Day

She wanted to travel and had been considering working abroad for some time. The only opportunity the bank could offer was South Africa and Pam had been looking into the possibility of a transfer. Sture suggested working as an au pair in Sweden. He offered to put an advert in the local newspaper as soon as he got back home. It was not long before a position came up in Malmo. Pam was to look after a little boy, the son of busy parents, a doctor and his wife. She was employed to teach him English. Queenie was sad to see her go. She enjoyed her company and the support that Pam gave to the business. Pam soon settled into her new life with the Doctor and his family. On her first weekend free Sture came to collect her and take her back to Tollarp to meet all the family. In the summer of 1952 Pam and Sture rolled up at the big house on the nursery. His mother Elin was there to greet them both. His eight siblings peered out of the windows. The little ones, only eight or so were fascinated by this English maiden. Pam was soon welcomed into the fold. Sture's older sisters looked after her and everyone put her at ease. On the day of Midsummer Eve 1952 Sture took Pam into Kristianstad. He bought her a ring and asked her to marry him. The pair celebrated with a special meal in a hotel. The excited couple began to make the necessary arrangements. It took some time to finalise all the required paperwork. There was much toing and froing between Tollarp and the Council offices in Kristianstad. The wedding was finally arranged for the 29th November 1952 in the beautiful church in Tollarp. By this time Pam was expecting! As an engaged couple it was quite acceptable, in Sweden, for them to share a bed and the inevitable happened. Queenie was anxious that Pam was making the right decision in planning a life in Sweden. Big brother Jack was sent over to check it all out. Pam was able to convince him that she did indeed know what she was doing and the wedding plans went ahead. Pam's Dad, Bert, was busy working hard at A B Stevens's pig farm. He had little interest in travel so Queenie was escorted to Sweden by Cecil. They travelled by train to the ferry and over to France, and on through Europe and across to Malmo and Kristianstad. They were picked up from the station and settled into a local home where bed and breakfast was provided. The wedding was a simple occasion. Pam, dressed in a smart blue dress and jacket, looked radiant as she walked down the aisle, with her handsome groom at her side.

After a week spent with the newly-weds, sightseeing and getting to know the family, Queenie and Cecil left early on December the 5th. Pam and Sture took them to Malmo and treated them to a smorgasbord lunch in a swanky hotel. Queenie referred to it as the, "*last word in food.*" She was impressed with the array of hot and cold meats and sausages. She was also surprised to find that the shopping was as good as London or Paris. After coffee and cream cakes in a swish coffee shop, Queenie said a sad goodbye to Pam. In a diary-type note, written on a manila envelope split open to provide two sides, she wrote, "*hated to leave her!*" But Queenie being Queenie, she soon settled down to enjoy her trip home. On the boat she conversed with the youngsters going home to their families for Christmas. She delighted over the beautiful gifts they had bought for their families. She commented on one sweet girl who had bought a pretty silver cream jug and bowl for her mother. In Denmark Queenie was determined to find time to shop. In the busy high street she was stunned by the elegance of the shop windows and all the Christmas lights. *"It was like being in fairy land!"* she wrote, *"lights and trees lit up wherever you looked."* As always Queenie was interested in food and before long she and Cecil were sampling delicious Scandinavian hot dogs served with mild mustard in sweet rolls by the street vendors. Queenie always had a soft spot for young men in uniform, and this trip provided the golden opportunity for Queenie to view the smart young men from the safety of the carriage window or interact with them at customs. She wrote as she crossed the border, *"Change here from Danish to German so now we shall have very arrogant smashers in grey-green uniforms." ---"There goes a uniform I have not seen before. Smashing light blue and grey cap."* There is no doubt that she was an old flirt!

Back home Queenie settled into a life without her daughter, and Pam settled into marriage and motherhood. Pam returned to England in 1953 for a visit, with new baby Johnny and her mother-in-law, Elin. In May, a year later, an anxious Jack phoned Pam in Sweden to explain that their Dad was seriously ill and that she should make arrangements to come home; Bert had lung cancer. He was wracked by a continuous cough that took all his strength. Pam, Sture and Johnny were on the first available flight back to the UK. After a few weeks Sture had to get back to work in Sweden but Pam stayed to support Queenie. Everyone rallied around to help her nurse Bert. She had the support of Jack, Dot, Cecil and Pam. They watched helplessly as Bert's health declined. Queenie had created a comfortable bedroom for him downstairs in the bright drawing room. The beautiful room had large windows that looked out onto the lush green lawns. A bed was made up and every night someone from the caravan site came in to be with Bert whilst Queenie and the family got some well-earned sleep.

As the weeks turned into months Bert badgered Pam into returning to Sture and Sweden. After a three-month stay she eventually gave in, and in August 1954 she returned. Sadly Bert passed away in October. Pam dropped everything and once again she and Johnny were back in England for the funeral. Dot looked after the children whilst everyone else went to the local service at the Methodist Chapel.

After Bert's death the house seemed empty and Queenie missed her daughter and grandson even more than she had before. She began to put pressure on them to set up home back in Goff's Oak. Sture was not sure at first but his relationship with his father was becoming increasingly difficult. Following from his education in horticulture, Sture had ideas to improve production on the nursery in Tollarp but his father Nils was having none of it. Sture felt stifled in the family business and began to realise that he could be his own boss in the UK. Queenie began to make enquiries and before long she had found two nurseries in the local area for Sture to view. He decided to rent a one-acre nursery in Crouch Lane. It had been run by Mr Sheppard. He grew a few cucumbers and a second crop of tomatoes but not very successfully. Sture was convinced that he could make it into a going concern and the little family settled back into life in Goff's Oak.

The young couple were keen to use Pam's inheritance from her grandfather to buy a newly-built semi-detached three-bed roomed house in, what we called, "The Service Road." But Queenie was having none of it! "Why do you want your own place when there is so much room here?" she asked. There were fewer paying guests at Goff's Oak House and Queenie offered to create living accommodation for them. Pam and Sture never had a convincing argument against this and so they made do with a couple of rooms in Goff's Oak House and got on with the job of improving the nursery and raising a family. With Dot and Jack doing the same next door, a unique family dynamic was being created with Queenie firmly positioned at the head.

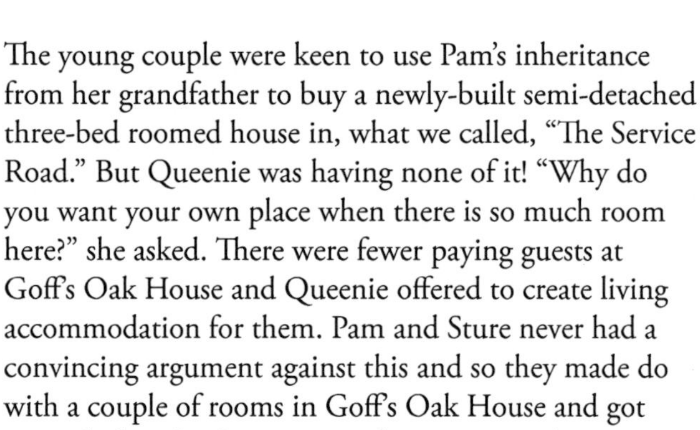
GOFFS OAK HOUSE,
GOFFS OAK.
Oct. 11th 1954.

Mrs. A. Fletcher and Family wish to express their sincere thanks for the kind expressions of sympathy received in their recent bereavement.

Caravans at Goff's Oak House

Caravans at Goff's Oak House evolved out of necessity. There was a demand from people needing cheap accommodation during difficult times and it provided a much appreciated income for Queenie. It began with Queenie's roll-along caravan. It had been brought back to the farm from West Bay with the onset of the Second World War. When Queenie moved to Goff's Oak House it came with her and was used for holidays and as an overflow for paying guests when all the rooms in the house were full.

Following the tradition of her father, Queenie had wintering circus folk to stay at Brook Farm. When she moved to Goff's Oak House they followed. Most brought their own accommodation and needed somewhere to park and space for their animals. Goff's Oak House was perfect for this; there was plenty of space for everyone.

In the 1940s a small number of professional people had their own touring caravans. Caravanning was becoming a popular recreational pursuit for those with money to spend. But with war raging, some people used them to escape the horrors of the blitz. They would drive out into the Hertfordshire countryside for some solace and solitude. For others life was less cosy. They had been bombed out of their London homes, and had bought a cheap van to stay in whilst they decided what to do. Goff's Oak provided an ideal location for many. It was close enough to London for commuters and yet felt remote enough to provide comfort and security away from the horrors of war.

The house and garden provided refuge for many of the circus performers and their animals. At the end of each season, or fitting in a visit between shows, the many gloriously colourful characters came. Carl Dane, the famous strongman was a distant cousin to the Stebbings, and lived in a caravan in the corner of the site. Carl began his circus career as a young acrobat. As he grew into adulthood it became obvious just how strong he was. This 6' 5" giant of a man could pull a double-decker bus with his teeth. In 1932 this circus strongman became the iconic figure of J Arthur Rank Films. With his torso naked and muscles rippling he graciously banged the gong at the beginning of all Rank films up to 1948. Every three years the sequence had to be redone due to the deterioration of the film. It often took several takes over several weeks. His body was bronzed with thick make-up and under the heat of his body and the lights it would run and require continual touching-up! It was said that this bad boy was often reported on in the News of the World for all the wrong reasons.

Most of the visiting artists were connected to the Fossetts. The world of the circus was a close-knit community. Jan Doksansky presented horses for Bette and brought his wife Sylvia, daughter June and son Johnny to live at Goff's Oak House. Sylvia had been a

Jan Doksansky with Nero, Soliman and Carmon. Shanklin 1947

Sylvia Doksanasky

talented rider and top mounter with the Baker Boys for the Cumberland's Troupe with Bertram Mills Circus since 1937. She was a petite, charismatic woman who fearlessly rode at the top of the human pyramid. Jan was a famous animal trainer, having worked with big cats, elephants, polar bears, horses and chimpanzees. Much of his work was with Chapman's Zoo Circus and when they opened a season earlier than Mills, Sylvia would help him present his elephants or perform a solo voltage riding act. Jan was very successful and took his act to Europe for a season or two. Such was his success that he went on to train other artists in the art of animal training. Jan and his family became good friends to Queenie. Jan gave Queenie a solid gold nugget that he got whilst in Spain and had it fashioned into a lion charm. A treasure Queenie was proud to show us.

June started her circus career as a teenage tumbler with Bertram Mills. Later her love of horses and riding skills led her to take over from her mother as an accomplished rider and she rode with the Baker Boys for many years. In the mid-fifties she met and married Doug. This handsome man did an impressive aerial act called 'The Flying Comets'. After they were married, Doug and June lived in a small caravan on the site with their baby daughter for a year or so before moving to a house in the local area. Doug continued to perform his aerial act around Europe. One year Pam and Sture travelled to Sweden for the double wedding of one of Sture's brothers and one of his sisters in their home town of Tollarp. After the celebrations Pam and Sture were able to stay in Stockholm in the flat of one of the happy couples whilst they were on honeymoon. Doug was performing his act at Grunalund open air theatre in Stockholm and Pam and Sture were pleased to be able to see him and enjoy the show.

Whilst the showmen and women were resting between engagements, they used their time to practise and perfect their skills, setting up their equipment on the bottom lawn. Much of their mastery needed to be polished and their routines perfected or reinvented. Timing was everything and there was much tumbling and juggling to be seen on the lawns at Goff's Oak House. They could be seen balancing on a low or slack wire. Some were seen riding around on a unicycle. Teenager Johnny Doksansky tried both. Try as he might he never quite got it whilst others made it look so easy! At eighteen he gave up and joined the army. He never went back to his act. After his service he travelled to New Zealand where he studied and created a new life for himself. On his return he and his new wife lived once again with Queenie. Queenie made a modest flat in the Ostler's Room. She put in a door where a window had once been and the patio flat was created. The couple lived a comfy life and raised their baby son for a few

Sylvia Doksansky and the Baker Boys

Queenie and the Hiymalayan Bear at Goff's Oak House

Queenie

years before getting a place of their own.

Goff's Oak House became home to a variety of animals. Bette made her little ponies comfortable in the stables and Jan, the famous lion tamer, brought Nero, Soliman and Carmon to Goff's Oak. The three beasts were housed in their travelling wagons in the yard.

One young local recalls hearing them roar at night as he was being tucked up in bed. After their extended confinement at Goff's Oak, Jan was a brave man to get in with the lions at their first show of the season. Bette often took her circus to Rye Park in Hoddesdon or Potters Bar for the opening show and Queenie and her family were always there to see it. Once Bette tried holding a show in Cuffley but the returns were not as good as she had hoped and so she abandoned the idea.

Sylvia's brother, Billy Dash, brought his black bear to the house where it remained caged in the yard. The beast was a vicious creature and bit an unsuspecting Billy on the heel. Billy found the animal impossible to work with and quickly sold him on. He had much better success with his chimpanzees, who were regular visitors to the house. I still remember coming home from school to find Queenie on the patio cuddling a chimp. The chimps had their very own room, the servants' hall, which became known as the 'chimp room'! Long after the chimps had

Queenie at Goff's Oak House with chimps

Jan Doksansky

Ethel and Pappa Glysson

gone and the room had been restored to a storage room it was always known as the 'chimp room'. The original PG Tips chimpanzees stayed in that room and had tea parties with Queenie on the patio. Before the "Dash" chimps were in residence in the servants' hall, a Dutch couple often stayed. Papa Glisson and his wife Ethel, a contortionist who could put her legs behind her head, had a variety act where Papa Glisson walked on his head! When this got too much for the elderly couple, Ethel took the bookings and sold ice creams for Robert Brothers Circus.

Most of the showmen and women were versatile performers and hard workers. Circus life required a good deal of flexibility and compromise. Many did seasons with a variety of different circuses and many worked the variety circuit as well. Queenie happily followed them from local shows in Hoddesdon, Potters Bar and Waltham Abbey, to London and Colchester. Queenie's door at Goff's Oak House was always open and visitors like Jacko Fossett or Recco the clown would often call in when they were passing.

Jacko was Britain's best loved clown and gave nearly 60 years of service. As a youngster, he worked with his sisters on the trapeze. When his dad died, he was packed off to school to finish his education. Then, when war broke, he joined the RAF and was posted to ENSA (Entertainments National Service Association) where he met Ralph Reader. Ralph produced shows to entertain the troops and Jacko honed his skills and performed comedy skits with Peter Sellers, Dick Emery and best buddy Tony Hancock. On leaving the forces, he joined Bobby and Tommy Roberts as their principal clown and tent master. His work took him all over the world and Queenie enjoyed hearing his fascinating stories. Queenie rarely stood on ceremony and Jacko was happy to do the same and sit like so many others at the big old kitchen table for a cup of tea and a chinwag.

Bette' son, Jimmy Fossett married his chorus girl sweetheart Alice and in the late 1950s he took his family out to America to start a new life in Sarasota. He had developed a unique swaying pole act. The rigging and design were all Jimmy's work. "The Swaying Stars" consisted of two vertical poles 70ft above the ground. Jimmy and his partner Evelyn gracefully moved from one to the other without a safety net. They toured the world with this breath-taking feat. His children grew up and joined the act. Then in 1970 disaster struck; Jimmy's seventeen-year-old son fell from a 100ft pole in Tivoli Gardens, Copenhagen. News of his death quickly reached Queenie. She was devastated. I never saw her cry but her face was etched with sorrow for weeks to

Goff's Oak House

come. Then five years later disaster struck again. Michael Fossett at the age of 26 lost his life in Denver, Colorado. He had been performing without a net and fell to his death witnessed by a shocked audience of 8,000 people. This second tragedy shocked Queenie to the core and a little bit of her heart was broken. Her love for the young was so strong, her empathy so powerful. It was one of the rare times that I saw her show real emotion. When Bette arrived for her annual visit, I remember hushed voices as the two grandmothers shared quiet moments together. There was such sadness between them.

In these early days, permission for a caravan site was not required. There were no rules or regulations for Queenie to follow and the site simply sprang up within the leafy confines of the glorious garden. With one draughty outside loo on the patio and another by the cottage, facilities were very basic. People's expectations were different in the late 1940s - early 1950s. Not every home had an indoor bathroom and some only had shared facilities. Queenie invited guests to use the bathroom in the house for a ritual soak once or twice a week but most made do with a stand-up wash in a bowl at their tiny kitchen sink.

By the mid-1950s the local Council had begun to make a fuss. Originally they had given outline permission for 34 hardstandings for temporary vans. The site had only twelve caravans but they had become a permanent fixture and the Council were not happy with these residential vans on the site in the garden, and it became necessary for Queenie to obtain a license and adhere to a few basic recognised standards. Queenie rose to the challenge and got herself organised. She appointed Mr F Hellings to act for her. He put her case to the Council stating that the site had been in use since 1940 and that it therefore had existing rights. But they refused consent.

In July 1956, Queenie was fined £2 for using the site without proper facilities with a continuing penalty of £1 a day running from October. Immediately Queenie began to improve the site. She began to make plans to have water laid and hardstandings nestled amongst the greenery of the garden. The Council were still less than happy! On the 4th October, they announced that whatever was spent on preparation of the site, they would not grant permission. Someone in the Council was definitely gunning for Queenie! Queenie was being asked to lay out a considerable amount of capital with the strong risk that it would be to no avail. It was not only her income at stake. There was the possibility that twelve homes would be lost and these belonged to her friends. She was not going to give up that easily! Together with Mr Hellings she organised the fight back and continued with the work.

On the 8th January1957, papers were resubmitted to the Council but once again permission was refused on the grounds that the site was adjacent to green belt land. They went on to say that the original outline permission for temporary vans should never have been allowed and no further work should be permitted to allow the site to become consolidated. But Queenie being Queenie went ahead anyway. By mid-January the works were well under way and on the 22nd January the site was inspected by the National Caravan Council. The site had twelve hardstandings with clear access via a roadway. There was a new drainage system, and running water from stand pipes was accessible to all the caravans. The site had three flushing toilets and met with all the requirements. The secretary of the National Caravan Council said "I would say that anyone who could get on that site for living accommodation could count themselves extremely fortunate." Still not satisfied, the Council sent Dr Garrard to the site in February to give his view. He came away very much impressed and announced it among the very best of sites he had inspected. When Mr Hellings put his appeal to the Council on March 21st he had the backing of the residents; eleven of them joined him at the Council offices to put forward their case. The Council had no grounds to refuse!!! And after much heartache and extreme cost to Queenie, permission was finally given. Unconditional consent was granted for a lavatory block, a wash-house and drainage for the twelve existing caravans, plus hardstandings and drainage for a further eleven vans. Queenie continued to rally a workforce and the additional hardstandings were finally laid amongst the tall trees and shrubbery. A year later the gents and ladies toilet blocks were completed by builder Mr Chapman, and in the 1960s the site was completed with the addition of another toilet block, and a shower block for the men and one for the women with a useful laundry room built in between. The site had a mix of residential vans; some were purchased second-hand by Queenie and others belonged to the residents themselves. Queenie had sheds built. One shed for each van. Little concrete blocks with black doors were tucked away at the edge of the site, giving the residents much needed space for storing all sorts of things, from bikes to furniture.

Gradually the circus performers retired to pastures new and were replaced by a different kind of resident. Many from the sixties were respectable people working in the city. They included doctors and other professional people between homes. Others were retired couples or singles looking for an economical residence to spend their twilight years. And where better than the village of Goff's Oak in a cosy, if not damp, van nestled between the greenery where you could enjoy the flora and fauna in peace and quiet.

Each resident had their own story; each had a unique character. Queenie had her favourites and if she liked you she made friends easily. She especially loved the retired show people and often popped in for a cup of tea, eager to hear their stories. Henry Vadden and his wife Gladys became family friends. On odd occasions Henry would babysit us youngsters, when all the grown-ups went out together. He performed his daredevil and dangerous juggling act, during the 1940s, '50s, '60s and occasionally the '70s. He balanced long bladed knives end to end on his chin or forehead, and balanced a full-sized cartwheel on a spiked helmet on his head. As a finale he would whip off the helmet and catch the cartwheel on his back. Together with his glamorous wife and assistant they toured the UK and beyond, earning enough to pay for their only son to be schooled privately and later educated in veterinary medicine. It was a proud day for Henry and Gladys when he graduated as a vet.

Henry was a warm-hearted man with deep clefts in his forehead and chin, scars from his days as a performer. His unusual show brought him fame and notoriety. He performed for King George VI, her majesty Queen Elizabeth II and the Queen Mum, on November the 4th, 1946 at the London Palladium Theatre. He found himself on TV more than once and performed on the ITV Variety Show in 1960 with Frankie Howard topping the bill. He got to meet many of the greats and went to Canada to perform with George Formby. He was loved and well respected amongst them all.

At Goff's Oak he became Queenie's handyman. He would keep the toilets and showers clean and tidy. He would paint and mend as he went along, maintaining the site and helping out other residents when they got into a fix.

Queenie's grandson John loved Mr Henry Vadden and at weekends or school holidays he would knock at the flimsy caravan door and ask Gladys: "is Mr Henry Vadden coming out to play?" Henry would find John a pot of paint and a small brush, and he would set John a task whilst he got on with the day's work.

Both Gladys's sister, Cynthia, and her mother had caravans on the site. Cynthia had also been a showgirl. Her juggling act involved another young lady and over time rumours grew as to the extent of their relationship. At Goff's Oak, Cynthia managed to stir up controversy

Caravans at Goff's Oak House 1960's

and scandal by having an affair with Mr Bird, a married resident. There was never a dull moment on the site!

The sixties definitely brought a special type of person to the site. Mr Millner, a composer confident in his success, sent his works to a London office and waited with bated breath for the reply. Each day he would check his pigeon-hole in the scullery for post. But the news he was waiting for never came. Sadly he never became famous! There was however one famous resident who stayed for a year or so, a member of the sixties pop group 'Unit 4 Plus 2'. The local band went on to have a big hit with 'Concrete and Clay'. Queenie had a talented milliner who made hats for the royals in London, living on the site. The middle-aged lady lived with her sickly daughter and then later on her own. She lived a quiet life at the bottom of the garden. She was so quiet; it was difficult to know whether she was in or out! Her neighbour across the way could not have been more different. At weekends, as soon as the sun began to shine, she would strip off! Dressed only in her white bra and skirt she could be found sunbathing on a reclined deckchair, her eyes tightly closed to the glare of the sun. I never batted an eye but some less liberal residents did grumble.

Bunny was another lady on her own. She had a 'big' caravan plot shaded by the spread of a tall horse chestnut tree. Retired, with time her own, she loved her little bit of garden. It became a passion and she spent all her time tending to it. She created a riot of spring colour where none had been. She never showed much tolerance to us children. Her haughty air spelt out "don't mess with me!". She never passed the time of day or acknowledged my friendly smiles like most other people on the site. She was sharp and unforgiving if we played too close or made too much noise, and often complained to Queenie, who only reprimanded us lightly. Queenie never forgot that it was our garden too!

Other residents were much nicer. On damp drizzly days, I would call in on old Mrs Gates. Her van was behind the abandoned tennis court beside the washing lines. She had brought with her a young Spaniard who had fled the Spanish Civil War and lived with her as her lodger. His English was poor and often on meeting him he would announce "Mrs Gates she cookie in the oily oil". Sadly he must have been deeply troubled because he took his own life by jumping from a high building.

I was oblivious of this tragedy as I made my way to her caravan. Two or three rain beaten pots welcomed me along the pathway and up the steps to her pale green aluminium door. Her face etched with life brightened when she saw who was at the door. The warmth of her van invited me in. Her snug home was clean and cosy. Small vases on lace doilies adorned the little table and sideboard. Everything was neat and ordered. The sweet, white-haired lady kept me entertained for a little while on grey days. She asked of school and the family. I took some of the little things I had made down to show her. She knew I had a firm interest in arts and crafts and gave me her old copy of the Big Book of Needlecraft which I still have to this day. Inside is simply written… 1959 H. P. Gates.

Another welcoming couple were a retired couple who used to perform a dog act. They had two white poodles, and then only one. The couple had bright open smiles. Her face was always made up with subtle colour that complemented her blonded grey hair, which she wore

Caravans at Goff's Oak House 1970's

neatly scooped up into a graceful chignon. They were both full of life and young at heart. They were happy to be settled in their retirement and spent a quiet contented life with the last of their dogs. When the sky was clear and blue and the sun warmed the air, they sat out on their step. I was often invited in as I passed. The van was packed with photos and memorabilia. I would sit on a low tapestry stool, nibbling biscuits and sipping weak tea. As I petted the dogs they reminisced, retelling their stories with references to the objects around me. They ask me of my future plans. Where was life going to take me? I had no idea but they felt sure a pretty little thing like me should be shown off. It bolstered my confidence but I was under no illusion.

The anonymity of the site attracted a small number of misfits and deviants. Mr Cooke was probably special needs. His mother had set him up in a caravan to live an independent life. He was often seen in the mornings aimlessly wandering around the site with a saucepan in his hand. As a child I accepted this and took no notice. It was all part of life!

Suave Mr Timms was from a well-to-do family with money behind them. In his hey-day he had been a famous photographer but sadly the demon drink got the better of him. He drove a smart blue Rolls-Royce and dressed in elegant jackets and slacks. Often on returning home from a bender he would stumble out of the car, unable to co-ordinate his legs, and land in a drunken stupor on the car park gravel. Once he arrived home dressed in full armour complete with helmet. Goodness knows where he had been but needless to say he was very merry. One year he went off to the south of France for a holiday in the Saint-Tropez sun. He came home weeks later with a young French woman half his age on his arm. Whatever she thought of the ramshackle site and its inhabitants, we will never know. Needless to say she did not stay long.

There was an alleged peeping Tom who prowled around the vans after dark and a knicker snatcher who helped himself from the washing lines. He was caught one evening. His wife came into the house in a panic; her husband had gone for a shower some time previously and not returned. She had been banging on the door but she could not get an answer from him. Queenie was down at Brightlingsea at the time and it fell to Pam and Sture to sort things out. They hammered on the locked shower door. The water was still running, hot and steamy. They ended up breaking the door down to find her husband, a big burly coalman, collapsed naked on the floor. He was surrounded by all the missing knickers, including a pair of mine. The ambulance was called along with the police who prosecuted him. As a child I was protected from all this drama but looking back, I can understand why I got mixed reactions from people when I mentioned that I lived at Goff's Oak House.

For me it was all very normal and most of the residents were just that. One or two were young married couples, with small babies, waiting to be housed. If Queenie took a shine to them she would bend over backwards to help them with furniture and whatnots for their new homes when they moved out. On bright afternoons, the little babies would be nestled into their prams to get some fresh air in the garden. I would offer to take them for a walk. The mums were happy to get a little peace and allowed me to push the big coach-built prams around the site path for a few circuits. I loved it! If Queenie was in the garden, she would come up to say hello. She was always interested in who I was taking for a walk.
Mr and Mrs Bates were a very normal couple. They became family friends. Their daughter Jackie was a couple of years younger than me. A timid little thing with silky brown hair and doleful brown eyes. She and I became playmates but it was Mark she wanted to spend time with. When she joined me at Mill Mead Primary School, it was her dad, Alan, who offered to take the three of us into school one morning when we were running a little late. We bundled into his old Commer van, the three of us squashed together on the one front seat. Off we set along Goff's Lane; the traffic was busy for a Monday morning, and we slowed to turn right into Robinson Avenue. The traffic cleared and Alan took his chance and swung the van across the oncoming traffic. As we took the turn, the van door flew open and I slid, as if by slow motion, onto the hard black tarmac. I lay stunned in the middle of the cold road; cars and vans seemed to be all around me. The oncoming traffic screeched to a halt and Alan, as shaken as I, jumped out and lifted me back into the van. I think he took the others to school. He certainly took me home. Mum and Queenie fussed over me until they were sure that there was no lasting damage, then packed me back off to school. I could have been only seven or eight but the memory of the oncoming traffic still remains and the

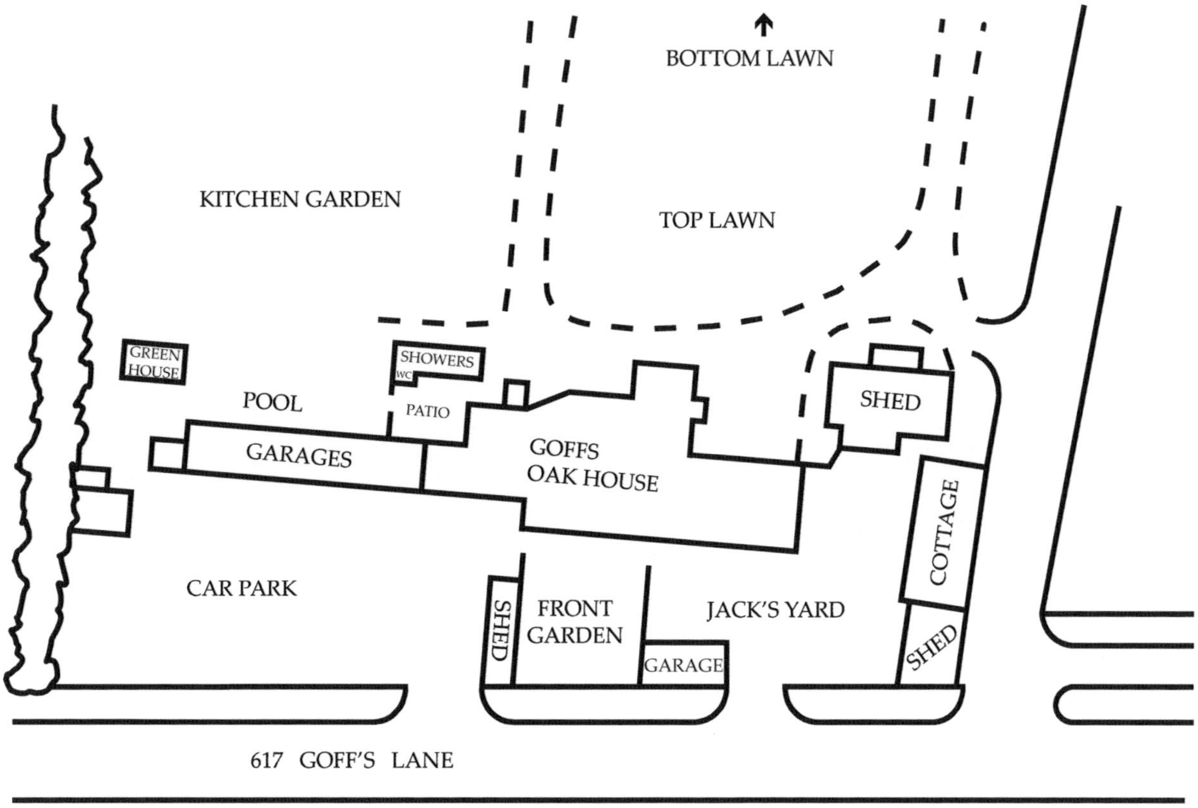

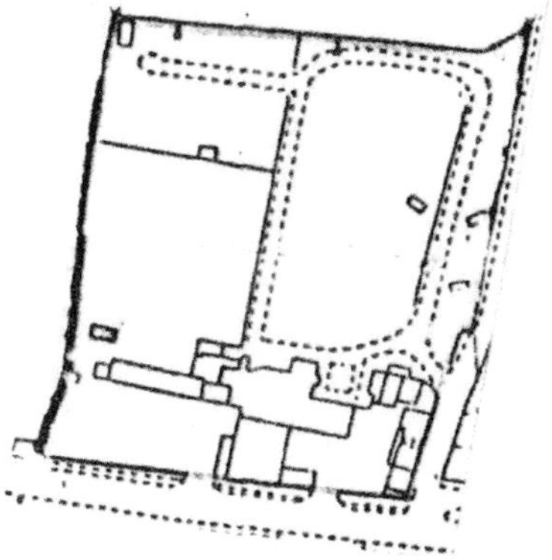

into the safe for security. The site provided Queenie with a substantial income over the years, which in turn she was able to share with us all through the treats and gifts she bestowed upon us. But more lasting are the unique experiences she provided and the enduring memories of them that make us who we are.

injustice of being sent back to school so soon still rankles!

In its heyday the site or 'Caravan Park' as Queenie liked to call it in later years, provided good accommodation for many people regardless of their circumstances. For some it was a haven. The door from the patio into the house was always left open. Residents would wander in daily to collect their post housed in the pigeon-holes in the scullery. Each and every Friday afternoon through to Saturday lunchtime, there would be a continual stream of rent payers. They would stroll in and knock loudly on the kitchen door or holler a "cooee" up the stairs to attract attention. If Queenie was not around, we took it in turns to take the rent. 'The Chart' was laid out on the red Formica table. It was an A1 sized sheet of graph paper securely Sellotaped to an old piece of brown packing card. Lines had been ruled with a black pen to provide a list of all the vans and their tenants down one side and the dates along the top. The cash was stashed into a wooden box and deposited

QUEENIE FLETCHER

JACK married DOROTHY **(DOT)** — **PAMELA** married STURE **(STUART) ELIASSON**

PAUL — CANDICE **(CANDY)** — **LEE** — JOHNNY **(JOHN)** — **ANITA** — **MARK**

1960s Goff's Oak House

By the time the book of life turned the page to a new decade we were living as an extended family. Jack and Dot in the wooden 'Cottage' in the yard, with their three children, Paul, Candy and Lee. Pam, Sture and their children in rooms on the first floor of the house. Queenie had the butler's pantry knocked through into the room next door to create a kitchenette, lounge and diner for Pam's family. Bedrooms on the same floor were provided for John, Anita and eventually Mark. Living independently but together, the family rubbed along amicably with Queenie as the matriarch.

Rooms in the house were still let out to paying guests but they were renting for much longer periods, most living with us for years at a time. Mr Fisk had the housekeeper's room at the top of the house for a time. He travelled to Silver Street each day to work at Gun Station as a caretaker. Mr Douglas stayed for many months in one of the rooms. His work as a SPY took him out at all hours of the day and night.

Miss Pratt had the big bedroom at the end of the passage on the first floor. She had lived with her parents until they both died. A true Victorian spinster, she became her married sister's responsibility. They paid for her lodgings at Goff's Oak House and left her to look after

Jack and Dot's Cottage

Jack Fletcher

herself. She was a pale, fragile old lady. As light as a feather, she would waft about the landing like a spectre in her long white nightdress and her dressing gown. She lived mostly on milk and eggs, and occasionally had tiny portions of white fish poached in milk which she prepared in the scullery and took quietly to her room on a wooden tray. Miss Pratt was of a very nervous disposition. Anything and everything would unnerve her. If the lights flickered or made a slight buzzing sound, she would complain that the electricity was leaking. During night-time thunderstorms Pam and Sture would be roused from their slumbers to find a ghostly Miss Pratt perched on the end of their bed. Spending much of her time indoors, Miss Pratt was an avid reader of the women's magazines of the day. She was happy to share them with the newly-married Pam but only after she had censored them. She carefully and laboriously cut out any article that may be too salacious for a young woman to read. Anything provocative or offensive had been snipped clean away.

Mrs Farest and her two grown-up daughters, Rosemary and Linda, lived in the nursery flat at the very top of the house in the eaves. It was quite spacious with a large lounge and separate dining room. Basic kitchen facilities had been provided behind a pair of painted doors in the dining room and a cooker had been connected up on the landing. The flat had two good size bedrooms and made comfortable accommodation for three. Much later Paul, his wife Anne and their young family used it when they were between homes.

On this floor there was a further room for rent. The housekeeper's room at the top of the house was let to a middle-aged woman who, for a time, was the leader of the local Cub Scout group. Years later when she finally left to live in a new flat, the room was redecorated with a coat of fresh paint and John moved in to create a teenage pad.

During this time the billiard room end of the house was let to an old lady and her two adult sons. The heavy door from the grand hall of the house remained firmly locked for many years. Access to the billiard room area was through a separate front door to the right-hand side of the house beside Jack's yard. Behind it was a stone-floored lobby which was used as a kitchen-cum-diner. It had three doors off of it. The first was the locked door back into the house. The second led to a small scullery with a butler sink and an oven, and from there you could access, through yet another door, a beautiful blue and white porcelain Water Closet. This set up would never be allowed by today's standards. At the time, expectations were much lower and people were more than happy to accept what was on offer.
The third door off the lobby opened into the billiard room, a gigantic room with an open fireplace and dual aspect. One window looked out onto the garden at the back and the second to the shrubbery of Jack's yard. The room was roughly divided by dark heavy furniture and served as both lounge and bedrooms for the three of them.

In the main part of the house, Norman Punshon had the master bedroom overlooking the lawns. He kept himself to himself, trotting off early each morning to work as a butcher in Waltham Abbey. Each evening he would come home smelling of raw meat, his hands red and swollen from the damp and cold of the butchery. With his tea neatly wrapped in white paper, then printed newspaper, he would slip in barely noticed. An old Navy man, he was quite capable of looking after himself. He would cook his chops or sausages on the stove in the pantry and quietly take it back to his room on a tray to eat.

On Sunday mornings, I was asked to knock on his door and invite him along for elevenses. He would join us promptly as the clock struck. Queenie, busy as ever, would join us after chapel for a swift cuppa before sneaking off to the garden before lunch. Pam busied herself with the roast lunch as the men chatted over the week's events. As a little girl I would curl up onto Uncle Norman's lap for a cuddle as he took a sip of his hot tea. When I was ill he brought home prime fillet steak specially selected from the butcher's just for me. All he ever wanted from life was a family of his own.

We welcomed him into our family as best we could but he was a sad man. Jilted by his bride at the altar, he never fully recovered his confidence. Poor old Norman took to the drink and became more and more reclusive. The alcohol finally killed him and he died in the 1970s of liver failure, a lonely man in his late fifties. His death shook us all. We felt a certain responsibility and it saddened us to think that maybe we could have done more.

All of us shared the two bathrooms and one toilet on the first floor. It never seemed to be a problem. On occasions we would brave the elements in the summer and use the showers on the site or the outside loo on the patio. For a house that was so busy, we never seemed to trip over each other.
The family meant everything to Queenie but she was not a cuddly grandma. I only remember a soft kiss on the cheek and the slightest of hugs. I rarely snuggled up on her lap but then she never sat still for long enough. Yet it is clear that she was very proud of all her grandchildren. She wrote to her Aunt Lizzie in Canada in the summer of 1963, ***"I have six grandchildren now. They are gorgeous."*** Then in February 1965 she wrote to Lizzie again this time including all the family. ***"Nellie's son and family were in a bad car accident just before Christmas. Albert is out of hospital and the baby but his wife is still in but doing nicely. Nice to hear from Bessie, must write her but I am always so busy. Pam's Mark now goes to school and Anita has chicken pox at the moment and Johnny is fine -- he is top of the Grammar school. Jack's children are lovely-- Candy is a ballet dancer and still at school. I don't think she will make a profession of it. Lee is very interested in sports and Paul is in the timber business."*** The warmth that she expresses is genuine.

Queenie was always most concerned if one of us was ill. When I was about six, I was taken into hospital in Potters Bar. I had some undiagnosed virus. My temperature remained high and the doctor was very worried about me. A year before I had been in the same hospital to have my tonsils removed, I spent my stay in the children's ward. Now I was put into isolation in the babies' side ward. There were two little ones there already, and they were wheeled into the adjacent children's ward, I watched the staff push their heavy metal cots into the next room. As I lay in my bed I could see the faces of the other children pressed up against the glass partition looking at me in my isolation. I knew it would not be too long before they would

Anita, Lee, Howard Bartrop, John and Candy

Lee, Queenie, Mark on her lap, John, Anita and Candy

be riding the magnificent rocking horse in the centre of their room, to recovery. I felt sad and lonely. There were no facility for parents to stay and visiting times were strictly adhered to. I was not happy and made my stand by refusing to eat! Matron in her starchy dark blue uniform pulled up a chair and sat down next to my bed. At first she pleaded with me to eat, and then she became forceful, explaining in no uncertain terms how serious it would be for me if I did not eat. Still the steamed white fish and mashed potato, as white as the plate it was served on, remained untouched. It was Queenie who came to the rescue. She made one of my favourites, plump apple dumplings. Apples fresh from the garden, covered in golden pastry and still a little warm from the oven. I ate the lot, turned a corner and was soon back home, once again in the nurturing midst of my loving family.

As year followed year we each celebrated our birthdays with a small party of friends in the big rooms at Goff's Oak House. Queenie always appeared around teatime, ready for a cuppa. Once she bought a cake from the bakery as Pam had not had time to make one. I remember it clearly. A dome of pale sponge made to look like a clown. I thought it was really special with its layers of vanilla cream and bright fondant icing. It was quite unlike anything I had seen before. Pam was concerned by the cost but Queenie was just happy to see the smile on my face.

My girlfriends were generally well behaved at party time but Johnny's eighth birthday party was, by all accounts, riotous. After tea the boys became overexcited and decided to bundle each other to the floor and fight. There was no stopping them. Queenie ordered them all outside onto the lawn were they continued to play boisterously. That was Johnny's last party.

For Queenie, family life would not be complete without a dog or two. She loved both pekingese and poodles. When Queenie was at Brook farm, years before, she had bought herself and Pam a pekingese each from Hampstead Heath. Queenie had a rusty brown bitch called Cheeky, and Pam a black one called Karla. When Pam moved to Sweden, Queenie looked after both dogs. When she returned, Queenie continued to have charge of the dogs and they lived downstairs with her and Cecil. In addition, Queenie had a toy poodle called Tina and a larger chocolate brown poodle called Coco; he was a favourite of Cecil's and was often by his side.

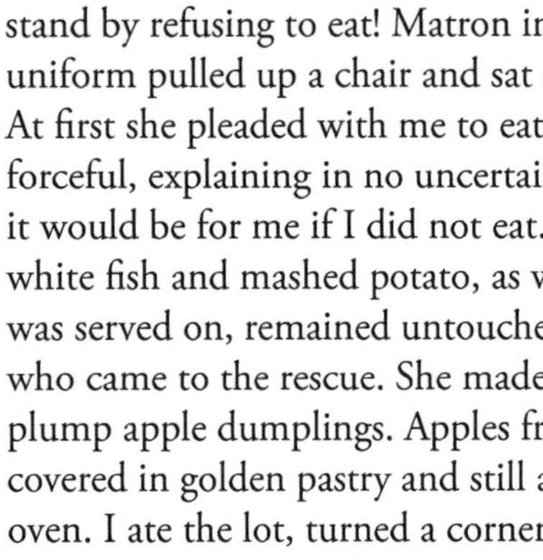

Karla

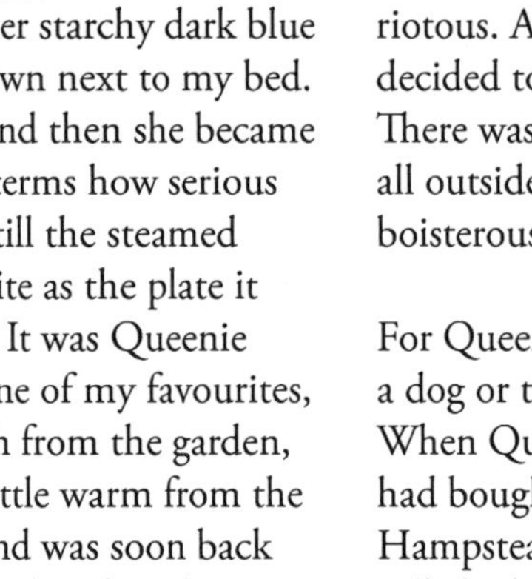

Cheeky

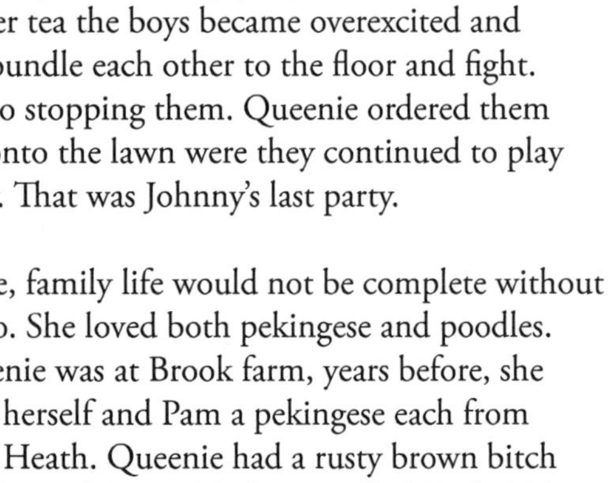

Queenie decided that Tina should have a litter of pups. I remember the makeshift cardboard pen of boisterous puppies in the corner of the warm kitchen. I recall with affection the time I was allowed to sit in the pen amongst the excitable bundles of fur, their warm bodies having that unique puppy smell. Queenie gave all the puppies away with the exception of one which she kept for herself, little black Lulu. When she was old enough, Queenie took her in the car to Brightlingsea for the weekend with Mark and me. We loved it! We used to put her in the old pushchair and wheel her around the lawns like a baby. Just like I did back at home in my dollies' pram. Early one morning some other children staying on the site decided to play with the dogs. Little Mark must have spotted them through the window; he was livid! Still dressed in his flannelette pyjamas, he rushed out onto the lawn, picked up the gangly puppy from right under their noses and gave them the angriest look his young face could muster. It said don't mess with my puppy.

One poodle Queenie rescued from a farm in Dorset. It was bedraggled and unloved. She bought the scruffy ball of matted fur home in a cardboard box. It was thin and shaking with fear as she lifted it out of the box to show me. She christened him Gigi and with a little love and nurture he was soon on top form. The dogs spent some of their day out in the patio, where the gates had to be kept firmly shut. I would often offer to take one for a walk around the garden or throw a toy for it on the lawn. The dogs were spoilt rotten and Queenie would buy offal from the butcher or ask Norman to bring scraps home. The meat was boiled in a saucepan on the pantry stove. The unpleasant smell permeated the whole house for days, especially when the pan boiled dry and the contents burnt to a black crust at the bottom of the saucepan. Every evening when Queenie eventually relaxed in front of the TV, she could be found with a little dog curled up contentedly on her lap. Queenie was never far from her beloved dogs. When she went visiting friends or holidaying in the UK, she would often take one with her. She loved the dogs and the dogs loved her. One year, after her month long holiday to the Mediterranean, Queenie was busy going back and forth to the caravan, emptying the cupboards and cleaning up after her trip when Lulu sneaked out of the house unnoticed. She jumped up into the caravan and made herself comfortable on the bench seat. She snuggled down into a deep sleep; no one could make her budge! She seemed to say … if you must leave again, take me with you! No amount of coaxing could entice Lulu back into the house. In the end Queenie had to pick her up and carry her back indoors.

Just like his grandmother, Lee developed a great love for poodles and when the time was right, he too had them as pets. He bought his first dog whilst on holiday with his wife. His passion was for standard poodles, Queenie liked toy poodles better, and over the years he too bred and kept them as loyal pets.

Queenie with pups

When all my school friends enrolled in the Brownies, I decided to join them. I donned my brown dress and solemnly took my vows. It turned out to be rather dull. Once, we were all asked to take in an item for washing-up. Queenie found me a cut glass bowl, crusty with sugar. I did a good job with the soapy suds and proudly received my badge. Brownies was not really holding my attention and I soon started to mess around. Fooling about during tasks, I would play up to an audience of giggling girls. Brown Owl was furious and asked me not to return. More defiant than upset, I decided to pluck up the courage and tell Queenie of the injustice. Needless to say, she came with me to the next meeting. I waited outside whilst she had a polite word with Brown Owl. I am sure that she brought up the fact that both her father and grandfather had been benefactors and ardent supporters of the Methodist Chapel in Goff's Oak. She may have even spoken to the vicar after Sunday service. Whatever was said between the two women, I was allowed back. I entered with my head held high. I never played up again out of respect but I soon became bored. Brownies had little to offer me. I had the freedoms of a Manor House with four acres of playground. I had Brightlingsea and West Bay full of exciting adventures. I had camped and I had cooked. I was constantly being creative and making things from nothing. I had met fascinating people and been to interesting places. I did not need anything else. So it was

Mark and Anita play in the paddling pool on the patio

not long before I left of my own accord. I think Queenie was a little disappointed but she soon got over it!

Over the years Queenie spent time with us all, taking each of us away on holidays and treating us to outings. It is true to say that as we were growing up, she took an interest in what and how each of us was doing. When Queenie went away to the Mediterranean for her bi-annual holidays, she would always buy each of us a special present. Often it would be something unusual to wear from France or Italy. Whatever she decided to buy, it was always perfect! The most amazing thing was that she always, without fail, managed to bring the right size. She did this purely from eye as the foreign sizing was completely alien to her. One year, she bought me a sweet little swimsuit in navy, red and white. It had a little skirt that was fashionable at the time. I felt so special in it! I still remember prancing around the garden, jumping in and out of the paddling pool with a splash for Queenie behind the camera. Another time, she bought Mark and me matching striped jumpers. They were made from fine ribbed cotton and very comfortable to wear. I loved mine but I do not think Mark was quite so impressed. When Queenie took us away to Brightlingsea for the weekend, we both wore them. I thought we looked really good; it made me feel like we were a team. Much later, when I was sixteen or so, she took a trip to Scotland and brought me a lovely brown and green tartan kilt. I wore that kilt for years and years, until eventually I had my first baby and never quite got back to a size 8.

When we got a bit older, Queenie started to take an interest in first, Candy's boyfriends, and then mine. She openly disapproved and tried hard to influence us! Most of her prejudices were based on class. Queenie could be so snobby. When I briefly dated a boy from Brookmans Park, Queenie was thrilled. I met the lad on his home turf, I think Cecil gave me a lift; the boy took me back to his modern home. His mother was waiting in the kitchen. She gushed a welcome and then immediately ushered me upstairs to see a wedding outfit she was planning to wear. Deprived of female company, in a family of two boys, she was desperate for my opinion. I politely made all the right noises but I knew that this was not a match made in heaven. We were so totally different. Like Queenie, I had something of the bohemian in me. When I got home, Queenie was eager to know when I was to see this lovely boy again. She was so keen to get the two of us together that she started to put pressure on me and would not let the subject drop. I had to make up a fib. I told her that he had tried it on. She was horrified! And thankfully the boy from Brookmans Park was never ever mentioned again. After this, I made the decision to keep my own counsel! My mum recently told me that she would never confide in Queenie and that growing up, her confidences were only shared with her dad.

Music morphed its way through the decades. From the big bands and big ballads in the 1940s, through to the rocking 1950s when a revolutionary teen culture emerged, Queenie who loved to party, always kept pace. She loved Turner Layton and swooned over Frankie Vaughn and his infamous high kicks. In the sixties the beat of the music got faster and louder and the freedoms of the youth became ever more relaxed. A sexual revolution hit the western world and with the sixties in full swing, Queenie was still holding her own in the world. With the slightest of tut's, she loved to see Candy dressed in a miniskirt and made up with dark smoky eyes for an evening out with her friends. The radio always played the latest hits from the top ten. Queenie liked to listen to the Seekers, Cliff Richard and the Shadows, and some of the Beatles. She thought Lulu was fab and that Candy bore a similarity. She was still interested in what made young people tick.

Late into the night when she could not sleep, she would tune her radio to Luxembourg, or Tony Blackburn on the pirate station Radio Caroline. For hours she would lie in her snug bed and listen to the hits of the day. For an old girl well into her sixties, she could still be quite with it! When the 1970s brought a feminist revolution and equal rights, she said nothing. With the slightest raising of an eyebrow she tolerated glam rock and platform shoes. But I think that by this time, a lady in her seventies, she was hankering after the old days, when music was not belted out at high decibels and accompanied by gyrating hips from boys that looked like girls!

Queenie and the Modern Chapel

Queenie was a long-standing devotee of the little Methodist Chapel in Goff's Oak. She had witnessed the good work both her father and grandfather had done. They had contributed to the building of the original chapel and she contributed to the new one. Because of her young-at-heart approach to life, she embraced all the changes. When after years of fundraising the new Modern Chapel was finally built in 1957, Queenie was there with an open heart once again. Typically, she enthused over the new young Reverends as they came and went. She loved their modern sermons and fresh looks. Over the years one or two were given temporary accommodation in the vast rooms at Goff's Oak House. Queenie made them very welcome and soon took them as family friends. She enjoyed the thought that they were staying in her home, to the envy of some small- minded parishioners who distrusted the carryings-on at Goff's Oak House.

Every Harvest Festival, the pantry would be scoured for tins of food for the less fortunate and Queenie would ravage her garden for suitable produce. A mammoth marrow was always found, as well as armfuls of sharp-smelling chrysanthemums. Mark and I would be asked to take them up to the Sanctuary on Thanksgiving Sunday. Queenie proudly watched us from the pews, a broad smile on her face.

The annual summer fête became a ritual for Queenie. Over the years all the grandchildren rode on a float and got involved with the Carnival. Many a time Mark or I were dressed up for the parade. Queenie was always there with suggestions and a needle and thread if needs be. Once grand-daughter Candy was in the Beauty Pageant and rode in the procession with the beauty Queen. Queenie was so proud! She was always there on the roadside to cheer us on.

The fête stall was Queenie's inspiration. Carnation heads and delicate green fern would be bought wholesale from a local nursery. Dot, Candy, Pam, Queenie and I would make them into buttonholes for the stall. In the evening before the fête, we would all sit around Queenie's red kitchen table, laboriously twisting squares of silver foil around each small sprig of fine fern and sturdy green stem of the tightly petal'd flower heads. We attached a shiny pin to each of them, ready for our customers to wear. The large trays of bright red and pastel pink blooms were kept cool in the cellar overnight. They would be brought out fresh the next day and carefully carried over to the fête when the stall was safely set up. We always sold out. Year after year the people of Goff's Oak would find our stall and buy a buttonhole. Queenie

Fete stall, Mrs Vaden, Queenie, Dot

loved it! Greeting everyone with a pearly smile, she enjoyed being part of this annual highlight of village life.

Supporter of the Chapel to the last, Queenie bequeathed £100 in her will to the chapel just as her father had done before her. A letter of heartfelt thanks was received from the Church. A small reminder of her quiet dedication over the years.

Anita and Candy sell their wares

West Bay, Dorset

It was in the 1930s that Queenie discovered the delights of the harbour village at West Bay as an annual holiday destination for the family. Initially, she chose to stay in one of the new chalet style bungalows springing up along the seafront. West Bay had been a holiday resort since 1887 when the promenade was first opened. Alternatively, in those early days Queenie would camp. Packing the basic old tent, Primus gas stove, blankets and other camping paraphernalia into the old Hillman Coupe, Cecil would drive Queenie, Jack and Pam down to the West Country. Aunt Nell and her young son Albert would make their way by train and be met at the station. Camping had been popular since the early 1900s, giving rise to the Association of Cycle Campers, founders of the Camping and Caravan Club of which Queenie became a proud member.

When war broke out in 1914, camping declined as a pastime but when the war was over there was an upsurge in popularity. During the 1920s and 1930s, a healthy outdoor lifestyle was considered to be of great benefit to everyone. In 1938 the Holidays with Pay Act made it compulsory for many employers to give their workers one week of paid holiday a year. By 1939, 11 million people were entitled to this benefit. Throughout her time at Brook Farm, Queenie had seasonal campers on her land and she was keen to enjoy the fun for herself. Often inviting friends and family to join her for a week and so a little party would set off for West Bay.

The early site at West Bay was no more than a muddy farmer's field, managed by Mrs Gates, who later went on to run a store in the harbour village. There were two cowsheds on the site, one had a makeshift toilet in the corner that was regularly emptied but often shared with the cows looking on.

It was not until the late 1930s that West Bay Caravan and Campsite was opened and operated by Bridport Municipal Borough Council. Even with the addition of mains sewerage to West Bay village in 1897, the facilities on the site were still very basic in the 1930s. As time went on they slowly improved to include flushing toilets and eventually showers.

After a year or so of sleeping under canvas, Queenie decided that the way forward was a caravan. The 1930s witnessed a revolution in caravanning. The few that could afford such luxury were nicknamed "Gentlemen Gypsies". They needed a big car to tow the heavy caravan and land on which to store both car and van. Queenie purchased a second-hand Roll-Along. It had been coach-built to its previous owner's specification for touring in Europe. The van was divided by way of a wooden concertina door into two bedrooms, one twin and one double. The floorboards could be removed to expose a bath fitted into the floor. It was the height of luxury and caused quite a stir when Queenie took it on a road trip to France some years later.

The Alvis and Roll-a-long caravan in France

At West Bay the family would spend happy times taking long, bracing walks along the coastal path to Burton Bradstock or Eype. When down at West Bay one of Queenie's favourite pastime was catching prawns. She would cast her heavy nets off the quayside and wait. Spending her time chatting to the old weather-beaten fishermen and sailors along the wharf and getting their opinion on sea conditions and the catch of the day, she loved to be outside in all weathers. Once, whilst Queenie passed the time of day with the locals, son Jack was fishing off the wharf. He cast his long trailing line into the water to catch silvery sprats for tea. Unfortunately, he got the sharp hook caught in his finger; attempts to free it were useless. Queenie was frantic and ended up taking him into Bridport to find a doctor who could remove it.

Caravanning was becoming more popular and holidays were fast becoming a business opportunity. Queenie could see a potential money-maker and opted to leave the Roll-Along on the site at West Bay for the summer months. She let it out to holidaying families to make a profit, making alternative arrangements for herself and

West Bay 1951

1951 West Bay, Sture,Cecil,?, Queenie

her family by returning to one of the wooden chalet style bungalows that continued to pop up along the front.

Queenie's husband Bert rarely joined her on these holiday jaunts. He tried it once but found that, in his own words, the sea disagreed with him. Once or twice he was asked to drive down with a vehicle-load of luggage but the sooner he could escape back to the farm the better. When war broke out in September 1939, Bert was putting the finishing touches to the dugout that he was building for the family's safety in the field behind the house at Brook Farm. Queenie was most anxious that her precious caravan be brought safely home. With Bert too busy and too muddy, it was down to Cecil to rush down to West Bay and retrieve it for her.

During the Second World War, West Cliff was billeted by the army and the population of West Bay village swelled. The houses on the cliff were used by the officers and their families. Surprisingly, it was still popular to camp during these difficult times. Many people were desperate to escape the horrors of the Blitz and leave the towns for short breaks when they could.

After the war, Queenie increased her standing at the West Bay Caravan and Campsite to two caravans. Buying and selling wisely, Queenie never made changes for the sake of it and kept her vans for many years. Eventually she had two static caravans, brought from the Goff's Oak residential site and moved to West Bay for summer lets. Each autumn these vans had to be laboriously pulled off the site and moved to a safer, higher field to be stored for the winter. It was paramount to get this done before the weather took a turn for the worst and the waves, wind and pounding rain hit the unprotected campsite and damaged the flimsy vans.
As spring approached and the risk of floods had finally abated, the site would be inhabited once more and the tricky process of moving the vans was repeated.

As the years passed, better positions became available and the caravans moved closer to the entrance and the amenities. By the late 1960s, the two vans were in a prime position five or six places in on the right-hand side.
Over the decades Queenie made herself at home in West Bay village. She shopped with confidence in the few local stores around the harbour, stocking up on the basics needed to feed her family. As she shopped, she chatted. She soon got to know the locals, passing the time of day with everyone that she met as if she had lived in West Bay all her life.

Prices were always a little higher in the village. So when it came to buying anything more than the essentials, Queenie would ask Cecil to drive her into Bridport, where she would take a leisurely stroll along the high street buying whatever was needed.

In 1969 I wrote home to Mum and Dad… ***yesterday we went shopping and Queenie bought us some health sandals and she bought rug, mats, cakes, bread, biscuits, trays, sweets, steaks, washing-up cloths, milk pans and the biggest tin of hot chocolate.***
As you can read we had a lot to carry back to the car.

At West Bay Queenie made friends with Lesley, an ex-circus dwarf who performed in pantomime under the stage name of "Lesley Laughing" during the winter. During the summer he served the holiday makers sweets and ice creams from his little wooden kiosk. The kiosk was originally positioned between the seafront and the harbour but it was moved due to the inclement weather closer to the campsite. Lesley married a tall girl from the chorus line and they went on to have a family. In the 1970s, another family of dwarfs worked in West Bay; they were not connected to Lesley. Both husband and wife were dwarfs and they had a daughter who was also a dwarf. Queenie always took a great interest in them and enjoyed chatting about the circus and the showmen she knew.

Sometimes on Sundays Queenie would rise early to attend a service at the little seaman's chapel down in the harbour. She would slip out before our eyes were opened and we had brushed away the sleep. By the time we were ready to leave our warm beds she was back, apron on and at the stove frying bacon.

Like the generation before us, we enjoyed the long, bracing walks along the cliff top to Eype and Golden Cap. It was usually with Cecil and the dogs whilst Queenie set to and cleaned the caravans for the next onslaught of paying guests. Many of our visits were weekend stays and often out of season; we always wanted to stay longer. When we could, we enjoyed exploring what the region had to offer. Portland Bill was a must! Queenie watched John fly his kite in the energizing wind, whilst Mark and I raced around, sucking in the salty sea air. We all ventured down onto the precarious rocks, waves crashing and pounding, sea spray lashing our faces, it was exhilarating and dangerous. Queenie loved it as much as we did.

Other times we journeyed out to neighbouring seaside resorts or places of natural wonderment like Durdle Door or Lulworth Cove. We would stop for afternoon tea in a dainty tearoom or eat fish and chips for supper in a seaside cafe.

On the Harbour

Year after year, Queenie continued to cast the same old prawning nets, caringly taken back home after each trip, to dry upon the front wall of Goff's Oak House. Each visit she would look forward to finding time to catch prawns from the quayside whatever the weather. I wrote to my brother John in April 1969... ***As I sit here Queenie is saying shall we go fishing even though it is raining. She is still determined.***

After several hours, when she had finally caught enough, she would bring a bucket of them back to the van to boil up in a big pan of hot water. As they turned a delicate shade of pink, Queenie tipped them out and cooled them ready for eating with thin slices of buttered brown bread. Sometimes she did not have time to cook the prawns before leaving for home. She brought them home to Goff's Oak in the boot of the car wrapped in smelly damp newspaper; everyone was horrified and not at all keen to eat them.

Whilst Queenie passed the time with the locals, John was also on the quayside fishing for crabs. Furnished

Queenie, Sture and Pam go prawning

with the rind from Queenie's breakfast bacon, John would dangle his orange reel over the edge and wait. Queenie was keen to cook the catch but the old fishermen looking on advised her not to.

On grey days Mark, John and I could still be found on the rocks of the man-made sea defences, jumping the waves and getting caught in the spray at high tide. Back to the caravan for a warm up, Queenie would fill us up on soft fresh white bread cut into thick chunks and spread with homemade raspberry jam and local clotted cream. Delicious!

As evening approached and the sun began to set, we could be found strolling along the shingle of West Bay beach under the shadow of Burton cliffs. Skimming stones and fighting the bitter sea breeze, we would make our way toward Burton Bradstock until our tired legs told us to turn back.

Homeward-Bound

Laden with pots of locally sourced clotted cream and a packet or two of Dorset Knobs, picked up from the bakery shop at Morcombelake, we headed home, always breaking our journey at Queenie's favourite, the Little Chef restaurant. We would tuck into a gigantic all-day breakfast or gammon and pineapple, and then finish off with American style pancakes and lemon. We could always eat exactly what we wanted when we were out with Queenie and Mark and I always did! With our tummies full we continued on our weary travels home and back to school the next day.

Paul fishing on the quay side

Pam and Queenie

Brightlingsea, as we called it, was technically Point Clear in Essex, a separate village south west of St Osyth Stone. The caravan site that Queenie eventually bought was situated on the south bank of Brightlingsea Creek, a branch of the River Colne, facing Brightlingsea proper.

Just before the War, when Pam was still in her teens, Queenie would arrange a family holiday to Point Clear, staying in either "Danbury" or "Colne Point", two of the wooden chalets lined up along the seafront. Queenie, with her eye for business, decided to rent the two for the whole year. She negotiated a reduced rate, and then sub-let them for a profit. In these early days sanitation at the site was basic. Once a week, Dan the toilet man had the smelly job of collecting the effluents from all the chemical toilets, pile it into his cart and empty it into the pit of water in the field next door.

When the Second World War broke out in 1939, the whole area was commandeered by the military. Historically, the area had always been used by the War Office for defence. The Essex coastline had many Martello Towers built in 1804 during the reign of King George III for defence against French invasion. One still stands, as a landmark, at the end of the road beside the Ferry Boat Inn.

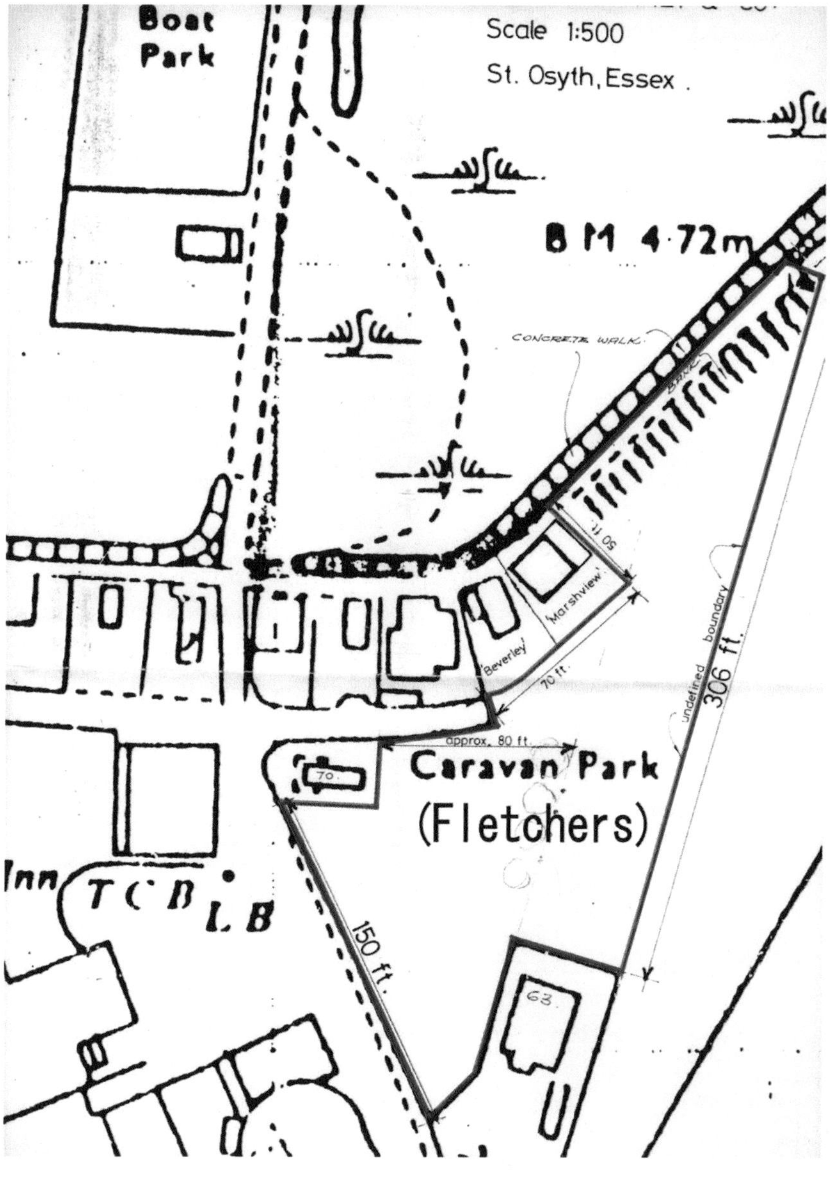

It was when war ended that Queenie returned to Brightlingsea, at first renting and sub-letting sea wall chalets as she had before the war. Building on her previous success, in 1951, she decided to buy into the fashionable holiday business. Billy Butlin had opened his first holiday camp in 1935 at Skegness. Both Harry Warner and Fred Pontin were making a successful go of holiday camps across the country. Queenie could see the potential and began the process of purchasing the caravan site.

The site had one access through the narrow concrete roads of Point Clear Caravan Park. Passing the Club House, Bingo Hall and small shop, the site Queenie bought was situated right at the bottom, opposite the Ferry Boat Inn and second amusement arcade. 'Fletchers', as

Fletcher's viewed from the Martello Tower

Pam on the sea wall at Point Clear

it became known, lay behind an impenetrable hedge. Its sweeping lush green lawn edged with only two or three large caravans was kept open and airy. Vehicular access was down a dusty unmade road that ran behind several sea wall chalets and through a gate into an open expanse of hard standing and thin grass. Much of the land belonged to Mr Wade. Over the years, Queenie added to her empire and acquired a two and a half acre site, two sea view chalets, "Beverly" and "Marsh View", "The Gift Shop" chalet and numerous caravans.

Sometime in the sixties the toilet block was added, complete with basic showers; it provided 'modern' facilities for both men and women. There was a continual battle with the resident spiders; Queenie would sweep and clean regularly but they were most persistent. With 'Izal', the tracing paper toilet roll, and the strong fresh smell of 'Coal Tar' soap, visits were always kept as brief as possible.

Queenie advertised "Fletchers" in the Daltons Weekly, a national magazine of holiday adverts. In her make do and mend fashion, Queenie worked hard to make the accommodation comfortable. She provided adequate blankets, mismatched china and basic pots and pans. The clients were happy enough and returned year after year. Each weekend Cecil would drive Queenie down to the site. He would laboriously cut the lawns whilst

Queenie

Queenie cleaned the vans and chalets for the next guests.

Around 1952, Queenie went to the Ideal Home Show and fell in love with and bought a single-roomed cabin. Made from dark Russian cedar wood, it affectionately became known as "The Dolls House". Using fitments from old caravans, she created a functional kitchen area and cosy bed-sitting space ideal for a couple. It provided novel accommodation and guests would ask for it time and again.

The Dolls House

By 1955, 96% of manual workers were entitled to two weeks' paid holiday per annum. The seaside holiday was at a peak and Queenie was turning a good profit and making a nice living. She wanted to maximize her potential and make full use of what she had.

In the late 1960s, "Marsh View" was improved and modernised by Mr Duncan. He was a St Osyth Stone resident. He and his family spent half the year in their spacious bungalow on the main road into the caravan park and the other half of the year in the sea wall chalet next to "Beverly". A "bit job" builder, he made alterations to "Marsh View" which included an open-plan living and kitchen space with clear views across the estuary, two upstairs double bedrooms, a small balcony and a miniscule bathroom that never functioned properly. He left the dank downstairs room as an additional bedroom and storeroom.

Facilities were always basic down at Point Clear. The site was never overdeveloped; the front lawn was prone to winter flooding and never used for caravans. Even when Queenie rented an additional acre, the site remained

Pam and Sture

open and spacious. She was most particular who stayed and only allowed the occasional touring van.

Over the years we stayed in them all. The caravans with their creaking floors and wooden lockers. The chalets with their linoleum floors and tiny rooms. All with mismatched china and a bizarre array of cooking utensils. Sleeping in narrow bunks with thin candy-striped sheets and scratchy grey utility blankets, memories were made. Sometimes Mum and Dad would accompany Mark and I but mostly it was with Cecil and Queenie on her many weekend trips to clean the vans ready for the next holidaymakers. Cecil was still working nights with the Railway and was often tired and grumpy after the drive to Point Clear. One Saturday afternoon, Cecil and Queenie had nephew Albert and his wife Margaret staying. They were all relaxing in the pink caravan having a cup of tea. Queenie opened a bag of buns enquiring, "What shall I do with these buns?". Cecil was totally disinterested and replied, "How should I know!". Queenie did no more than take the bag in her hands and playfully launched them into the air! Brooke Bakery's finest sticky buns flew everywhere! Cecil was furious and loudly voiced his disapproval in a torrent of profanity. He leaped up out of his chair and stomped off to cool down. Everyone sat in silence. They were so stunned that they dared not break into a laugh or even crack a sly grin!

For me, one of the most vivid recollections of Brightlingsea was the sound of the old petrol mower. Each weekend Cecil would be expected to mow the acres of long lush grass with the ancient mower. My nostrils filled with the pungent smell of petrol mingled with new mown grass as he guided the mower up and down and around the vans. The air was spiked with the salty ozone of the marsh, the continual cry of the seagulls overhead and the rhythmic clang of metal on

Nell and Cecil

metal as the ship workers toiled across the estuary. Looking back, the days were always warm and busy. Despite her workload Queenie always managed to find time for us. On Sundays the harsh industrious sound of the ship workers was replaced by the gentle tinkling of the breeze upon the spinnakers of the sailing boats moored across at Brightlingsea. It was a day to relax and find some fun before the drive back home.

Messing about in boats

Queenie loved boats and the water but she never learnt to swim. Despite all our efforts as children to get her afloat and moving, she never made it and only ever paddled. If we were lucky enough to be down at Brightlingsea during a regatta or race day, Queenie would find a comfy place to sit by the window of "Marsh View" or take a cushion onto the sea wall to watch. She would enjoy the ease and speed at which the small sailing craft would glide across the water. Watching them leave to the sound of a shot, she was always eager not to miss their return later in the afternoon.

Queenie always made sure that we had a boat to mess about in. Over the years I recall two clinker-built dinghies both with small outboard motors that would "p-hut, p-hut" us sedately about the marshes or over to Brightlingsea. In the 1970s, Queenie bought an Avon rubber dinghy from the Boat Show. Complete with its powerful Fletcher outboard motor, it would skim the

Queenie with family and friends

Jack, Cecil, little Paul, Mr Bowls and Queenie

Cecil and Queenie

waves at speed and create a foamy wake across the inky water. It was such excitement pulling the boat out from the shed, getting it down onto the beach and finally with the tides right, into the water. With Queenie as skipper and Cecil at the helm, we would negotiate the tides and set off on an adventure. Her smiles were as broad as the youngsters. Sometimes we would venture out to Mersey Island where we would land the boat on the shingle beach, and would picnic and play until the tides forced our return.

Other times we would take a jaunt around the headland at Colne Point. This was fraught with dangerous currents and large craft. Queenie was always the one to push us on a little bit further. As a child, it was exhilarating; the blood pumped and the adrenaline flowed as the fear inside of me mounted and I begged for them to turn back.

Once, as we sped around splitting the sea behind us in a foamy white wake, Queenie lost her favourite hat. It flew off behind us and lay tantalisingly close on the top of a wave. Queenie gave the order to swing around and pick it up before it was sunk for ever. Swiftly, Cecil manoeuvred the craft, all of us watching the hat as if we could will it to stay afloat. As we pulled up beside it, Sture precariously lent out across the wide rubber wall of the boat and just managed to get a grip and pull it safely out of the sea to loud cheers and a round of noisy applause. The hat once home and dried had shrunk two sizes and Queenie could never wear it again. Many years later, my son Aron, as a toddler, took to it and wore it for a couple of summers. After that, it was given to Bengeo Playgroup where it may still be.

Queenie

Since the early 1940s Queenie had been taking the ferry from Stone Point, across the estuary to Brightlingsea with friends and family. I remember in the 1960s handing over the shiny sixpence to "Frenchie", one of the old sailors who would ensure our safe crossing. All the 'old boys' looked ancient, their leathery faces tanned and weather-beaten. Their white heads topped with an old blue cap nodding the time of day. Queenie knew most by name and would chat leisurely, eager to know the forecast and times of the tides. I loved the gentle lapping of the water and the melodic dipping and creaking of the oars as we made steady progress across the waves. A little bit of me was always disappointed when we reached our destination. Queenie would go on a shopping trip purchasing items of particular importance to her but there was not much to interest a young child beyond the boat trip itself and I was always eager to return.

One of the highlights for all of us was a trip up the estuary to find crabs. Whilst Queenie attended to the chores of the caravan site, it was Cecil and sometimes Sture who took us. We went armed with our orange crabbing lines rescued from the shed and lovingly detangled whilst we waited for high tide. Queenie would furnish us with bacon rind from breakfast. We scrambled around in the dirty shed to find our largest buckets, put on our life jackets and set off.

Getting the heavy wooden boat down to the shore was always tedious but Queenie was always on hand to help.

The boat was pulled by hand onto the trailer. First it had to be manoeuvred slowly and carefully out from under the chalet, through the narrow gates and out onto the road. Next it was pushed up the steep incline of the sea wall and safely down the other side where it was pushed along the concrete road and onto the sandy shingle of the beach.

It took a lot of effort; all the grown-ups pushed and pulled to get the boat over the unforgiving sand. There was many a time when a stranger or two would help us to negotiate the beach. The pace was slow; I could hardly contain my frustration at the never-ending process. Mark and I would romp about the beach annoying each other and everyone else. Eventually it was in the water and afloat. With the outboard motor safely fitted, we clambered aboard whilst Queenie stood on the shore waving us off as if on an epic voyage. One of the men would row out a little and try the motor. This was not always successful but after much swearing and cursing we were off, up towards Flag Creek.

Crabbing is an art form. You need to catch the tide just right. Exactly what that should be was disputed on every trip. But we did agree that the best crabs were to be found in the muddy banks of the estuary edge. Stopping the engine, we rowed in closer and closer until we could hear the bottom of our boat scraping along the seabed.

As soon as we could, we were fixing bacon to our hooks and casting our lines into the murky depths. In quiet anticipation we waited, keeping our bodies still, least we should miss the ominous tug on our line. Now, there are two methods for landing a crab: the 'slow pull' which can backfire when the crab loses interest and lets go or the 'yank and land'. The first style has the advantage that you can see what you have caught and prepare yourself for a safe landing. But of course the older and bolder preferred the yank and land, giving rise to much squealing from the youngsters.

Some of the crabs were fairly big by a child's standard and once we got underway the buckets soon became overcrowded. The bigger crabs would clamber up onto the smaller ones and topple out of the bucket onto the bottom of the boat. Before we knew it, there would be more than one scampering about the boat. There would be more squealing (mostly with delight) and jumping as they angrily scurried about, pincers up and ready to nip anything, especially fingers and toes. I pulled my legs up onto the seat and tucked my feet in, clasping my knees tightly. Fuelling my fear, someone would edge a big one closer towards me or pick it up to give me a closer look at the angry pincers. I verbalised my horror with more squeals and fake tears.

Beaten by the ebbing tide, we began to make our way back. There was always a need to row part-way because the sea level was too low for the outboard. It was at these times that we learnt to row. At first Mark and I would take an oar each. We made good headway as I counterbalanced his smaller strokes. Later I took both oars and enjoyed the systematic rhythm of oar and water, loving the physical challenge until Mark pleaded for his turn.

Most times, after our adventures, the crabs were simply tipped back into the murky depths of the sea to be caught another day. Occasionally, I would insist on taking the largest specimens back for Queenie to see. She was always duly impressed, exclaiming that some of our catch was 'big enough to eat' but we never did. Sometimes Mark and I would keep one or two of the smaller ones in a large bucket of smelly sea water for a few days but in the end they all found their way safely back to the sea.

A little bit of luxury at the Seaside

Sometime in the early 1970s, Queenie bought a second-hand residential van for family use only. It was well appointed with its fashionable Ercol furniture and teak fittings. The kitchen, by caravan standards, was a nice size with its built-in cupboards and sink unit. It was far more modern than anything at home. It had a lovely teak dresser which Queenie filled with matching plates. In the centre of the room, there was a modern circular table, laid with a clean green cloth and a jug of fresh fragrant sweet peas, their sweet smelling, pink and lilac heads bobbing as we moved about the van; a reminder

Anita, John and Mark go Boating

of Goff's Oak House and Queenie's lovely garden. The table was just right for Queenie to serve up one of her substantial meals on. Queenie as always made sure that we were all well fed. She would cook thick slabs of prime beefsteak, either purchased from the local St Osyth butcher or brought with her from Ripley's in Cheshunt. She always served this with home-grown onions fried to succulent perfection and piled on top, with deliciously buttery new potatoes on the side.
The potatoes were freshly dug from Goff's Oak House garden late Friday afternoon just as we were about to leave. With Cecil snapping at her heels, eager as always to get away before the busy weekend rush, Queenie would take her time to dead-head the sweet peas and pick a fresh bunch of them to take with her.

Sitting in the sun on the steps of the van or in a fading deckchair, with an old washing-up bowl of water on her lap, Queenie would scrub the muddy skins of the potatoes clean. Lastly, she would cut one of the massive green marrows growing in the composting warmth of the grass clippings on the site and would cook it with a peppery white sauce.
The van had an inside bathroom, which unfortunately

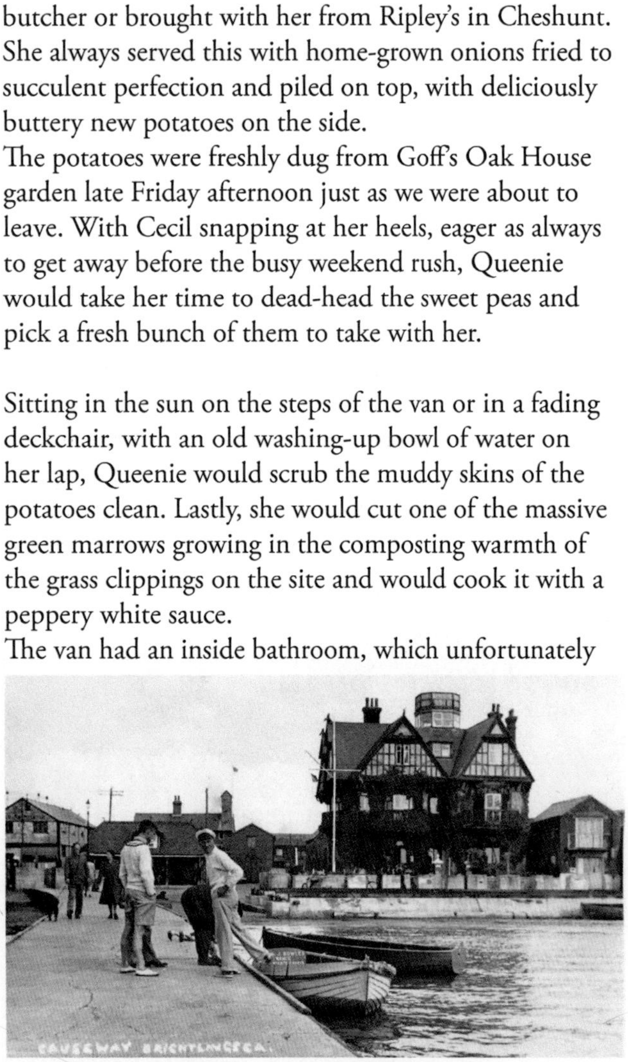

Brightlingsea causeway and the Ferrymen

Queenie

was never fully installed. It had cold running water and provided a private space to wash and clean our teeth in without having to venture out to the shower block in all weathers. The toilet was never plumbed into the mains sewerage system and consequently never used but on rare occasions; the bath was filled with a little warm water from a kettle or two for Mark and I to have a wash in.

Queenie and I would share the master bedroom at the end of the van. Mark and Cecil would share the double put-you-up in the lounge. From the antiquity of Goff's Oak House, it was all very modern and efficient. We all enjoyed staying in it.

Alone I snuggled down into my sleeping bag. With the window open to the balmy night, I lay listening to the sounds of the late night revellers as they spilled out from the Ferry Boat Inn. The neon lights from the amusement arcade shined through the inadequate curtains. Music, laughter and the commanding voice of the bingo caller wafted through the warm air to me. I lay and wondered if Queenie was taking her chances with the others at Bingo. She could never stay away from the amusements for too long. Aware of the distant waves ebbing and flowing over the sandy beach, I was lulled into a pleasant slumber with thoughts of tomorrow's adventures. Walking the sea wall or sliding down it at great speed on the old tin tray. Maybe clambering over the marshes or venturing out over the smelly mud at low tide to collect cockles and winkles for Queenie to cook and eat. With an expert hand she would winkle out the tiny black crustaceans with a pin and enjoy them with delicate slices of buttered brown bread for her tea.

In the morning there would be another shiny tray, vase or chalk figurine on the kitchen table. More Bingo spoils! Queenie would be her smiling cheery self, ready to face another day and eager to make sure that we were well fed and happy.

In The Garden

The entire area of Goff's Oak House was approximately three acres in total. Looking at the front of the house and to the left-hand side lay the old stable block, having long ago been converted into garages. In front of them, a potholed and uneven car park for residents, visitors and family.

On the opposite side of the house were Jack's yard, office and workshops. Tucked into that was the black timber cottage, an original workman's cottage from the estate, where Jack and Dot brought up their three children.

Between these two areas there was a front garden. Relatively small, it spanned out from the principal front door and up to the pavement and road. It was laid with gravel paths, borders and oval beds of spring and summer bulbs. Each spring scillae would poke their tiny heads up through the gravel in a carpet of pale blue and white. A wide metal Victorian rose arch spanned the main path from the front door. Its massive fragrant blooms in shades of pink lasted all through the summer. On either side of the arch sat more pathways. Beside them were two broad beds of mahonia bushes, the dark glossy foliage catching the late light and clashing with the vibrant yellow of the flowers.

The back of the house looked out onto two massive lawns. The top lawn was soft with moss and mown bowling-green-flat each week by Cecil. The bottom lawn was left to grow longer. Daisies and buttercups grew amongst the tangled green and danced in the summer breeze. Gigantic, hundred-year-old trees shaded the edges of both lawns, twelve of which were protected by a tree preservation order. Their spreading canopy hid the caravans nestling within the shrubs, bushes and flower beds. A broad yew-lined, U-shaped path, just wide enough for a vehicle to pass through, gave snug access to over thirty residential caravans.

When a van had to be moved or a new one was brought on site, Queenie was frantic. The process was never straightforward. She was most particular about the garden. She hated to have to cut down overhanging boughs or damage any of the shrubs. Woes betide anyone who trampled on an emerging daffodil or snowdrop. And if the van had to be manoeuvred over the top lawn… well!!! Great heavy metal grids were placed under the tiny wheels of the van. Men, women and children were deployed to slowly inch it into its final position. With sweated brows and tempers ragged and frayed, the job could take all day.

Away from the residential area and to the left-hand side, was the kitchen garden. Its two long, wide beds of rich loamy soil were partly encircled by orchard trees and used to grow the vegetables and soft fruit bushes. For a short time Queenie kept a clutch of monochrome guinea fowl for their eggs. An ark and run was set up at the bottom end of one of the wide beds. All went well until one night, under the cover of darkness; a wily

Goff's Oak House, Top Lawn

Dot's Cottage Garden

Goff's Oak House the Garden

Lee and John enjoy lollies on the patio

Roller-skating

John archery practice

old fox helped himself to the lot. Queenie hadn't got the heart to try again and so the venture was dropped but she did miss the fresh eggs. The vegetable garden needed a lot of work but provided the kitchen with an array of fresh produce throughout the seasons. The composting waste and grass clippings were piled high in a heap to the side of the main bed and provided the ideal environment for marrows. Queenie grew them to mammoth proportions and I was proud to display them at the annual harvest festivals in school and church.

Situated on this side of the garden were Queenie's greenhouse and our play area. We had a climbing frame, a swing, an old butler sink for newts and a proper tree house. Built by Jack in an old elm on the boundary of the land, it gave us a great vantage point from which to view the world. An eight-foot ladder had been nailed to the trunk and ascended the dizzy heights up to the canopy of the mighty elm. A platform of sturdy planks approximately six foot square had been made between the spreading arms of the tree. A timber chalet in the sky had been built on top. It had an open doorway, a window and a roof, and made a cosy den. Jack had built it for Lee and John. They even slept in it for a night or

Roses In Bloom

two. What an adventure! It was fun but did not suit me so well. I struggled to get my dollies and tea service up the precarious ladder. I wanted to set myself up with table and chairs but it was impossible. Once I fell from near the top rung. I had become cocky and simply failed to hold on tightly. I lost my footing and fell straight back to the ground below. Thankfully, it was damp and forgiving and I lay for a while winded and stunned but unhurt.

With their hideaway places and forbidden adventures, Goff's Oak House and its environs were a child's paradise. Sharing the garden with paying residents meant that we were given rules and regulations to abide by.

We were kindly asked not to be too noisy, especially at weekends, but we were.
We were asked not to play too close to the caravans, but we did.
We were asked not to play around the residents' sheds, but we did.
We were asked not to cross the moat, encourage the horses from next door or walk along the boundary, but of course we did.
With so much in the garden to tempt us, the urge to be outside whatever the weather was too strong to resist.

Both Queenie and I could always be found in the garden. Queenie, dressed in shabby old trousers, a well-worn quilted anorak and a pair of turned-down black wellies, she could be spotted pottering about the beds and boarders. It amused her when visitors asked her to direct them to 'the lady of the house' and casually enquired what she was like to work for!

With ground to dig, seeds to sow and plants to plant, even with the dependable help from the weekly gardener and Henry Vadden the resident handyman, Queenie would be found outside in all weathers. Bent double to her chores, dressed in an old pair of Bert's Oxford bags, she never once complained. Openly enjoying herself, she forgot all concept of time. She was reluctant to stop for anything, only interrupting her labours for meals. Cecil often cooked. Throwing meat into a pot, along with whole onions and large portions of vegetables dug fresh from the garden, he left it on the stove to simmer all morning to a thick tasty stew.

Cecil Harriss

While Queenie busied herself in the garden serenaded by birdsong and befriended by robins, I was enjoying the freedom of my childhood. Taking my dollies for endless walks, I pushed the pram around the labyrinth of pathways which surrounded the beds and lawns. I was totally absorbed in my own private world, and Queenie never questioned my childish chattering.

The garden's many beds and borders were full of beautiful bulbs and flowering perennials needing tending and nurturing. Queenie adored her flowers, sweet peas being one of her favourites. She grew the pretty pastel blooms on tall canes set in a long row between the flower border and the vegetables. Queenie regularly picked an armful of vibrant, colourful blooms for the house. She filled great vases with them, making the rooms smell fresh and fragrant. Other times she would pick smaller, sweeter blooms to make one of her famous colourful posies, reminiscent of the Edwardian posies of her youth. She gave them with love to family and friends for all manner of occasions. She would take one as a simple gift when she went visiting for afternoon tea or give one to cheer up a sick friend. Often she would make an extra one and give it to Dot or Candy in the Cottage. It was her way of saying I love you. They were always warmly received with generous thanks. With so many trees, shrubs and bushes to keep tidy, a great pile of brushwood grew high at the 'dump', an out-of-the-way spot in the garden where everything and anything burnable was dumped. Queenie loved her bonfires; she could spend all day prodding and poking a good blaze. Meanwhile, Mark and I played on the rope swing hung from a nearby tree. With much hooting and hollering we would spin around at speed, testing our strength, and daring each other to try out new stunts. Queenie was too absorbed in the fire to worry about our antics, the whiff of woodsmoke lingering on her clothes and in her hair for days afterwards.

I loved to play with Mark and our friends in the derelict summer house situated out of the way on the bottom lawn. In its Victorian heyday it had revolved to face the sun but now it stood motionless, its blue paint faded and flaking. Inside it was cobwebby and musty; an old car bench seat all split and torn had been left by someone. We would sit for hours on wet days, chatting and using it as an HQ for our secret games. Designed for summer use, it had a wide window flap that became an awning when opened and no door. It was really draughty and when Queenie bought herself a lovely new tool shed, smelling of fresh clean pine, and erected it near to our play area, I was quick to act. Before Queenie had a chance to organise her forks and spades, like a squatter I moved in. Putting up a makeshift curtain at the window, finding a disused bedside cabinet to use as a cupboard and bringing my children's table and chairs down from the bedroom, I made myself at home in 'The Little House'. Each week my friends and I would sweep out the bugs, rearrange the furniture and place a new jam jar of fresh flowers on the table. Once we invited Queenie in for a dolly's cup of weak squash and a pretend cake. She accepted graciously and never once complained about her forfeit shed.

The "Little House"

For us the fun and games went on and on. Riding around and around the yew-lined broad walk on our bikes up past the back of the house then once again round for another lap. Taking the same route with 'the trolley', made from a sturdy plank and four old pram wheels, we would furiously push each other around until someone grazed a knee. Then play stopped, in floods of tears, whilst we waited for first aid to be administered.

Queenie was never far away. Once, whilst she pottered in the greenhouse, we dangled upside down from the climbing frame. Legs hooked under the bars we hollered

Mark and Anita play with their friend

out a pop song at the top of our tuneless voices. Queenie never batted an eyelid and left us to our childish fun, unlike a resident who, coming from around the corner from the car park, was cutting with his remark. Stopping us dead with embarrassment he made us so self-conscious that, sadly, we never sang in the garden again.

Of course there were complaints from the residents but Queenie never seemed too bothered. She would tell Pam if things got out of hand and she in turn would reinforce the rules to us once more. But Queenie very seldom reprimanded us herself, even though, at times, she had cause. Our childhood was blissfully free and we knew it. Before long we were back out in the garden, the lure of its delights too strong to resist, and refusing to come in even after several calls for bath and bed. Staying out late into the summer evening, until the light faded and the last songbird had trilled its final evensong, we enjoyed every day to the full.

Then in the 1970s Queenie bought us the ultimate gift, a swimming pool! We could not believe it when she came home from the Ideal Home Show with the news that she had bought a Driclad pool. The pool was to stand three feet above ground level. There was much preparation needed before we could swim. Queenie decided to give up the big flower border behind the stable block. The old brick wall provided shelter from the wind and proved to be quite a sun trap. The flower bed had to be cleared and everyone was enlisted to help. Once it was clear of roots and stones, a thick protective layer of fine sand was laid. Now the pool itself could be erected. It was so exciting to see the progress. The flimsy blue sides were slid together to create an oval on the soft sand. Next the enormous liner was laid over. We all took our shoes and socks off to smooth out the wrinkles as best we could. We needed to fill the pool as soon as possible. The fragile structure relied on the pressure of the water on its sides to give it stability. The tap was running for two solid days and nights! Even then, it was only half full. Water pressure was dropping and it was decided that we would have to pace the filling. As soon as I got home from school I would rush out into the garden to see the progress. At last it was full! The purifying pump was fitted and with a bit of technical help from Sture it was running. The chlorine was added and the water tested. We were ready for our maiden swim. Queenie announced that we should have an opening party for the family at the weekend. Thankfully, Saturday was bright if not warm. Everyone arrived. The patio flat, devoid of any residents, was to be our changing room. Queenie was very strict and ordered us NOT to enter the house dripping! Dressed in our bathers we shivered our way up the metal steps and onto the slatted sides of the pool. Some of us foolishly jumped in. It took our breath away; the water was freezing! The pool being so newly constructed, the sun had not had a chance to raise the temperature of the water. After a tot of something warming, we braved the elements again and allowed adrenaline to keep us warm until we turned a vivid shade of blue and with teeth chattering we gave up for the day.

John

Dot, Cecil, Paul and Jack

Each and every day at four o'clock sharp the old copper kettle, converted to electricity, would be plugged in. Queenie would lay the red Formica table in the cosy kitchen with cups, saucers and plates for afternoon tea. When all was ready, she would ask one of us to pull the rope on the old brass bell that hung in the stairwell to summon the stragglers with its loud peel. The massive bell had been brought back from Canada by Albert Wombwell, a souvenir from his trip. It had been removed from the front of a steam train. Queenie had it stored for many years before she found the perfect place for it to hang.

As the grandchildren wearily struggled home after a long and arduous day at school, Queenie would quickly knock up a batch of potato scones. As we popped our heads around the kitchen door with a tired "we're back", the oven door would be opened, the warm aroma of new baking hitting our nostrils as the hot, golden discs were brought out and set onto the wire rack to cool. It gave us just enough time to nip upstairs, change out of our school clothes and wash our hands before we were back in the warm kitchen and sitting up at the table. The scones still hot from the oven were thickly spread with rich yellow butter that melted into a dripping gooey deliciousness that ran down our chins.

Other days Queenie would instruct Cecil to call into Brooke Bakery during his morning chores in Cheshunt and bring back a selection of cakes. Cecil knew all our favourites. He brought back macaroons, rum truffles and an assortment of buns including Bath and Chelsea. We sat around the old red table chatting over the day's events whilst the tenants would call in to pay their rents. Queenie had her particular favourites. John Dean was one of them. He would be invited to sit down and join us for a cup of tea and a cake. At Queenie's request we would scramble around to find another stool and make room at the table. Queenie was always eager to hear his stories and happy to accept complimentary tickets for the cinema in Leicester Square where he worked as a projectionist. In contrast, others tenants were dealt with more briskly and moved quickly on.

Patio before pergola

Pam under the Clematis Arch

On Fridays Jack would often pop in requesting cash for the men's wages. Generous as ever to family, Queenie would ease his cash flow problems without question. She would trudge up the narrow back stairs to the big old safe and get him what he needed. On her return she would offer him a cup of tea from the pot, which was often refused with a, "I must get back to pay the men". And with a slight draught from the door he was gone!

On warm afternoons the family sprawled out onto the secluded patio. A 1960s addition, Queenie had it laid in pink concrete inset with grey stepping stones. Whilst the concrete was still wet she had all our names written into it for posterity. A novelty that made me feel safely bound to the family. Some of the ground around the patio had been left bare and planted with billowing hydrangeas of pinky blue. There was a variety of pots overflowing with nodding blooms and Queenie's pride… large blue faces of morning glory clambering up the black downpipe.

In the seventies a white pergola, reminiscent of Queenie's many European trips, was built over the table and chairs. A grapevine was planted to trail and climb the white frame. It gave us dappled shade from the summer sun but, to Queenie's disappointment, no grapes.

Sitting under the shade of the spreading grapevine we contemplated our day. Queenie pushed out the wobbly tea trolley, heavily laden with cakes and clattering cups, saucers and plates. The big brown teapot was filled to the brim and covered with the old tea-stained cosy to keep its contents warm. A newly boiled copper kettle of water was brought out ready for seconds. Sometimes we

Afternoon tea with friends

would be joined by Jack and Dot or one of the children from the Cottage.
Teas would be poured and plates passed around. Wasps would be attracted to the sweet stickiness of the fresh buns. Quick as a flash, Queenie would snap them up between thumb and forefinger, instantly despatching them into the flower bed behind her. We just sat in awe.

As the residents returned home from work, they must have looked on at this relaxed afternoon ritual of three generations enjoying each other's company in the lazy afternoon sun with certain envy.

Sunday brought a different teatime treat. Most Sunday morning's Queenie went to the Methodist chapel. She encouraged me to join her with the enticement of a trip out, to visit her old friends and have afternoon tea. Strangely, I enjoyed these visits. Sitting quietly in unaccustomed rooms, I dutifully listened to the adult conversations and answered only when spoken to. I never tired of the fascination of other people's lives and looked forward to these random visits with Queenie.

Often, on a whim, she would gather all the family together and ask Cecil to take us out in the 'Chevy'.

John

The seaside was always popular. Not just Clacton and Brightlingsea. But sometimes we went to Southend or the south coast for an out of season adventure. After a long breezy walk along the seafront we would seek out a little café still open on the front to take tea in. At Southend we would enjoy fish and chips and end up in the amusements, with Queenie generously doling out pennies for the slot machines. Once we went to Brighton to enjoy all the fun of the fair on the pier. The carousel was the only ride that Queenie would join us on. We galloped round and around, up and down on our golden horses, manes and nostrils flaring, until it got late and we were forced to make our way home in the dark with another tale to tell, waiting for the next exciting adventure.

Tea with Royalty

Queenie's most prestigious teatime guest was introduced to her by her cousin Bernard. Bernard was a highly regarded estate manager for the Luton Hoo Estate.
In the early seventies, the Luton Hoo family had the esteemed house guest Prince Albert of Liechtenstein staying with them. Bernard was instructed to show the dashing young prince around the estate and soon the pair built up quite a rapport. Bernard suggested that he take the Prince to his cousin's for tea. The young prince agreed. When Queenie found out, she was thrilled!
She began polishing and dusting everything in sight. The gleaming drawing room was prepared with vases of sweet smelling flowers on every sideboard and table top. She dressed herself in one of her glamorous Nina Ricci dress suits and waited for her guests to arrive. The Prince was a handsome man no more than twenty-five. He was very debonair in his well-fitting suit. He looked a little uneasy at first as he sat in the archaic splendour of Queenie's drawing room. His English was very limited but he smiled a broad smile at Queenie and I could see her heart melt! She enjoyed every minute as she fussed over her renowned guest with English tea and homemade cake, privately wishing that it would never come to an end.

Queenie's grandest room the Drawing room

Auctions and Sales

Queenie loved to make a little extra cash. She was an advocate of "look after the pennies and the pounds will look after themselves". All through the 50s, 60s and 70s she would sell her autumn garden surplus on the roadside at the front of Goff's Oak House.

Passing traffic coming up Goff's Lane from Cheshunt would stop and buy from boxes of wasp-worried apples, overgrown marrows, scruffy tomatoes and buckets of sharp-smelling chrysanthemums. Even the 242 bus driver, on his journey to Potters Bar, would draw up once a week for home-grown tomatoes, his passengers peering out of the steamy windows wondering what the hold-up was all about.

Queenie would display her wares on the old circus stand, a strong, low, small, wooden circular table that had been used by performing lions in days gone by. It had been left by Jan the lion tamer after one of his many stays at Goff's Oak House. Customers would lustily ring the old brass hand bell left on the stand; the deep loud clangs would resonate over the garden, echoing to where Queenie worked, and penetrate the thick walls of the house summoning one of us to play shop and take the money.

Frugal as ever Queenie loved to go to an auction and pick up a bargain. From time to time she would take a trip out from Clacton and into the depths of the Essex countryside to Thorpe Market, where all manner of old and dilapidated farming equipment could be bought. Try as he might, Cecil could not restrain her. Many a time she would come home with a box of rusty, dusty, old stuff hoping to find a little gem hidden within its depths, but mostly there was nothing either useful or ornamental.

Another favourite were the railway sales up in London. Here a crazy array of oddments could be bought in the freight terminal at Kings Cross goods yard. After 1948 traders sent goods by National Carrier via the depots at Welwyn Garden City, Harlow and Hitchin. At the time goods were simply put into the truck with a rudimentary address label. Quite often the label would simply fall off. If the goods were not claimed, they went into the railway sale. Every three months a sale was organised and advertised. It was Albert Cooke who first saw the advert. Both Queenie and Cecil were keen to go. The goods were organised into small lots and the pair often came home with chairs, settees and step stools. It proved to be an enjoyable day out for all of them.

Items that had been left on trains and never claimed were also sold. It is amazing to think of the variety, and at times quality, of goods left on trains, their owners simply walking away and never thinking to claim them. On more than one occasion, Queenie came home with a box of assorted umbrellas. Typically, they were all shapes and sizes. The good ones were kept in the hall stand for general use. Others were riddled with holes. Bent and buckled against a gusty wind, they were of no use but Queenie kept them in a shed just in case!

Once, she came home with four bicycles. On another occasion she bought a lot comprising of four boxes of assorted china and kitchen wares. Queenie enjoyed the pretty green tea set, frequently using it over the years. Other items were not so practical. The family laughed for years over the enamel cooking pot tucked into the bottom of one of the boxes. It was found complete with crusty, cold, grey porridge! Ugh! What on earth was that doing on a train and how could you possibly forget it?

Doing a deal was Queenie's forte. When Lee showed an interest in learning to play the drums and struggled to find the money to put together a set, it was Queenie who offered to loan him the money to buy them. Together Queenie, Cecil and Lee took a trip into London to Drum City in Shaftesbury Avenue. It was the place to be seen and the place to buy drums in the 1960s. They started to look around the shop but before Lee had even a chance to decide what he might be interested in; Queenie was straight in, negotiating with the "nice young man"! Lee had to rein her in…"No, not that set Queenie, let me check them all out first." After careful consideration, Lee decided on his drums and Queenie began her magic. By the time she had finished, Lee came away with a brand new set of drums complete with cases worth more than £150 for the sum of £120. In those days this saving was quite a coup.

Queenie loved the 'shows' in Olympia. Annually she would attend one or another, the Ideal Home Show with Pam and Dot and later with me, the Caravan and Camping Show with Cecil and then Albert and Margaret, the Boat Show with Paul, the Motor Show, or the Boys and Girls Show with John, Mark and I. I was always so excited waiting for her return. One never knew exactly what she would come home with.

Back from a long day at the Ideal Home Show, still bright and breezy, Queenie would enter the welcoming kitchen after a tiring day, heavily laden with bags of all shapes and sizes. She had collected samples from just about every food stall in the show. Slowly she would begin to unpack, everyone eager to taste her wares. One of our favourites was Melton Mowbray pork pies with their meaty filling and rich pastry crust. Next to come out of the bags was soft fresh bread. The mini Hovis rolls were so cute. Even if we had just eaten our evening meal, we had to have one of them cut into tiny, dolls sized slices to eat with butter.

We tasted all manner of delights from around the globe. I remember my first Ski yogurt. Flavoured with delicious fruits, we tried them all. But our 1960s palates found the taste sour and not nearly fruity enough. Queenie encouraged us to add sugar by the spoonful but Pam put her foot down with a firm no!

Queenie was always full of surprises; each visit she brought back the next latest gadget. Over the years she must have seen them all! Her early memories must have been of blackened ranges and gas lighting for the wealthy. How things have changed! The new innovative labour-saving devices that sprang from the invention of electricity gave her freedom from many household chores. The vacuum cleaner, the gas cooker, the refrigerator and the washing machine were exciting additions that Queenie added to her home. She was always keen to impress. We got to sample the 'Susi Matic', the early Kenwood food mixer, and a doughnut and waffle iron set.

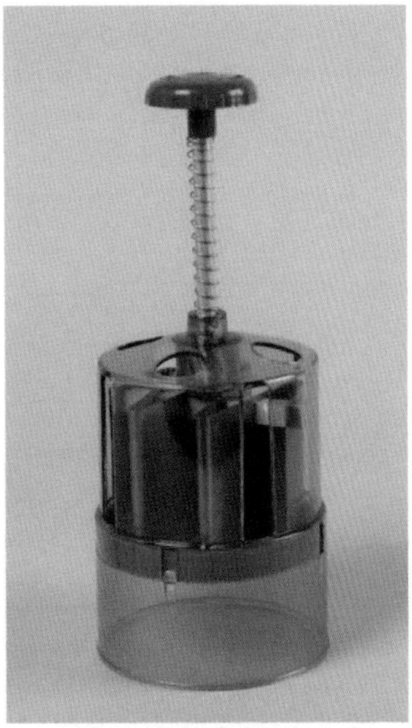

Susi-Matic

Working the first soda stream was a challenge. That Easter one of the men tried it out. Somehow, in all the excitement, he managed to soak Pam's friend, Norah, who was staying for the weekend. Poor Norah was wet through to the skin with sweet fizzy pop. Unlike us, she was not at all amused. We never heard the last of it.

Most of Queenie's purchases were useful additions to the kitchen but some were a total waste of money. They ended up tucked out of the way in a cupboard and never seen again. One good example was the contraption that churned unsalted butter into cream. We all took turns to pump the churn up and down, up and down. After what seemed like hours, Queenie turned out the meagre offering. It was disastrous, with no flavour other than buttery fat; we did not know what to do with it. We certainly did not fancy it spooned onto our pudding. Needless to say, that gadget stayed in the cupboard for a very long time.

Soda Stream

These shows were another arena for Queenie to practise her negotiating skills and clinch a deal. Once she bought a beautiful white metal patio set. It had a lovely circular glass table where all the family could enjoy their summer afternoons sipping tea and eating cake.

Another time Queenie ordered a piano from one of the shows, she rented it for a year or so. No one could play and there was no money for lessons. I tried some scales with the help of a friend who was learning and Candy taught me to play chopsticks. Still I amused myself in the cold billiard room sitting at that piano until it went back. By this time Queenie had struck a deal with someone else and bought the pianola. It opened up a whole new world of music. There were three large trunks of reels. Sture, Cecil and John fixed what they could and I went through them all until I found my favourites, La Bohème, Peer Gynt, Day Break and The Toreador. Now I had some real music to play and I would sit for hours on wet cold days pedalling away, belting out the notes with gusto. Queenie would pop her head around the billiard room door from time to time, probably interested in who was playing, giving me encouragement, as always, with a simple smile.

The last two touring caravans were bought through contacts made at the Caravan and Camping Show. The final one was a beautiful but massive 18ft five berth tourer, complete with a chemical toilet; it was the largest van permitted for towing. Bought when Queenie was in her seventies and Cecil in his sixties, Pam and Sture questioned her wisdom. It never got the use it deserved. We did enjoy it on 'safari' once or twice. It was fantastic to stay in but not so practical for Queenie's choice of venues and campsites down long narrow muddy tracks. Driving the Chevy with that monster of a caravan towed behind, it is not surprising that Cecil needed to vent his frustration from time to time.

Pianola still working today

One Friday afternoon, back in December 1967, Mark and I came home from school to find Queenie eagerly awaiting our return. She was as excited as a child, with a glint in her powder blue eyes; she said "I have a little girl for you to see". We looked at her blankly. Whatever could she mean? Impatiently she beckoned us into her cosy little sitting room next to the kitchen. "Come on, come see who is here." Expecting to find a visitor sitting on the settee, imagine our surprise to find a colour TV, reputedly the first in the village, sat in the corner with the test card playing. Queenie was so happy she bounded around the room, her excitement infectious. Keen to show off her new addition to the family, she instructed Mark to run around to the cottage and get Dot and Jack. Uncharacteristically, all evening she invited selected tenants in, as they paid their weekend rent, to view the new wonder that was colour TV. Together we spent many a happy evening watching the "box". Queenie's cosy little sitting room was soon christened the television room!

On Saturdays Nell and Harry were invited to spend the day with Queenie. Harry rarely ever came; he preferred his own company. By this time he was becoming quite a recluse. Life had been tough on Harry. He had returned home after the war, damaged by mustard gas and traumatised. Nell had miscarried late into a pregnancy sometime before little Albert was born and it had left them both grief stricken. At home Harry took to eating his meals crouched on a low stool, his eyes just level with the table top. Probably keeping his head down to avoid attack! At Goff's Oak, once the supper had been eaten and cleared away, Nell and Queenie would settle down to an evening's viewing. Queenie would settle herself into the corner nook of the settee. Nell would sit next to her, her head of fading auburn hair wisped up into a loose bun, and Queenie's strawberry blond curls contrasting with the dark green of the sofa. Amicably they sat side by side, their faces aglow with the light from the TV; their full attention on the small screen. If the content of the show became anything close to risqué, the quiet Nell would exclaim, "Ooh err, Queenie!" then the channel would be swiftly changed and something more suitable found, bearing in mind it was early evening and I was sitting with them. Viewing at the time was geared for families and hardly salacious. But Nell was easily offended and Queenie was respectful of her older sister's sensitivity. So she gave the impression that she too was shocked. I wonder how they would both have coped with the content of today's programmes!

Harry and Nell in the early years

Clacton

It was around 1964 that Queenie bought the flat at 18 Marine Court East, Clacton. I remember one dull winter Sunday she took Pam and Sture to Clacton for their opinion and of course I went along for the ride. We drew up outside and Cecil parked the Chevy along the front. I begged and begged to go in with them. I'd been cooped up in the car for far too long! Pam and Sture did not think I should join them and urged me to stay in the car with Uncle Cecil. But Queenie was confident that my conduct would be nothing less than perfect and said a resolute "yes".

We were shown into the living room. The light was fading in the winter's afternoon. The green of the grass and the blue of the sea were melting into grey. The stuffy, warm room was overfilled with furniture; amongst it sat a small grey-haired lady. Whether we had arrived unannounced I do not know. But she did not rise from her seat and we were not invited to take our coats off or sit down. Queenie stood and chatted, making her negotiations and explaining the ins and outs to Pam and Sture. The meeting was brief but it was the start of another string of adventures and wonderful memories for us all.

The next day I was keen to tell my friends at school. "My Grandmother has bought a flat." I announced. This received little interest, nothing new there! "Ohm!" came the reply, "My Granny lives in a flat.", "But this is only for holidays!" I proudly replied.

Mark and I spent many a happy time with Queenie and Cecil down at 'The Flat'. On cold wintry Sundays Queenie would impulsively announce that we should all go to the flat. After Chapel Cecil would be requested to prepare the car and off we would go on a trip to the seaside. We would arrive in good time for lunch at 'Cordy's Restaurant'. Cecil would drop us off, then park the Chevrolet back at the flat and walk back to join us at the table. The large two-storey restaurant with its starched linen tablecloths and heavy silver cutlery was always popular. Even off season there were times when we had to join a queue of hungry customers waiting for a table. The classic three course menu, served by ladies in tight black dresses and spotless white starched aprons, was well worth the wait. With its heavy patinated wood and solid furniture it was a 1930s time warp. Cordy's was no more than half a mile from the flat. Pam, Sture, Cecil and we youngsters were happy to take a leisurely stroll back but Queenie often insisted that Cecil walk back for the car and drive us the short distance.

Visits often included a walk along the pier. In winter, with the attractions closed, we would stroll along its length and take in the sharp fresh salty air. At the pier end we would look at the lifeboat in its house and check out the view across the turbulent grey sea with its galloping white horses, listening to the cry of the gulls and the crash of the waves on the beach.

When we stayed for the weekend Queenie loved to play the slot machines but not the ones on the pier. Come the evening or late afternoon on dull days she could be found in the arcade at 'our end' of the seafront. Here she would while away the hours with her hands full of coins. Never once did she refuse us extra pennies when our supplies ran out. Goodness knows how much she spent but she loved it. In the afternoons Cecil would stay in the flat reading his newspaper. Mark and I would join Queenie for a while then pop back when we had had enough. Quite often Cecil would need to go looking for her in the dark. Queenie was never keen to leave; the next coin may just be the lucky one. She protested like a petulant youngster when Cecil told her that she had been out long enough.

If we were staying for any length of time, especially in the better weather, the big boot of the Chevy was loaded to bursting. All manner of essentials and non-essentials were piled in. Copious amounts of food were carried out in brown cardboard boxes. Food was always a top priority for Queenie and she always packed exactly what we liked. As visits became more elaborate, the quantities of stuff became well… just more copious. For example, Queenie was more than happy for me to take my new dollies' pram and all the paraphernalia that went with it.

Flat 18 was on the ground floor of the block and it was on the busy seafront road. Stopping to unload was a nightmare. Parking was around the back and it was quite a trek to carry everything into the flat. Until one day we used our initiative, opened the bedroom windows at the back and started to ferry the boxes and bags in. The gentile neighbours looked on in annoyance. Nets twitching at every turn. It was not long before us kids discovered that this was by far the easiest and most fun route for general ins and outs to the back. Queenie was very tolerant of this for quite some time until one day the residents, retired and staid, complained a little too loudly and Queenie had to take notice of them. Using the window was not quite, banned but discouraged in daylight and always accompanied by the warning of… "Keep the noise down!"

Queenie organised the flat to sleep eight. The copious master bedroom at the back had a double and a single bed in it. The small front bedroom had bunk beds with a single divan snuck in as well. With the settee in the lounge making another double, there was room for a family party. There were times when all the beds were taken. With three generations, we were quite a crowd and at times we must have made somewhat of a din but I never heard Queenie complain, just the neighbours. One Easter weekend I remember being there with Lee and Candy. Queenie bought us each a chocolate Easter egg wrapped in shiny gold and silver foil paper. We lined them all up on the long low windowsill of the lounge for the passing world to see.

Our mornings at Clacton were early; Cecil, Mark and I would take the dogs out for a long breezy walk toward the Martello Tower and beyond. Trotting along in the fresh early morning air, our only companions were other dog walkers and beachcombers out before the crowds. Queenie rarely joined us. Instead she welcomed us back with the smell of eggs and bacon cooking in the pan and the table laid with soft fresh white bread and a pot of home-made jam.

Sunny days were spent on the beach. Thanks to Queenie we moved in lock, stock and barrel. Staking our claim with windbreaks, deckchairs, rugs, and buckets and spades. We made ourselves comfortably at home. By mid-afternoon we were ready for some refreshment. It was not unusual for Queenie to nip back to the flat to make a pot of tea. She would bring it back to the beach on a large tray, the cups rattling loudly as she stepped onto the uneven sand. Someone would jump up to rescue the milk and sugar. With the big brown pot still steaming hot, we would gather around for a welcome warm up and a sandy biscuit if we were lucky.

On days when the weather was not so nice the evening often calmed with the promise of a new weather front. Queenie would always support us in our desire to night bathe. It was heavenly! The wet beach was deserted in the fading light. With the tide fully out, the sand lay flat and clean in front of us. The sea was as still as a millpond, and in contrast to the cool drizzle of the evening, was as warm as a bath. With the tide at its lowest, the sea level remained a continuous safe level for what seemed like miles. Mark and I had such a good time splashing and swimming under the watchful eye of a grown up. We would race our mini Lilos. A special gift brought back from France by Queenie on one of her holidays. We had so much fun. With the sky darkening and the night drawing in cold, Queenie would always be there with a dry towel and a restorative cup of something hot to warm us up when we had had enough.

Days were happy and long, culminating in a walk to the pier where we would enjoy all the fun of the fair. With Queenie keeping a watchful eye over us we would ride the ghost train, the dodgems and the carousel. Queenie enjoyed the spinning horses of the carousel, with their flaring nostrils and golden manes. Often she and I would take a ride together, gliding up and down, and round and round to the hypnotic music of the organ. Her pale blue eyes captured the laughter of a time gone by, when she was young and innocent.

Tired and happy we took a slow stroll back along the promenade to the flat. Here and there the sea twinkled as the electric street lights spilled out over the dark water. The waves softly lapped the beach with a rhythmic ebb and flow as we walked our weary way home. The foam gently rolled over the noisy pebbles and shells as we made our way slowly back to our beds with the promise of another glorious day just around the corner.

I remember that one year a young mother and her small children moved into the flat opposite. With most of the residents being retired old fuddy-duddies we all thought that she would be a welcome addition. After one or two instances where the Flat key got left behind and domestic arrangements had to be moved to Point Clear while "good Ol" Cecil drove home to collect it, Queenie decided to entrust a key to this young woman. Until one evening Queenie and Cecil turned up unexpectedly to find that she had borrowed every chair in the place for a party. Queenie was furious; needless to say that arrangement did not last. From that time on, remembering the key was paramount and everyone did their best to remind Queenie.

Queenie was always very protective about who should be allowed to use the flat. Steve and I were privileged to stay there for our honeymoon, a beautiful warm week back in the spring of 1979. We went on to use it for more than one occasion to entertain friends for long weekends. I was able to relive the memories of my childhood and create some new ones. It was a sad day for all of us when it had to be sold.

The Flat Clacton (ground floor left)

'Safaris' started with the purchase of the 'Paddy' wagon. Bought in the early seventies it was a four berth Bedford campervan complete with awning. It had a roof that opened up and two narrow canvas bunks that precariously pulled out from above the windows. The bench seats down either side made up into two comfy beds. It had all mod cons, a cooker, sink and fridge. Queenie loved to caravan and this latest addition bought new from the Caravan and Camping Show proved to be a lot of fun.

Sitting on those elevated bench seats, everyone had a fantastic view of the countryside as it stretched out in front of us. We could see into private gardens, over drystone walls and beyond. Suddenly our world of travel became bigger and more alive.

Safaris were taken during half-term holidays as a mid-week break. Previous to the Paddy wagon we would travel in the Chevy and tow a caravan. Queenie, Cecil, Pam, Mark and I would be excitedly bundled off for an adventure. However we travelled, we were always accompanied by Cecil's two Reader's Digest books, 'Book of the Countryside' and 'Treasures of Britain', to be used as a reference along our unknown trail. Pam had her head stuck in the pages. She was always feeding us with interesting facts about the countryside and the towns we visited. She planned our stops to include museums, castles and other places of historic interest. We zigged and zagged our way across Britain, north, south, east and west.

Bedford CF Campervan

Many times we ventured down to the West Country. Exploring Dorset and Devon was a favourite with all of us. Often we would incorporate a drop into West Bay or a stay with Queenie's friend, Aunt Bertha. Passing Stonehenge on our way, we would take a break from our travels to stretch our legs and climb upon the mighty stones for a few photographs.

Bertha was Queenie's oldest and closest friend. A little older than Queenie, they had known each other since childhood. She married Ernie Chapman and had two children, Tony and Audrey.

In the 1930s the children were both married and had left home. Young Pam was a bridesmaid at Audrey's cold January wedding, wearing a little cape made of white fur. Queenie was so proud of her. Bertha and Ernie lived between Enfield and Palmers Green, moving into a modern 1930s new-built semi. It was at the end of the road and had nice gardens both front and back. When Pam was young she loved to stay for holidays. In the early 1940s, during the war years, Bertha moved to Bell Bar. The bombing spooked her and each evening she would travel out to Cuffley and sleep under the kitchen table at Brook Farm. She had many contacts and could always be relied upon to supply Queenie with the odd bag of sugar or extra supplies when rations were short.

It was at the end of the war in 1953 that Aunt Bertha moved to the West Country. She found a beautiful rundown home in Ferndown, just north of Bournemouth. It was not long before she was on her way once again, like Queenie, a woman before her time. Bertha would buy a home, do it up or modernise it with basins in the bedrooms for example, then sell it on and make a profit. In the early days she bought a rambling old farmhouse set in acres of rolling green pastures. Facilities were a bit basic and Pam recalls the oven heated by burning wood that had to be raked out before cooking could commence and the bread could go in.

Aunt Bertha seemed to have moved each time we visited. She lived with her husband Ernie and Uncle Bert. Much like Uncle Cecil, Bert had lodged with Ernie and Bertha for many years previously and had stayed as part of the family. Ernie was a Plymouth Brethren and had experienced a strict upbringing. Bert had worked for the Customs & Excise. He was not a well man; he had pernicious anaemia. Both men were quite old and fragile by the time I was visiting in the late 1960s and 1970s but we were always made welcome.

Her homes were always interesting. Once, we all stayed, including Sture, in a lovely big country house. Each of the many large and grand bedrooms was named after the colour in which they had been decorated. Pam

and Sture stayed in the yellow room whilst Mark and I shared the twin blue room which overlooked the garden and the churchyard beyond. Some of her homes were deep in the countryside with stunning views sweeping across green meadows; others were tucked into quaint villages or hamlets. Each had a unique charm and there was always plenty of space for Mark, John and I to run around and explore.
I wrote home in the 1960s, ***"You walk out through a shed into a large field of lush green grass. It's just like a secret garden!"***

After a day or so with Aunt Bertha we would move on to the coast in search of pirate coves and rock pools. We would scale the heights at Jacob's Ladder. Chasing through the precarious muddy pathways, we would suck in lungfuls of salty fresh air, with Queenie shouting after us to take care! Alternatively we would travel over the barren moor to Cornwall where we could explore the enchanted Castle of Tintagel. Later that night, tucked up in our cosy sleeping bags, we would dream of Merlin, King Arthur and the Knights of the Round Table. It was a magical time.

Other times we would visit towns and cities. At Bristol we drove over Clifton Bridge. At Bath we saw the roman splendour of the baths and sampled the waters. At Brighton we watched in awe as the dolphins were put through their paces. At Portsmouth we clambered over the Victory, imagining ourselves to be sailors on the high seas.

Taking in the many sights along the way we travelled up and down the country, each evening stopping at a different campsite, finding places to eat out at every opportunity.

Thanks to Queenie, Mark and I enjoyed places like Longleat, Cheddar Gorge, Wookey Hole, Beaulieu and Blenheim Palace, our knowledge and imaginations enhanced, our lives enriched with tales of pirates, knights, witches and highwaymen.
One year, on the recommendation of Jack, who had been working and staying there, we went to the Wye Valley and Symonds Yat, a place of sheer natural beauty. We camped on sites surrounded by trees and took long walks through the many trails of the Forest of Dean, always keeping an eye open for wildlife, especially deer. Daringly we walked on the swaying rope bridge over the river Wye; the view was spectacular! The charms of this region beckoned us back and we went more than once, discovering the delights of Monmouth, Ross-on-Wye and the mighty castles at Goodrich and Ludlow.

Once, when we were older, we ventured into Wales and on to Liverpool where John was at university. Queenie was most interested to see his shabby digs and meet his new friends. Cecil took us into the hills to find the spot where John and his friends went potholing; he took us onto the beach where the boys had raced on a car bonnet towed behind a car. Pam was quite concerned about John's safety but Queenie found it all thrilling.

Now in her seventies, Queenie showed little sign of slowing up. I do not know where she found her boundless energy. But she did and we treasure all the magical times that she gave us on safari!

River Wye, Symonds Yat. Q1L

Hairdos and High Society

Queenie nearly always started her weekend with a trip to the hairdresser's. Saturday morning she would nip out for a shampoo and set, especially if there was a 'do' to attend. I remember her using two hairdressers: one in rooms over Cheshire's the butcher's shop in Goff's Oak and one in Cheshunt.

As always Cecil would be asked to bring the car around. On rare occasions I would be invited along. From the depths of my distant past I can recall climbing up the narrow grubby stairs into a large room furnished with back to back dressing tables, each with a tall mirror. There was a hint of black and pink décor from the fifties and an abundance of dust laden plastic flowers in arrangements upon the windowsill. It was warm, smelly and noisy with dryers and female chatter. As they trimmed and preened, Queenie was in her element. Holding court with the 'girls', she laughed and joked with them, sharing topical conversation and catching snippets of gossip to pass onto Pam and Dot. Tipping generously on her exit, with her bubbly blonde curls held high, she gave them a broad farewell smile as she stood up to leave.

Once at home she would slip into something more comfy. After a cup of Cecil's tea, she would find herself drawn to the garden, with just one more small job to complete before she went out. Digging in a few rows of spuds or pruning back an annoying hedge, Queenie always found something to do. More often than not she would end up stoking the bonfire with a fork or big stick, trying to resurrect the smoky grey embers into dancing flames. Fire was always a draw and Queenie could spend all day just messing about burning things.

Queenie and Cecil

At teatime she would come in, remove her smoky headscarf and get into a hot bath for a sweet-smelling soak. Once dressed she would apply a little bit of powder and paint to her sun-beaten face. Then with a generous spray of Channel No 5 she would be ready for any grand occasion.

Usually dour and practical, Queenie loved to dress up. Like a drab cygnet turning into a beautiful swan, she emerged as an elegant lady. Her wardrobes, and she had a few, were full of elegant evening dresses and beautiful Nina Ricci dress and jacket suits, bought in London or the Pearsons store in Enfield.

She had coats and stoles of fur. And matching hats, shoes and bags for any and every occasion. Her jewellery boxes were full of pretty pieces that had been collected over the years. As I watched her dress, she let me touch and try some on. They glistened and sparkled like her bright blue eyes. I was fascinated by her brooches. The diamante-incrusted lizard always took my fancy and I was allowed to borrow it on a few occasions, proudly pinning it to my coat or dress for a party.

As she stepped into our living room for help with a tricky zip or necklace catch, she came alive. The years fell away and through the eyes of a small child I was in the presence of royalty. Her destinations were always glamorous: dinner dances, shows and Masonic do's. Since the death of Bert it was Cecil who escorted her. He loved dancing and social events just as much as she did. They made a dapper pair out on the dance floor. Many of the events were in top London venues. Queenie's show business friends had given her many contacts. The 1940s and 1950s had seen an explosion in self-expression and cutting loose. The London scene was becoming far more liberal, especially Soho where foreign restaurants and drinking clubs were springing up. Queenie relished this side of life. Eagar as always to sample something new she embraced the changes that these different cultures brought to society.

Next morning I was eager to ask about their evening and find out if they had had a good time. I anticipated a small treat and was seldom disappointed. Often Queenie managed to discretely slip a cracker trinket or sweet treat into her jewelled evening bag. I was delighted. She was my special Grandma like no other older lady that I have met then or since.

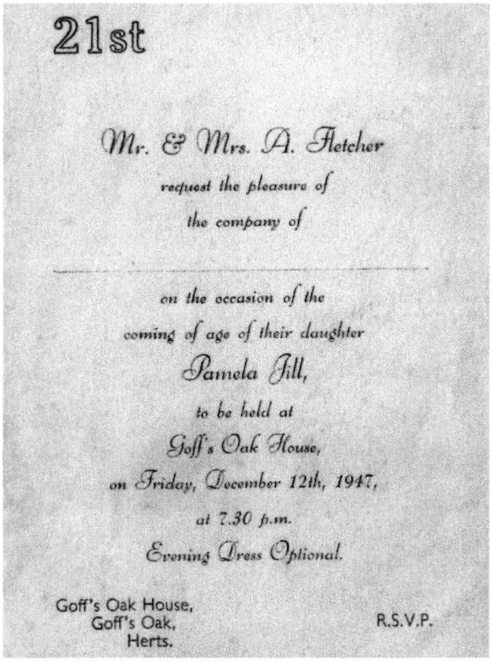
21st

Mr. & Mrs. A. Fletcher
request the pleasure of
the company of

on the occasion of the
coming of age of their daughter
Pamela Jill,
to be held at
Goff's Oak House,
on Friday, December 12th, 1947,
at 7.30 p.m.
Evening Dress Optional.

Goff's Oak House,
Goff's Oak,
Herts.

R.S.V.P.

Queenie was a true party girl; the grandest party she organised was for Pam's 21st Birthday in December 1947. Rationing was still in force and it was a challenge to obtain all the ingredients needed for a successful party but despite all the hardships, it turned out to be a glamorous affair. Queenie and Pam shopped in London for their ultimate outfits. Queenie found an elegant long, black, designer gown with gold encrusted braid trailing down one of the slender shoulders. It fitted her figure beautifully. Pam wore a floaty voile dress in blue. It had soft capped sleeves and frills at the bottom of the long hemline. A butler was hired for the evening from the swanky Mayflower Hotel in Hertford. A bar was set up in the morning room and a three piece band played in the drawing room. The carpets were removed to expose the well-worn oak floor boards ready for the dancing.

The Butler acted as maître d' insuring that everyone had drinks and was well fed from the buffet supplied by the hotel. The smartly dressed men in their suits or military uniforms drank beers whilst the sophisticated young ladies, in their long evening dresses, sipped damson crème. Against all the odds Queenie got her hands on some Champagne. Everyone was gathered in the grand hall and a toast was raised to Pam. The guests danced into the early hours, too tired to go home many stayed over, finding any suitable spot to get some shut eye. When early riser Aunty Nettie got up for her morning cup of tea she was horrified to see servicemen sprawled on all the settees. The party was such a success with everyone that Mr Cheshire the village butcher and friend of Bert's asked to use the house to host a home coming party at the end of the Second World War. Once again the house was filled with young service men and women. A group drove from North Weald in their service Jeep. Letting their hair down after the ordeal of war the partying went on well into the early hours and once again the house was the talk of the village!

Queenie needed little excuse to gather her friends and family together, find the old records, open the bar and put together a buffet. Back in 1960 Queenie held a Wombwell family reunion. She set tables in the big hall with its inglenook fireplace, for over thirty lunch guests. The tables were laid with crisp white linen. Silver candelabras alternated with vases of chrysanthemums down the centre of the tables. Chairs were brought in from all corners of the house for this rare occasion. Queenie and her cousin Barbara cooked a meal in the large farmhouse style kitchen. Three generations of the Wombwell family wined and dined together; the house rang with laughter and the excited chatter of a reunited family thanks to Queenie.

The house was made for parties and after Pam's 21st and the Cheshire's Second World War party, Queenie hosted three wedding receptions at the house. The first wedding party was for Bette's daughter Belle, and Tauge. The second was for grandson Paul and his new wife Anne in 1971. The disco was held in the billiard room. Coloured lights lit the walls and ceiling and the floor throbbed from the beat of the music. I can remember us all in the crowded room dancing the night away. Queenie was there at every turn, helping guests and partying into the early hours with the rest of us. The final wedding was my own in 1979. It was my dream to be married at home. I would have loved to have taken my vows in the drawing room, standing in front of the big leaded window with its stained-glass top, the lawn laid out behind me. Unfortunately back in the 1970s this was not permitted, so I made do with a simple ceremony in Saint James Church and a reception back at the house. Queenie gave us free rein of the downstairs rooms. After the church service she opened the wide front door to her home and I proudly stood with my new husband beside me, receiving our guests as they entered. Queenie, now aged 81 years, took more of a back-seat approach. I know she made her feelings felt to Pam, but she never openly interfered. We never forgot that it was her house and that she was ultimately in charge and loved to be in control. Thankfully she only guided us through the preparations and left us to make all the final decisions. The reception was catered by a team of professionals and Queenie let them take over her kitchen. We ate in the billiard room seated on antique 'thrones' at the top table, surrounded by the people we loved the most. After the wedding breakfast and speeches the guests spilled out into the vast rooms of the house and relaxed in their splendour. Everyone remarked on the beauty of the old house. Shabby as it was, Queenie had arranged for all the rooms to be cleaned and polished and decorated with flowers. She created a warmth that we all appreciated and that I never forgot.

left hand side from the front, Vi (Pittkin)Lewis, Ted Lewis, Cecil Harriss, Laurie Pollock, Dot with Lee and Candice.
head of the table Eileen and Bernard, *right hand side from the front,* Pam, Ken Perry, Jill Perry, Nell, Anita, Sture *with* John *behind.*

from the left back, Eileen Wombwell, Bernard Wombwell, Ethel Wombwell, John Curran, Clarence Mardell, Rene Bittleston

left hand side from the front

Vicky MacDonald (Pollock),Margaret Moon, Glen Moon, John Pittkin, Janet Pittkin, Leslie Pittkin, Olive Pittkin.

right hand side from the front

Barbara (Pollock) Dale,Martyn Bittleston, Ken Wheeler, June Wheeler, Chris Mardell, Paul, Jack and two unidentified.

Guy Fawkes Night

Guy Fawkes Night was celebrated each year at Goff's Oak House on or around the 5th of November. Queenie ensured that it was a great success and guaranteed that we all had a fantastic time. Other people had bonfire parties but none like ours. From the moment the day broke and the first rays of autumn sun shone through my bedroom window, I wanted it to be dark. The excitement mounted throughout the day and I could hardly wait for the evening to fall.

From early afternoon the large warm kitchen bustled with the preparations. Queenie scrubbed endless potatoes ready for the oven. Up to her elbows in flour, she knocked up catering-sized apple pies for all of us to enjoy. I'd look in from time to time checking on progress and asking "when will they be here?".

As the sky darkened to a shadowy black and when I could contain my excitement no longer, our guests began to arrive. Each year the same friends came. First to arrive were Aunty Rose with her children Douglas and Julie. Whilst waiting for the others, Mark and I would race around the lawns chasing them in the dark, flashing our torches and squealing with joy. Mr and Mrs Carter from the corner shop with their son Tony and in later years his girlfriend Maureen were next to arrive. Occasionally Albert and Margaret would come with their youngsters Pauline and Peter. The children were young and often the family left early. All the extended family from the cottage came, Dot, Jack, Paul, Candy and Lee each with their partners and friends. We made quite a crowd wrapped up warm against the November chill in our heavy coats, gloves and hats.

With everyone assembled, some twenty of us would make an informal procession to the bonfire, now burning brightly with red and gold flames vivid against the night sky. Sometimes the fire was at the 'dump', Queenie's spot in the garden for burning rubbish, at other times it was next door on Logy Joe's land. Jack and he were both in the tree business and had an arrangement for November the fifth. Either way, the bonfire was always spectacular. High as a mountain, roaring red and yellow it was so hot that you could not get closer than a few yards for fear of burning your face. The Guy, made by John and Lee, was dressed in Cecil's old clothes and took pride of place on top of the twelve-foot high bonfire. It lasted only a few minutes in the inferno before the red hot flames engulfed it forever.

The fireworks would begin immediately. Rockets flew into the black sky bursting with a loud bang into a thousand jewels that lit the heavens. Catherine wheels span uncontrollably with a high pitched whiz. Roman candles showered their glittering sparkles to the ground, popping and crackling all the way down. We danced about with sparklers, writing our names in the air and making great arcs of silver. Lee and John let off bangers behind the unsuspecting grown-ups, scattering everyone in all directions. It was difficult to know who was having the most fun, the children or the adults. As the final rocket sped away, Tony Carter would bring out the grand finale… his home-made firework! It was enormous and potentially lethal. I can remember standing well back… In fact, I can remember everyone standing well back! Often the whole thing would go up in one almighty bang and billow out great volumes of unimpressive smelly grey smoke. In raptures of laughter, arm in arm we trekked back up to the house and the warmth of the patio.

The patio would be lit with coloured lights. A large brazier glowed warmly in the centre. Music from the record player rang out into the starry night. Hot jacket potatoes split and loaded with butter were handed round. Spit-roast beef was thickly sliced and served in doorstep slices of bread. You have never tasted anything like it… Sitting out in the cold autumn night, eating with your fingers... It was paradise! Queenie always made a punch, sloshing this and that into the big glass bowl with no consideration for alcoholic content. It had an almighty kick that warmed us right through. When we had had our fill of beef and potatoes, the hot apple pie was served with a generous dollop of fresh cream whipped to soft peaks. It was an enormous pie, deeply filled with apples from the garden; the wide tin only just fitted in the oven.

We sat out there in the darkness talking and laughing, enjoying the food and each other's company, until the embers of the brazier began to die and we all began to feel the sharp nip of the November night.

Now we moved inside. The hats and scarves, the coats and boots all came off and we went into the 'billiard room'. Music was selected and the record player was turned on. Still in our old jeans and jumpers, we danced in our thick woolly socks and played silly games until we could take no more. Exhausted, I slipped away to bed, the faint hum of the music wafting up the stairs to my room.

From the very first day that Queenie opened the door to Goff's Oak House, she was a generous hostess. Christmas was special. It was Queenie's birthday and always a time to celebrate with family and friends. Old Aunty Nettie would come year after year to enjoy the festivities. She would share a bedroom with either Pam or Queenie. A Victorian relic, she would dress under her copious nightgown which covered her from neck to floor in white linen. With practised dexterity she would prudishly put on her garments completely hidden from sight. Each morning she would emerge from the billowing white linen fully clothed. At bedtime she would reverse the process, never once revealing her naked form.

Christmas in the dining room.Left to right back row, Dot,Sture, John, Jack, Lee,?, Queenie, front left to right, Nettie, Paul, Pam

Circus friends staying on the site were always made welcome and encouraged to join Queenie's celebrations. One year Pam and Queenie's circus friend Bette found a bottle of peach schnapps in the bar. They drank most of its contents whilst catching up on gossip in the cosy morning room one Christmas morning. The conversation grew louder and gigglier as the level in the bottle lowered. When afternoon came and the rest of the party were relaxing in the drawing room, Pam and Bette were not having quite such a jolly time! Both were definitely feeling a little worse for wear!

The large old house called out for big parties and in 1950 Queenie had a houseful, with Nettie, Bette, her daughter Belle with her new husband Tauge, and various other guests who were staying in the house. Her welcome was always generous and her parties memorable. Everyone always had a good time relaxing in the informal grandeur of the large rooms. By the time I arrived in 1958, the routine and family customs for this special time had been well and truly set!

Christmas 1960s - 1970s

Getting Ready

Queenie's Christmas preparations were traditionally early. First, the dark brown chutney was made using fresh autumn fruit and garden vegetables. Throughout the morning the vinegar slowly evaporated into the steamy kitchen, leaving the richly spiced mixture perfect to accompany the Christmas ham. Next, the mincemeat was made, well in advance, and then left to mature to its full rich flavour in jars alongside the chutney on the pantry shelves.

Mid-1960's Christmas morning
John, Queenie and Jack with Anita and Mark

Once the fifth of November celebrations had been enjoyed and put behind us, the Christmas puddings and cake had to be made. Sitting on a high stool up to the solid kitchen table with its turned pine legs and its red Formica top, I watched Queenie dressed in her wraparound apron, long wooden spoon in her hand, and a large earthenware bowl in front of her. Not a classic good cook, Queenie had an innate way of bringing ingredients together without recipe or measure and triumphing with yet another culinary marvel. Puddings were generously laced with alcohol. I needed no second invitation to stir the dark brown glossy mixture; close my eyes tight shut and make a wish. With the puddings left to steam in the pantry, the whole house would be enveloped with the sweet smell of dried fruit, freshly grated nutmeg, heady spices and spirits. Next, the dark rich cake mix was prepared and spooned into a large square tin, wrapped in copious layers of protective brown paper and newspaper tied with string and placed in the oven for its long slow cook.

Throughout the years Queenie employed a 'daily' three times a week. In the later years we had Mrs Johnson who, like all the rest, doggedly attacked her chores with Queenie tireless by her side. The build-up to Christmas brought a frenzy of activity often resulting in extra hours. Together, Queenie and her 'help' would toil over the silver and brass. The big reception rooms had to be dusted and cleaned. All of the old wood was polished to a gleaming shine. The guest rooms had to be prepared and aired. The house and its heavy antique furniture in all its tired splendour had to look bright and clean for the coming festivities. The pungent aroma of mansion polish followed their progress as they worked their way through the substantial rooms.

Hall inglenook

You could smell the coming of Christmas. Over the weeks that Christmassy smell would swell with the introduction of the greenery. Mistletoe was found and hung in the centre of rooms, the same old red ribbon used time and time again! Big buckets of dark green prickly holly were brought into the house; the holly was graced with ribbons or bells as it hung on every nail and post. Finally, each picture was adorned with a simple sprig. The freshly cut tree was proudly supplied by Jack from one of his friends; it was always the tallest tree ever seen! Often the pointy top had to be chopped to fit the ten foot ceiling. With the waft of pine so fresh and fragrant, Christmas was truly on its way.

Mark and I often helped put up the decorations. Each year the same dusty boxes would be brought out. Cecil and John would be expected to make the ancient lights work for yet another year.

All four of the major fireplaces were furnished with coloured lights. Illuminated paper stars hung in the two tall windows of the hall. There were bright decorations hung, draped, and twisted all around the house. Two musical golden bells hung in the doorways to the billiard room and the drawing room. The tall tree was an eclectic array of glittering baubles, bells and assorted miscellany all lovingly collected across the decades and safely stored for the next year. Complete with its trusted Angel at the top, the tree shone its glory for all to see from its position in the corner of the large hall.

The final addition to the Christmassy scent were armfuls of dinner-plate-sized chrysanthemums, placed not in vases but umbrella stands and enormous jugs. Grown professionally by Sture, these beauties were hand-selected and the best money could buy.

A day or two before Christmas, Queenie insisted on the fires being lit. She loved a good blaze. With the wood in good supply by Jack, the inglenooks were soon stoked and roaring with enormous logs that took two adults to lift in from the frosty outside. We would sit warming ourselves, changing sides with our companions when our faces glowed scarlet on one side from the penetrating heat!

John's wife Renee and Anita enjoy the fire

At around this time there would be a loud knock at the imposing front door and a choir of carol singers would be invited into the hall by Queenie. She would request her favourites, and the angelic sounds echoed throughout the old house. Shyly drawn down the stairs by the heavenly voices, I would listen with joy to 'Silent Night' as I sat undisturbed on a step in the shadows. Even as a small child a hair would raise on the back of my neck. Queenie's smile was broad; her blue eyes twinkled in the firelight as she enjoyed the first magic of Christmas. She showed her appreciation with her famous hospitality. Generous glasses of liquor and hot mince pies were handed around before the troupe went back out into the cold of the late afternoon air.

Visitors arrived. Aunty Bette came each year. Travelling by train, she arrived a few days before Christmas. Just 4'6" tall, dressed in her classic curly brown bear of a fur coat which touched the top of her trim leather ankle boots, she celebrated her birthday with us on Christmas Eve and stayed through to the New Year.

Queenie, Bette and Pam

Christmas Eve

Eventually Christmas Eve came… The smell of woodsmoke mingled with pine and Christmas spice filled the warm rooms. The presents started to arrive and were secretly placed under the spreading green boughs of the Christmas tree. Many were tucked in behind the saggy old blue velvet chesterfield, away from small prying eyes. It was a most exciting time. I could feel the anticipation as the adults busied themselves with last minute preparations and the atmosphere became tense building up to the big day.

Tucked up in bed trying to sleep against the restless excitement fluttering in my chest, I would be aware of Queenie preparing to go out to the local Methodist chapel for a midnight service with Pam, Dot, Bette and Cousin Candy. It was an important part of Christmas for Queenie and she always made the time. Afterwards Queenie invariably found jobs to do. Vegetables needed to be prepared, another batch of mince pies made, or last minute wrapping. Sometimes Candy would be invited to stay over and share Queenie's large bright twin room with its uneven white walls. Queenie had an eye for design and colour, mixing the thoroughly modern with the antiques of the house. She decorated the white walls with a broad, bold floral border of vivid reds and greens.

The Big Day

Everyone was up early…I can still visualise Candy ballet dancing in the window of the drawing room, the early morning sun pouring through the panes capturing her lithe form through the transparency of the sheer fabric of her nightie as she pirouetted, toes pointed and arms held elegantly. Queenie was sitting in her dressing gown and apron, sipping hot tea and enjoying the spectacle of her eldest granddaughter gracefully gliding around the beautiful old room. She had high hopes for all of us, speaking proudly of our modest achievements to whoever would listen.

Pam in the kitchen

Breakfast was Christmas ham, and home-cooked brawn for the more adventurous. Jack would pop in for a 'wee dram', wish his mum a happy birthday with a swift kiss on the cheek, then announce his departure to the pub before confirming his return to carve the bird. The turkey was always enormous; with at least eighteen expected for dinner it had to be. Goff's Oak House had three 'good' cookers: one in the kitchen, another in the pantry and one upstairs in Pam and Sture's kitchenette. All three were deployed to provide the vast quantities of food needed, the turkey in one, a joint of pork in another, roast potatoes and Yorkshire puddings by the trayful in another. The Christmas puddings bubbled merrily under the watchful eye of no one in particular and ran the risk of boiling dry. Gravy was made by the gallon and vegetables were carted up and down the back stairs. Everyone worked together, under Queenie's watchful gaze. She insisted that copious portions of traditional home cooking were the order of the day.

As children all we wanted to do was open our presents. Back and forth, back and forth into the hot steamy kitchen to ask the same question. "When can we open the presents?" Finally everyone assembled in the cosy warmth of the hall. But before a single gift was handed out, glasses were filled with champagne and held high in a toast "To Queenie!". Birthday hugs and congratulations were given for another year. Queenie never ever let us know her age; it was a closely guarded secret until after her death. Queenie stashed her birthday and Christmas presents into a neat pile; then proceeded to capture the scene on her cine-camera before slipping back to the kitchen. If she did stay longer, she was seldom coaxed into opening her presents with the crowd, preferring a quiet time in the late afternoon or evening all to herself.

As my presents piled up around me I knew that the largest, most expensive one would come from Queenie. One year she was exceptionally generous buying me a beautiful, Silver Cross, twin dolls pram. Complete with twin baby dolls brought back from a holiday in the south of France. I instantly fell in love with them. She had also hand knitted two identical layettes complete with vest, pants, dress, coat, booties, hat and mittens. All crafted by her own fair hands from scraps of wool with no pattern. Queenie was a talented needle woman. We all had particularly big presents that year; Mark had a pedal car, John got a much needed desk, and Lee had a walkie-talkie set. I cannot recall the others but it was a joyous time.

One by one the cooks slipped back into the kitchen to help with the meal, leaving the children to play and explore their new toys and the grown-ups and teenagers to sit in the warmth of the inglenook to discuss the politics of the day or simply catch up.

As promised Jack returned from the pub. With eyes twinkling like his mother's, he was soon dressed in a clean stripy apron and tall white chef's hat. He would soon have everyone in the kitchen at his bidding, ordering the clearing of the kitchen table, and with a flourish of steel on steel he would sharpen the long blades. Taking the knife in his confident hand he would adeptly carve the bird without fuss or ceremony.

Serving dinner was an art form. All the plates were warmed; each had a little paper name label on it. The mums were enlisted to help workout who would eat what and how much. The plates were piled high and topped off with lashings of hot gravy. The leftovers were put into the hot hostess trolley and left handy for seconds. All the dinners were kept piping hot until the last one was ready for the table.

Christmas table in the 1970's. Left from front to back, Cecil, Sture, Steve, ?, Dot, Paul and Pam at the back and Candy behind the candles Bette ,Anita and Mark to right front

One year Jack brought back two unknown guys from the pub. With whisky on their breath, bleary-eyed and ruddy-cheeked from their brisk walk, they entered the hot kitchen. As always Queenie generously opened her home to the newcomers. Places were hurriedly set at the table and plates found for our unexpected guests.

The tables were laid with the green Christmas cloths and placemats, red paper napkins were folded at each place setting. Three silver candelabras adorned the table, a large one in the centre and two smaller ones on either side. Down the length of the tables laid flowers, holly and Christmas crackers. The red candles were lit making the polished glasses sparkle in the drab afternoon light.

If there happened to be thirteen of us to sit down for lunch, the superstitious Queenie would either sit on the corner of the table or sit away from the main dining table on a small table to the side. As we all prepared to sit down, the inglenook fire was fed and stoked to a generous blaze of golden warmth. The lights twinkled around the mantle of the inglenook and on the tree. The two paper stars in the windows shone against the dullness of a winter afternoon. That room glowed with the warmth of a family brought together by a generous grandmother for Christmas.

Christmas 1979 in the hall

Everyone had their plate and their place at the table. The wine flowed along with the congenial conversation, and we all tucked in. Toasts were made; Queenie, with a tear in her eye, raised a glass to "Absent friends!" Crackers were pulled and the jokes shared. Queenie relaxed and enjoyed being in the bosom of her family. Back in the kitchen the Christmas pudding was prepared. Shiny sixpences were pushed into the rich sweetness; a small sprig of carefully selected holly adorned the top; warmed vodka was poured and lit; the flaming pudding was brought through to the table with a chorus of "We wish you a merry Christmas". The pudding was served with hot brandy custard. The portions were carefully orchestrated so that all the youngsters received a shiny sixpence. With our tummies fit to bursting, the coffee percolators would then be switched on. We adjourned to the antique majesty of the drawing room where we enjoyed liquors, chocolate mints, petit fours and various unusual delicacies brought back from Queenie's foreign trips.

At just before three in the afternoon, Queenie would insist that the TV be turned on. All the adults moved into the TV room where they sat in silence and watched the Queen's speech. Queenie, a strong royalist, absorbed the words of our monarch, expecting full respect from everyone gathered.

Later a cup of tea was served. Those with room would indulge in just another tasty Christmas treat. In the darkness of early evening Cecil would be employed to set up the projector and screen for a slide show or cine film. The subject… footage from previous Mediterranean holidays, bits and bobs of family life, including past Christmases and family events. The style was always fast and furious. Taken from moving vehicles or panned too quickly, we felt every bump but we loved them. Over the years we watched ourselves play and grow. Queenie gave us so many memories to cherish.

Christmas Cheer. From left to right Sture, Pam, Cecil, Anita, Queenie. Dot, Jack and Mark in the front

I remember, with fondness, Queenie's recording of Paul and Anne's wedding. Dressed in their wedding finery they strolled hand in hand out of the front door at Goff's Oak House and under the rose arch with everyone waving their farewells. They were no more than a few steps out onto the gravel path when a ruddy great speedboat raced through the crowd, up the path past Paul and Anne and out of shot. Queenie had recorded her med holiday on top of the wedding party. We laughed and laughed! This family favourite was revisited many times over the years.

Slowly the night drew in. Gradually we would disperse to our own interests, new toys, the television or a chat with a favourite aunt or uncle. I drifted off to bed happy, beyond happy and pleasantly sleepy. Queenie would stay up late into the night quietly chatting and winding down after yet another busy but much enjoyed Christmas. With her little pile of gifts still waiting for their unwrapping!

Boxing Day

On Boxing Day I was always up late but Queenie had been up since the early hours. For me it was a relaxing time to look again at all my lovely new books and toys, to play and have fun. For Queenie there was a beautiful joint of beef to cook for lunch and a party to prepare for. It was not unusual to see Queenie still knocking out pastel coloured coconut pyramids at four in the afternoon. For me it was time to get ready for the evenings fun. First, a bath run deep and warm with Queenie's luxuriously scented bubbles or bath salts. Smelling sweet I would dress in my new outfit, either lovingly made by Pam and Dot or bought by Queenie on one of our many shopping trips into 'town'. One year I wore an emerald green corduroy dress. Another time I had a lovely dark purple velvet dress made from an old dress of Queenie's. I always wore thin grown-up tights and special glittery party shoes. My golden hair, now clean and shiny was adorned with a matching ribbon. At my neck, either my little pearl or crystal necklace, both gifts from Queenie. But what I liked best was to borrow the diamante lizard brooch from Queenie. It was my favourite piece of jewellery in her vast collection. I thought it looked like a newt and I loved newts. I felt like a princess and was quick to skip down the stairs to find Queenie and show her how I looked just the same as she did before a big night out. In the warm glow of the kitchen I was met with approving smiles and positive comments fuelling that safe warm glow deep inside of me.

Boxing Day left to right, Julie, Judith, Lynne, Anne, Queenie and Rose

As evening approached the guests would arrive, Mr and Mrs Carter always joined us, along with their son Tony and his girlfriend Maureen, Aunty Rose and her children Julie and Douglas (contemporaries of Mark and I), and of course all the family with their partners or friends. We all had so much fun in the big old billiard room! The drinks flowed easily and the music played loudly. We would dance and play games all evening. We would do the Lambeth walk and the hokey cokey, sing old-time songs to the record player and laugh and joke.

Queenie and John enjoy a Christmas knees up in the drawing room

One year all the men dressed in Queenie's undies. Putting her old corsets, long johns and bras on top of their clothes, with "The Stripper" playing, they did a mock striptease to hoots of laughter, tears of joy rolling down our faces. Even Nell saw the funny side to their antics and joined in with the hilarity.

Mr Carter, Queenie and Cecil

As the evening drew on we would sit in a circle and play 'the moon is round'. Mr Carter got increasingly red in the face as he struggled to make the connection

Boxing Day Tea 1977
Anita, Candy, Queenie, Mark, Lee and Pam

between word and action and get it right. Next we tested our expertise at 'sitting on the bottle'. A fat earthenware cask was laid on its side. One had to sit upon it, one foot on top of the other. With matches on one side and a candlestick on the other you were expected to pick up the candle, balance it on your lap, pick up the matchbox, take a match, strike it and light the candle to complete the task. It was a hoot watching the tipsy attempts. There was always someone who could do it with ease and this made male competition even fiercer.

Tony Carter on the bottle

At some point Queenie would slip away to lay an impressive buffet on the long tables in the hall. Out came the little pots of brawn, the cold turkey and the Christmas ham. The now matured chutney, rich and dark, smelt delicious as the jar was opened. Laid out to tempt us were the iced Christmas cake, mince pies and the pretty coconut pyramids along with many other tasty treats. The grown-ups continued their merriment well into the early hours. I took my leave and drifted up to bed, the sounds of the party echoing through the big old house and wafting up the stairs to my cosy room where I listened for a short while before slipping into a deep, peaceful sleep.

New Year's Eve

After all this Christmassy fun you may think that Queenie would consider slowing down, but no! New Year's Eve came and if Queenie was not out at some splendid reception or party for the night she would see the year in quietly with her close family. Queenie always had to find a 'stranger'. She was very superstitious and became quite agitated if a suitable one could not be found. Either Norman from upstairs or a mate of Jack's from the pub would be enlisted to fill the role. At the stroke of midnight there would be a loud, deliberate knock at the big front door. The door would be opened to the dark 'stranger' who would throw a piece of black coal into the house for good luck. He was welcomed in for a drink and warmly shook everyone's hand wishing each of us a Happy New Year.

New Year's Day

New Year's Day brought a different gathering. Each year Queenie would invite her cousin Bernard and his wife Eileen to tea. This would be quite refined and a more genteel affair. The afternoon was spent in the opulence of the drawing room. The conversation was often dull and I excused myself after a polite period of time. If Queenie considered me to be on my best behaviour I would be invited to join them for a sumptuous tea laid out on the long hall tables, the splendid candelabras once again lit for the occasion.

One of our last parties at Goff's Oak House
30 Decemeber 1989

Show Time

At some point around the time of Christmas and the New Year Queenie would treat us to a show. I remember the pantomimes, circuses and ice shows with such pleasure! We would dress in our Sunday best, wrapped up warm against the winter chill, excited with anticipation. Cecil would drive us into London and often Queenie would insist that he take us on an additional excursion to see the magnificent lights on Oxford Street and then on for a spot of tea or lunch somewhere nice.

If we were going to the circus it was probably at Olympia with the big top cleverly erected inside. The tickets were often complimentary and sure to be ringside. As we settled into our seats Queenie, with an air of confidence, acknowledged people she knew and name-dropped wherever possible. The show would be glitzy and glamorous. With the bellowing authority of the ringmaster, the acts would be welcomed into the ring. Dogs, sea lions, horses, high wire, big cats and clowns, Queenie had interesting stories about most of them. But the small girl beside her was hardly listening, too spellbound to say anything, mesmerised by the sparkly costumes, the gaudy make-up and the daredevil antics. After the show there was always someone to meet and be introduced to. Queenie had plenty of conversation, congratulating old friends on their performance and recollecting the old days. She reminisced with clowns; their leathery faces masked with white make-up unnerved me but Queenie's pleasure was tangible. She was as excited as a child as she offered hospitality to whoever she met; inviting them to Goff's Oak House should they find themselves in the area.

New Year

With the New Year safely in, it was time for Queenie to get back to business. Her first job was to prepare her charts. One for the rents from the caravan site situated in the three-acre garden behind Goff's Oak House, the other for the holiday lets at Brightlingsea and Bridport. Soon the phone would be ringing at all hours of the day and night. The big brass bell would swing out a peal around the house and garden in an attempt to summon Queenie. Before long all the little boxes would be filled in with the names and addresses of families keen to get away for a week or two by the sea. The year had begun to roll around once again and Queenie's thoughts turned not only to business but to her own holiday…

For all her life, Queenie loved to meet new people and visit new places. Witnessing the nomadic life of her circus friends and seeing the many holidaymakers enjoying time away from their mundane domesticity must have inspired Queenie to seek adventure. From a young age she enjoyed sleeping out in the tent with her cousins and taking short trips to the coast. But it was not until she was in her early fifties that she was able to realise her plans to travel abroad.

Queenie sent this postcard home from Ilfracombe on the 8th September 1916.

It read...

Dearest Mother and Pa,
Can you find anyone you know out there. Someone took this on the sly
I was drying my hair after bathing but it is so not very plain
Hope to be home Saturday night.

With love Queenie xxx

Her first great adventure began on September the 8th, 1950 when she took the Roll-Along caravan on a road trip to the south of France. Cecil towed the heavy van behind the old Alvis. It was an exciting time for Pam who took time off from working in the bank to make the epic journey. They left Goff's Oak at 2:45 in the afternoon, probably later than Cecil anticipated, and headed off for Dover. Arriving four hours later to board the 'SS Hampton' ferry that evening, the little party would have been buzzing with anticipation. On board Queenie made sure that they had inspected every part of the ship before finding the bar. After a bite to eat and a drink, she and Pam settled down in the caravan for the night. Cecil opted to stay on deck. At four in the morning he woke the girls excitedly, with the announcement that the crossing had been wonderful!

France 1950

Back on solid ground they began the fifteen-day journey that was to take them through the towns and villages of France to the Mediterranean. They drove deep into the French countryside and marvelled at the long, straight, tree-lined roads that cut right through the open fields where farmers still ploughed the land with horses. Europe was still reeling from the devastation of the Second World War and the cratered dusty roads were testament to the poverty of the people. Pam used her basic schoolgirl French to navigate the small shops, markets and garages where she and Queenie managed to pay for petrol and essentials. The old Alvis, already nearly twenty years old, needed coaxing into life. Pam often sat next to Cecil with instructions to bang the floor when the petrol pump failed! After their early start from Calais the group decided to pull in for the night. Their very first on French soil!

France 1950

Following a comfortable stay, they were all up early and enjoying breakfast in the French sunshine. Back on the road the terrain was becoming a little less potholed if not a little steeper as they headed south. Cecil pulled over after a particularly steep hill to cool the engine and before too long two English chaps had pulled up beside them. They wanted some engine advice. Without a second thought Queenie invited the men to join her for morning coffee, a pattern that was to repeat itself time and again. The next stop was for petrol just outside of Montmirail. Cecil watched as the attendant filled the car with fuel but to his horror as he looked under the Alvis he spotted that the tank had come adrift and petrol was running out everywhere. What were they to do deep in rural France? Luckily for Queenie, a mechanic was standing nearby. With no English he directed them back to his farm where he worked for hours tackling the problem. Queenie's hospitality got the better of her once again and she invited the guy to eat lunch with them. Conversation flowed remarkably well with a little pidgin French from Pam and much gesticulation from the Frenchman and Queenie. The mechanic ended up taking the petrol tank out in order to fix it. He worked from eleven in the morning until seven at night. Queenie paid him the few francs asked and they set off once again to a little dirt track just outside of Troyes for their second night's stop.

After an early start Queenie often asked Cecil to pull up beside the road for a cup of very English tea or very French coffee. She would eagerly pick primroses at the side of the road and put them into a vase for the van. Driving through the dense sloping vineyards Queenie would demand that Cecil stop the car. Queenie and Pam would jump out and gather bowlfuls of beautiful grapes to munch on the journey. Cecil did not approve. He sat behind the wheel of the car in trepidation and ready for a quick getaway should the girls be caught. The expedition took them further south as they attempted to follow the Rhone Valley. After a wrong turn they strayed from their route and began to climb higher through the mountains. The roads became treacherous! They travelled for nearly eight long slow miles up the steep mountainside. With serious brake fade, Pam had a wooden block at the ready and strict instructions to jump out quick and jam it under the back wheel. Cecil's eyes never left the road as they made the perilous ascent. Queenie sat unhelpfully reciting all the ghastly possibilities. Something nobody wished to be reminded of! After what they calculated to be a 3894 ft. ascent, they were finally able to make their way back down to the bottom, where they found the first suitable pull-in and stopped for the night.

The next morning they found themselves in a very quaint village. They took a walk by the small school. The villagers were in awe! Queenie's was the first caravan that they had ever seen! They marvelled at the little self-contained home with all its comforts. Queenie went into the school and asked the Headmaster if he spoke English. He did not but he got his assistant who did. Queenie, Cecil and Pam were made to feel so welcome! The Head instructed the whole school to stop lessons and come and see. The children were ordered to line up in front of the school for Queenie to take a photograph. She loved it!

France 1950, village school

Driving through the French countryside was always eventful. They were stopped on more than one occasion by the French police. Cecil would get quite uptight and irate but Queenie used her easy charm to glide her way through adversity. On one occasion they had not put on the headlights and on another they were directed off the road. The balmy day had closed in. The sky had darkened and the heavens opened with a barrage of hailstones the size of thumbnails. They were directed onto a side road and recommended the food at the Hotel. It was to be their first meal in a French Auberge. The waitress came over to take their order. Even with Pam's rudimentary French it was difficult to make themselves understood. They opted for chicken and salad. The waitress came back with a plate of sliced cucumber and tomato dressed in vinegar and olive oil. A real novelty for the 1950s' British palate. Queenie and Pam sat patiently and waited for the chicken to appear but nothing happened. Queenie looked at Cecil quizzically then waited a little longer before giving the ok to dig in. Despite the unorthodox serving, the salad was deemed delicious by all. The waitress came back with clean plates and left the cutlery in readiness for the chicken, which eventually arrived piping hot and with its head still on! Despite her country upbringing Queenie was initially quite shocked by what she saw. As were Cecil and Pam, but hunger got the better of them and soon they were all tucking into hot chicken and lettuce. Topped off with huge slices of melon and cups of strong coffee. A momentous first French meal!

Monte Carlo, casino

Monte Carlo, casino at night

Up at 6.30 the next day they headed off to their ultimate destination. By 10 o'clock they had reached Saint-Raphaël and the Mediterranean. The water was the brightest clear blue, warm and inviting. Pam and Cecil swam for the rest of the morning whilst Queenie wandered along the front, chatting to the people she met. At lunch time she brought a picnic down to the beach for them all to enjoy as they sat drying on the rocks. But Queenie was restless; she was keen to get the caravan parked up for the night and return by car to explore the delights of the Côte d'Azur. That evening they drove the car into Cannes and strolled along the harbour. Queenie found a delightful street café where they could all sip Cinzano and watch the world go by. She was completely at home in this new culture.

Queenie and Pam promenade

Next day they pushed onto Nice and Monte Carlo with another great storm chasing them. As they settled down to a late lunch in the best hotel in Monte Carlo, the rain fell in torrents and the storm raged all around them. During the meal Queenie broke a glass. The headwaiter just smiled and offered "good luck, madam". After the best eats that they had ever had, Queenie announced that they should go to the casino. Back in the car Cecil drove around to the most impressive building they had ever seen. He pulled up to the door where a black commissionaire sprang into action. He raised his large umbrella over Queenie's and Pam's heads and guided them inside. The place was amazing. It was lavish and ritzy, and Queenie was completely in her element! She watched in awe as people played with a hundred and some with a thousand franc stake. It was not long before Queenie had 10 francs' worth of chips in her hand and was at a table playing. Her first five attempts were useless. The numbers were not going her way! But she was persuaded to continue and slowly lady luck began to smile upon her. She came away on cloud nine and with 50 francs in hand. There is little doubt that she would have been buzzing with excitement and eager to repeat the experience!

South of France

The south of France was Queenie's ultimate holiday experience. She loved to dress up in all her finery and find a show to enjoy in one of the casinos. Alternatively she was happy to stroll along the seafront and look at all the glamorous hotels, stopping to take a drink in a waterside bar and watch the passers-by as they too enjoyed the delights of the Mediterranean. This first taste of the south of France was to ignite a passion that brought her back time and time again.

Queenie sunbathing 1950

Each year, for as long as I can remember Queenie and Cecil would set off twice, once in the spring, then again in the autumn, for a three-week holiday to the Mediterranean. In the early years, shortly after the first trip in 1950, they took Queenie's first grandson, Paul. The little lad had the time of his life; his pale skin and fair hair turned golden as he spent all day playing on the beach with his new friends. Conversing as children do, he came home with more than a little French.

Paul and Queenie enjoy a break

Cecil would motor down to the south of France. With each trip the roads improved. He was much more confident than during the very first trip. He made his way around Paris and headed straight down to the south. Paris was usually a nightmare and Cecil was always happy to finally be out on the open road. Making use of the newly built fast roads, he was often chased by the police who pulled him over for speeding. Queenie tried her inevitable charm but it was not always successful and often there was a fine to be paid.

Sometimes Queenie would prefer to take a large tent and pitch it on the sands of the Med. But most times Cecil would tow a caravan. Over the years the Roll-Along was replaced with a more modern touring van. The old Alvis changed to a more suitable model with power, space and comfort. Every few years Queenie would replace both the car and the caravan with brand new models. She loved to have the latest thing from the Caravan and Camping Show and she was always eager to show them off. There were always one or two caravans parked at the front of Goff's Oak House, ready to be taken on an adventure.

1961 Cecil and Paul

Often Queenie's nephew, Albert, and his wife Margaret would join them in the Mediterranean sun. It became a regular event and year after year they went, going for three weeks at a time, once in May and then again in September. Each year they would meet up with the same people and Queenie made friends with everyone. On leaving France she always extended an open invitation to her friends to drop in at Goff's Oak House should they be in the area. And occasionally they did!

Albert and Margaret took their own car and tent or caravan. Albert and his family often travelled down by train; as a Railways employee he was entitled to free travel and it made sense to let the train take the strain. Cecil usually drove the eight hundred miles. The journey began with a night-time ferry crossing from Dover to Calais. Queenie and Cecil would settle down for the night just outside of Calais, ready for an early start the next morning. They would motor on throughout the day, occasionally stopping for one more night before hitting the final stretch to the Med. Queenie would meet up with Albert and together they would set up camp as near to the sea as possible. Their days would be spent leisurely strolling the golden beaches and bobbing about in the warm blue sea. On the beach Queenie loved to spot the then larger German people swimming in the sea. It was her aim to get a sneaky snapshot to look back on and show how slim she looked in comparison. Taking time away from the sun, Queenie would sit under the caravan awning and watch the speedboats and their water-skiers as she wrote her postcards.

Queenie would stock up with tinned supplies and take as much of what was needed for the stay as she could. She would shop in the local markets and restrict her buying to foods that she recognised or essentials like bread, milk and fruit. It is not that she was unadventurous. If she felt peckish she would find a kiosk and order a tasty snack of crêpes flambéed in Cointreau and she happily bought sweetmeats for us to sample at Christmas. For all her generosity Queenie did like to be frugal wherever she could be. Saving the pennies was important but spending the pounds was fun! Each evening Queenie would find somewhere different for dinner. She would ask her new friends for

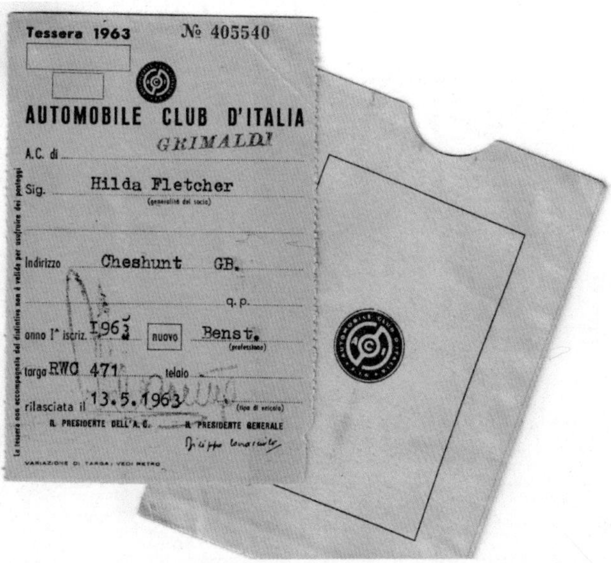
Tessera 1963 № 405540
AUTOMOBILE CLUB D'ITALIA
A.C. di GRIMALDI
Sig. Hilda Fletcher
Indirizzo Cheshunt GB.
anno 1° iscriz. 1963 nuovo Benst.
targa RWC 471 telaio
rilasciata il 13.5.1963
IL PRESIDENTE DELL'A.C. IL PRESIDENTE GENERALE

recommendations and try out the posh hotels. After a fantastic meal Queenie loved to walk by the quayside, listen to the fabulous music that entertained the crowds and ogle at the millionaires' yachts. Once, in St Tropez, Cecil saw Richard Burton, whilst Queenie was convinced she had spotted Liz Taylor. A tale she was eager to tell and retell.

1960 Paul and Queenie

Strolling along the promenade Queenie often popped into the colourful shops, making full use of the late opening establishments. One year she nearly missed the ferry home because of one of her late night shopping trips. She had just popped into a shop to buy a last minute gift. The shop was just about to close for the night but she insisted on making her purchase. In her haste she left her big document purse on the counter. By the time Queenie realised her mistake the shop was firmly shut and the proprietor long gone. She pressed her anxious face up to the glass. Her cream-coloured purse was sitting in full view. It held everything she needed: her passport, traveller's cheques, and ferry details. Cecil had hoped for an early start the next morning; as always he wanted to miss the traffic and get underway as soon as possible. Both Queenie and Cecil were up early; neither could sleep. They were pacing the pavement for quite some time, waiting for the shop to open and the opportunity to retrieve the purse hit the road and head for home.

1960 Paul and Queenie enjoy the sun

Although the south of France was Queenie's favourite destination, she often ventured further afield when the mood took her. Over the years she visited Spain, Portugal and Greece. She travelled to Italy where, in Naples, she saw Mount Vesuvius. With daughter-in-law Dot she travelled to the holy city of Jerusalem to sample the biblical sights. With Cecil's commitment to driving, she ventured all the way to Istanbul to take a dip in the Black Sea. And all of this was long after she had reached the age of fifty plus! For her age she was quite an adventurer. She never forgot us when she was away. Postcards regularly came for one or the other of us. Each carefully tailored to suit its recipient. Mention of guitar players for John, police chases for Mark, and flowers and nightingales for me.

Cecil in Venice 1961

Paul and Queenie take a shower in Venice 1961

Her travelling continued into the 1970s when Queenie herself was over seventy. One such trip was in the spring of 1970 to Catalonia, northern Spain. Queenie, Cecil, Jack, Dot and Candy were all invited to Vic and Enriquetta's wedding. In the summer of 1963 Jack had taken his family to Spain for an extended four-week holiday. This is where they met young Vic. He was only in his late teens and expressed an interest in learning English. Jack and Dot invited him to stay with them. It was not long before Vic was living in a small caravan in Jack's yard. He was soon taken into the hearts of all the family and when he returned to Spain he kept in touch. When he decided to get married, he invited everyone. The wedding was held in the green volcanic mountains of Olot. The little party took tents and camped in a large site on the beach at the fishing port of Rosas. From here they travelled the winding mountain road to the ancient town of Olot. Queenie wrote home to say what a fabulous time they had. "*There were 150 guests packed into the little Catholic Church*". Afterwards the reception was held in a typical Spanish restaurant. She wrote, *"all eight courses were delicious and served with either wine or champagne"*. The merriment went on into the early hours. "*Cecil and Jack were swept off their feet dancing with all the girls! Dot and Queenie were happy to settle for bullfighters and Candy had the time of her life with all the youngsters.*" Everyone was so nice to them and they were even invited to another wedding! Which reminds me of a story Queenie told us of a time in France when she was out strolling the area one evening, looking for entertainment. She came across a lively gathering in one of the restaurants. The music sounded good, the

Austria 1962

Queenie

wine was flowing and there was a lot of laughter from within. Queenie, enthusiastic as ever, urged Cecil to go in. They found a table and were offered a drink. They began to enjoy the party atmosphere and were soon up and dancing with the locals. Both Cecil and Queenie were having a lot of fun until they realised with a shock that they had gate-crashed a private party! They were at a wedding! Cecil was mortified and could not leave quick enough but Queenie was much more philosophical about it and would have loved to have stayed longer.

Queenie takes a stroll

Back in Spain, Jack, Dot and Candy made their way back home but Queenie and Cecil stayed on. They took full advantage of their extra time and explored the area famed for its natural beauty. One evening they travelled further round the coast to the fishing village of Cadaques where they listened to the talented young men playing Spanish guitar late into the balmy night.

Spanish Guitars

Queenie's last genuine adventure was in 1975 when she and Cecil took the campervan on a final epic road trip with Candy. Queenie had been inspired by the tales Candy had told on her return from Morocco the previous year and Queenie was keen to see the country for herself. Cecil drove the campervan, following their familiar route across the English Channel, down through France and on to southern Spain. Candy remembers them stopping at Granada and all enjoying the palace of Alhambra before they needed to move on. Cecil always liked to gain as much ground as possible during a day, so stops were often kept short. Back on the road, they travelled on down to Algeciras where they took the ferry across the strait of Gibraltar to Tangier. Queenie, now well into her seventies, took it all in her stride. The days travelling were long and tedious in the dusty Mediterranean heat. Stops were made for essentials but Queenie always packed well, stowing garden produce for a quick meal and a variety of tins. She would prepare food four times a day in the miniature kitchen. Queenie offered a slice or two of toast with home-made jam before they set off early in the cool of the morning. Then, after a couple of hours driving, a full cooked breakfast. Later, a sandwich lunch around midday and a full cooked supper in the evening once they had settled at a campsite.

Moroccan Market

As they rocked along in the tiny campervan Queenie often organised herself and Candy to peel potatoes or shell broad beans ready for supper. As a member of the Caravan and Camping Club, Queenie could always find somewhere interesting to stay. Conditions in the van were snug. Candy was not comfortable on the bunk in the space created when the roof was raised. Instead she opted to sleep on the floor between Queenie's and Cecil's narrow beds. They did not seem to mind, it was all part of the adventure.

In Morocco the sites were dusty areas with little more than two or three huge sinks and taps on standpipes. The toilets just smelly holes in the ground. With her never diminishing energy Queenie embraced the remarkable culture. Her first taste of Morocco was at Chefchaouen, between Tangier and Tetouan. All of the little square buildings of the town were painted in beautiful shades of blue. Nestled amidst the green of the mountains, the town was bathed in the harsh desert sun and looked like a magical haze of shimmering blue and white as Cecil drove into Chefchaouen. Queenie instantly loved the romance and announced it her favourite town!

The ultimate goal was the coastal town of Agadir some five hundred miles away. So they pressed on with their

Queenie

ten-day trip to Rabat, then Casablanca and Marrakesh, enjoying the sights, sounds and smells along the way. Posing for photos in her bright red T-shirt at the oasis, Queenie was relaxed and tanned as she positioned herself by the low wall of the well and nonchalantly rested one foot on the brickwork. They travelled on, each day gaining as much ground as possible. Every now and then Queenie would shout to Cecil "Stop, Cecil, stop!" "Bloody hell, woman!" was Cecil's reply, "What now?" Queenie would have spotted a roadside stall selling edible treats which she had to investigate or an unusual plant which she had to take illegal seeds or a cutting from. Her spontaneous actions infuriated the travel-fatigued Cecil. But he always conceded and reluctantly turned the campervan around to let her explore. In the markets she would have looked at all the leather goods with interest. I remember the bag she gave me on her return and the many pairs of pointy-toed slippers she brought back in all sorts of sizes for whoever they would fit.

Queenie loved the small children and animals that gravitated to the market places. She had a knack of communicating with everyone, her smiley personality shining through. At the camel market, both Queenie and Candy created quite a stir with their white, blonde heads. The blue-clad Berbers at the market were happy for them to pet their tiny black baby goat, whilst they attempted to make a deal in camels for the golden-haired Candy. Queenie was having none of it and turned her back on them and walked away. Retelling the story back home, it was Cecil who saw the danger. Surprisingly, the usually business savvy, Queenie could be quite naïve and a little too trusting at times. Because of this she was fearless and never afraid to try something new. Over her lifetime it took her to some fascinating places and enabled her to meet some interesting people who enriched her long life. Giving her a plethora of stories to kept us all entertained!

Queenie and Candy pose for the camera in Morocco

Queenie, the final Chapter

After years of being the lively centre of attention, age finally took its toll on Queenie. Her mind began to slip and she became more forgetful. One morning she was found aimlessly wandering around the village in her nightgown and slippers. On another day she tried to boil the electric kettle on the gas hob. Her bright blue eyes glazed over with glaucoma and her sight failed. She began to spend endless hours sat in the armchair, confused and quiet. A fragile shadow of the vibrant matriarch we had all grown up with. Pam and Cecil rallied to make her as comfortable as possible at home but eventually she was admitted to Highlands Hospital, Enfield, where on the fifth of November 1985 her heart gave up and she died. A great void was created in our hearts. Queenie had been the kingpin to so much in our lives. Her funeral was held a week later. A touching tribute was conducted at the Methodist chapel that meant so much to the Wombwell family. The coffin was then transported to the Cheshunt Crematorium. After a brief service the mourners returned to Goff's Oak House where a sombre party was held in her honour. The atmosphere in the house was never quite the same. On the morning of the funeral, a bat was found in the house hanging upside down in the small corridor outside the closed morning room door. Something that had never happened in all the years since Queenie's arrival in the 1940s. Such a bizarre occurrence… Was it a sign? And if so, what did it mean? Finally Queenie's ashes were laid to rest alongside her husband Bert at the Cheshunt Crematorium.

Three Generations, Anita, Queenie and Pam

Queenie, Christmas morning 1981.

With 87 years of life Queenie had come into the world at the end of the Victorian era and left a twentieth century world where Mark and Jack had mobile phones the size of house bricks and John was working with computers. She had boldly trod each and every step the modern world took. She had never once looked back. She had approached life as if she would live forever, eagerly embracing whatever the future had to offer next. She died a wealthy independent women and a true inspiration! We really do have so much to thank her for.

1981, Queenie with Cecil and family on her Birthday

Cecil Devoted Companion to the End!

Minister
Rev. Colin W Letchford
11 Keswick Drive Enfield Middlesex EN3 6NY
Telephone: Lea Valley 762317

GOFFS OAK METHODIST CHURCH

Newgatestreet Road . Goffs Oak . Herts

please reply to

Norman T. Cox
17 Jones Road,
Goffs Oak.
Waltham Cross
Herts EN7 5JT.

Dear Mrs. Ellisson.

Colin has passed to me the cheque for £100 being the legacy left by your mother to the church. I'm afraid that I never knew your mother myself but I have heard how she used to support the church activities and that was much appreciated. May I, on behalf of all the church, say how much we appreciate your mothers' thought in leaving a legacy to us and express our continuing sympathy with you & your family in the loss you suffered.

Yours sincerely.

Norman Cox.

№ 3 21st September 1986

Received from Exors. Mrs. H.A. Fletcher decd.

the sum of One Hundred Pounds - 00

Norman T. Cox

100	00

Goffs Oak Methodist Church.

1. From Acorn to Sturdy Oak...
The First Century of the Goff's Oak (Herts) Methodist Church (1868- 1968)
By Jim Priest

2. Theobalds Through the Centuries
The changing fortunes of a Hertfordshire house and estate
Edited by P.E.Rooke

3. Goff's Oak and Theobalds Past
A selection of photographs and engravings with notes

4. A London Family between the Wars
M.V.Hughes

5. Northaw Great Wood
Its history and natural history
Edited by Bryan L. Sage

6. Menageries, Circuses and Theaters
E.Bostock

7. Bertram Mills - The Circus That Travelled By Train
By David Jamieson

8. Tales of the Old Horsemen
Jennifer Davies

9. The Love of the Circus
Bookmark

10. Catalogue of Bostock and Wombwell's Royal Menagerie

Web sites visited

wombwell@eurobell.co.uk

chasb67@hotmail.co.uk

soba-stosyth.co.uk

Uttlesford district council

http://wombwell.net/wombwell/index2.htm

Frames Designed by Freepik.com

The Hatfield Rural District Council.

1935-36.

HOUSING URGENCY SUB-COMMITTEES.

Hatfield.

J. Lockley (*Chairman*).

E. C. Berry. A. Crowe. J. Lang.
J. A. Sinclair. H. Storey.
E. T. Tingey.

North Mimms.

J. Crawford (*Chairman*).

E. C. Doust-Smith. J. C. Newton.
H. J. Tilbury. F. N. V. Winckler.

Northaw.

A. D. Bishop.
C. G. Maynard.
A. L. Wombwell.

Essendon.

J. B. Healing.
S. Wallace.

COUNCILLORS.

Walter Clarke, J.P., *Chairman*.
Samuel Wallace, J.P., *Vice-Chairman*.

	Year First Elected
Essendon.	
John Burton Healing	1930
Samuel Wallace, J.P.	1904
Hatfield.	
Edward Charles Berry	1935
Walter Clarke, J.P.	1907
Albert Crowe, J.P.	1922
James Lang	1922
John Lockley	1927
James Angus Sinclair	1935
Harry Storey	1929
Edmund Thomas Tingey, J.P. ...	1919
Ralph Edward Whitby	1927
Northaw.	
Arthur Duvall Bishop	1935
Charles Gordon Maynard ...	1935
Albert Lewis Wombwell ...	1925
North Mimms.	
James Crawford	1913
Ernest Charles Doust-Smith ...	1934
Joe Campion Newton	1934
Herbert James Tilbury	1935
Francis Norman Vernon Winckler	1935

Under the County of Hertford Review Order 1935 all Councillors retire on the 15th April, 1937.

COMMITTEES OF THE COUNCIL.

FINANCE COMMITTEE.

R. E. Whitby (*Chairman*).

A. D. Bishop. E. C. Doust-Smith.
J. Lang. J. Lockley.
H. Storey. F. N. V. Winckler.

FIRE BRIGADE AND AMBULANCE COMMITTEE.

J. B. Healing (*Chairman*).

A. Crowe. C. G. Maynard.
J. C. Newton. J. A. Sinclair.
E. T. Tingey. A. L. Wombwell.

HEALTH AND GENERAL PURPOSES COMMITTEE.

H. Storey (*Chairman*).

E. C. Berry. A. D. Bishop.
E. C. Doust-Smith. J. Lang.
J. C. Newton. H. J. Tilbury.

REPRESENTATIVES.

Barnet Assessment Committee.

E. C. Doust-Smith.
J. C. McCowan, J.P.

Local Education Sub-Committee.

E. C. Berry. J. A. Sinclair.

Local Pensions Sub-Committee.

J. Lang. H. Storey.

Barnet Guardians Committee.

E. T. Tingey, J.P. A. L. Wombwell.

County of Hertford Playing Fields Association.

E. C. Doust-Smith.

Hertfordshire Society.

E. C. Doust-Smith.

DATES OF MEETINGS.

COUNCIL.

1935.	1935.
23rd May.	19th December.
27th June.	1936.
25th July.	23rd January.
19th September.	27th February.
24th October.	26th March.
28th November.	23rd April.

COMMITTEES.

1935.	1935.
15th May.	10th December.
18th June.	1936.
16th July.	14th January.
10th September.	18th February.
15th October.	17th March.
19th November.	14th April.

PLANS AND TOWN PLANNING COMMITTEE.

J. Crawford (*Chairman*).

E. C. Berry.
J. B. Healing.
C. G. Maynard.
H. J. Tilbury.
E. T. Tingey.
A. L. Wombwell.

RATING COMMITTEE.

J. Crawford (*Chairman*).

A. D. Bishop.
J. B. Healing.
J. Lockley.
C. G. Maynard.
J. A. Sinclair.
H. J. Tilbury.
R. E. Whitby.

Printed in Great Britain
by Amazon

11664639R00074